D0712916

THE REAL LIVES OF ROMAN BRITAIN

THE REAL LIVES OF
ROMAN BRITAIN

GUY DE LA BÉDOYÈRE

YALE UNIVERSITY PRESS
NEW HAVEN AND LONDON

For information about this and other Yale University Press publications, please contact:
U.S. Office: sales.press@yale.edu   www.yalebooks.com
Europe Office: sales@yaleup.co.uk   www.yalebooks.co.uk

Typeset in Minion Pro by IDSUK (DataConnection) Ltd
Printed in Great Britain by Gomer Press Ltd, Llandysul, Ceredigion, Wales

Library of Congress Cataloging-in-Publication Data

De la Bédoyère, Guy.
The real lives of Roman Britain : a history of Roman Britain through the lives of those who were there / Guy de la Bédoyère.
pages cm
Includes bibliographical references.
ISBN 978-0-300-20719-4 (cloth : alkaline paper)
1. Great Britain—History—Roman period, 55 B.C.–449 A.D. 2. Great Britain—Social life and customs—To 1066. 3. Great Britain—History—Roman period, 55 B.C.–449 A.D.—Biography. 4. Great Britain—Antiquities, Roman. I. Title.
DA145.D456 2015
936.2'04—dc23

2014047962

A catalogue record for this book is available from the British Library.

10 9 8 7 6 5 4 3 2 1

CONTENTS

INTRODUCTION

No story should begin quite where the reader expects it to begin and this is no exception. This one begins in Italy a few miles to the south of Rome. The Appian Way is the best known of all the Roman roads. For several miles outside the south-eastern walls of Rome it can still be followed, lined with trees and the crumbling remnants of Roman tombs. It makes for a striking, if exhausting, walk and takes the traveller past the vast Circus of Maxentius overlooked by the drum-shaped tomb of Cecilia Metella, a noblewoman of the late first century BC. Around 3.5 miles further on is a funerary inscription, still wholly legible and commemorating the burial and wishes of Gaius Ateilius Euhodus, a dealer in pearls (*margaritarius*). Euhodus probably lived in the second or first century BC. He might have heard about Caesar's invasions of Britain in 55 and 54 BC but if so, he makes no mention of the fact and nor would one have expected him to. Indeed, on the face of it there is no good reason why he would be mentioned here in a book about Roman Britain.

But there is a very good reason to start with Gaius Ateilius Euhodus. He exemplifies the emergent sense of self in the Roman world and, most importantly of all, of the sense of self in the ordinary man and woman and the desire or need to express it in a durable medium. This does not mean that other peoples, British tribes included, lack a 'sense of self' – such a judgment would be absurd. What it does mean is that in the

Roman world the means existed with which to express a sense of self in a form that endures in the record. In Egypt, for example, private individuals were quite capable of memorializing their lives in their tombs. Both also reflect the desire in their cultures, a commonplace need, to express oneself that way. However, in the Britain the Romans invaded there was no obvious durable means for people to express that sense of self, and nor was there apparently the desire to do so. The arrival of the Roman world changed the nature of the record dramatically.

Euhodus was from any historical perspective a nobody. He left no obvious legacy of any sort and we have no idea whether or not he was thought well of by his family and descendants, though he certainly thought well of himself. We know about him because he recorded himself, and his words in his funerary inscription are a direct message to us. It reads:

> Stranger – stop and look at this mound to the left where the bones of a good, compassionate, benevolent man of modest means, are contained [or: a good, compassionate man and friend of those of modest means are contained]. I ask that you, traveller, do nothing bad to this tomb. Gaius Ateilius Euhodus, freedman of Serranus, pearl seller on the Via Sacra, is preserved in this tomb. Farewell traveller. Under the terms of the will, it is not lawful to preserve or bury anyone in this tomb except those freedmen to whom I have granted and assigned [this].[1]

Euhodus' name was Greek (its literal meaning is that of a road that was easy to travel along) so he may have come from the eastern half of the Empire, perhaps being sold in a Rome slave market as a child or youth. We learn that the freedman Euhodus made his living as a dealer in pearls on the Sacred Way, a road in the forum of Rome, and was successful enough to free his own slaves and offer those whom he specified in his will a place in his tomb too.[2]

Euhodus' inscription is certainly unusually specific and conversational in style but in other respects it merely serves to communicate his ordinariness to us. Unlike many other great ancient civilizations, Rome provided its nonentities with the means to escape the anonymity of death. The money Euhodus made, the language he spoke and the customs of Roman society meant that this man, about whom otherwise we would know nothing, was able to tell us a little of himself in a medium we can access. His sense of self was communicable and transmissible because of the nature of Roman civilization. In Italy in the first century BC this was a fact of utterly no consequence; there were, literally, hundreds of thousands of such memorials as well as untold quantities of other written records. Euhodus' inscription just happens to be one that has survived intact and is also more or less still where he asked for it to be erected.

In Britain at that time all this would have been inconceivable. That it ceased to be inconceivable was the real revolution of the Roman invasion. The world that someone like Euhodus took for granted in Italy was imported to Britain as it had been to so many other provinces. Just as Euhodus recorded himself, so certain people in Britain began to record themselves in their own ways too and thus opened a new type of window to us on Britain's past. It is too glib either to curse the Romans for their imperial oppression or heap plaudits on them for their beneficence. What they did provide for British history are the first manifestations of the sense of self among the ordinary, though just who those ordinary people were is one of the focuses of this book because the vast majority of those who did this were immigrants.

Roman Britain is the label we apply to several centuries during which the most conspicuous forms of cultural expression were derived, all or in part, from the classical world of Rome and other peoples in its orbit. They range from altars dedicated to Jupiter Optimus Maximus on the northern frontier by soldiers, to the names and Latinate tags engraved on late Roman silver spoons found in treasure hoards buried in the late fourth or early fifth centuries. But they also include the rebuilder of a temple to Egyptian Isis in London and a tilemaker with a Latinized name who worked in what we call Kent. The inscriptions and other records of the men, women and children for whom Roman Britain was part of their experiences, whether as immigrant or native, are the first ordinary people in British history that we can name. That is, above all, why the Roman era in Britain is of such great importance to our history, however imperfect that record is. Roads outside the forts and towns of

Roman Britain became lined with tombs and inscriptions. To this we can add graffiti, wooden writing tablets and other memorials and records. The revolution began with the coming of Caesar in 55 and 54 BC. It is given to few moments in history to be really decisive. The moment Caesar first stepped ashore in Britain was one of them, even if that was not obvious at the time.

Roman Britain has been a part of my life ever since in 1963 my parents took me, aged then around five, to see the excavations at Fishbourne Palace near Chichester. At the time the discovery of remains of the palace had caused something of a sensation. I can, surprisingly, still recall that vivid experience, no doubt helped along by the photograph taken at the time of me and my brother sitting beside the Dolphin mosaic. It had only just been exposed and a fresh spoilheap sat beside the elegant and colourful floor to prove the point. I remember even then being fascinated by the idea that this had once been a house (plate 1). Around a decade later we visited the Lullingstone Roman villa in its quiet refuge beside the River Darenth in north-west Kent. It is still a peaceful and secluded place, making it easy to see why the location was chosen.

However interesting Fishbourne and Lullingstone are today, it is easy to forget that they were once homes, three-dimensional buildings in which all sorts of personal dramas and histories were played out. Hundreds of Romano-British villas are known, while modern excavation and survey work has shown that there were tens of thousands of simpler rural farmsteads and settlements across the green and pleasant land of Roman Britain, where the vast majority of the population lived, many little differently from before the Roman era. The villas and all these myriad settlements must have been places where children were born, played, grew up, experienced happiness and sadness, had their own families, grew old and died and were fondly remembered or otherwise by their descendants, who themselves wandered through the corridors with their own families and used the rooms to play out their own existences. Whole family dynasties passed through these places, experiencing joy or tragedy, success or failure, depending on the circumstances. At Lullingstone a young couple were buried below a specially constructed mausoleum a few yards from the house. We can never now know who they were, the tragedy that befell them and the impact it had on their families, but as human beings ourselves we can sense the evident despair their family or families must have felt.

All this and more is silently attested through the wear on mosaic tesserae and graffiti on pots. Roman Britain was also, of course, home to dozens of towns, large and small, and many more fortresses and forts. Here untold numbers of unique personal stories were played out against a backdrop of the broader Roman world and its extravagant, exotic, erotic and extraordinary history. That is the central point. Roman Britain was a human experience but we can all too easily forget that among the generalities of military campaigns, the antics of emperors, the arid plains of statistical models and typologies of pottery, the skeletal remains of buildings, and theoretical archaeological agendas which seem obsessed with refuting one abstruse dogma and replacing it with another, none of which appears to have much to do with real life. The nature of the record is such that it is easy to see why these dominate our understanding and why whole centuries are passed over or dismissed casually in a sentence, or why we fixate on events involving a handful of people in an imperial court and ignore everyone else.

This is not a 'history of Roman Britain'. There are plenty of those and therefore I make no apology for doing no more here than briefly summarizing or alluding to the comings and goings of emperors, governors and legions. This time it is their turn to lurk in the background, though inevitably some force their way in – after all, their experience of Roman Britain is as valid as that of a potter of indifferent skill who tried to make his fortune in the province.

No attempt has been made to come to any general judgments about the benefits or deficiencies of Roman control. Today it has become more usual to regard the Roman era in Britain as one during which an oppressive regime exploited and abused the population as part of an Empire-wide policy of systematic larceny. Far from being a source of opportunity, the Roman Empire in this revisionist paradigm is a malicious, greedy and destructive force that created and exacerbated social inequalities; it also fragmented society into disparate groups, defined by their very different experiences of life under Roman rule. Such a judgment is as simplistic as the Victorian perception of the Romans as being their beneficent imperialist forbears, in confident possession of a 'superior' civilization they were generously endowing on the rest of the world. The reality, inevitably, is altogether more blurred. Roman rule was neither invariably an idyllic induction to the pleasures of life in an imperial system and nor was it exclusively an oppressive nightmare characterized by merciless exploitation and cultural totalitarianism.

For around 360 years in Britain, Roman rule was a fact of life. It is self-evident, as it is with any regime, that the people involved would have included those who exploited their advantages and those who were oppressed. No doubt there were plenty of people who both exploited and were exploited in equal measure. A broader perspective on the historical tradition shows that all human societies involve elements of both and that these are in a constant state of flux. All human beings seek an acceptable accommodation between individual liberty and control since most of us crave some sort of order and security. It is obvious that there was great inequality in the Roman world, but it is also true that social mobility existed to some degree, that there was a significant component of elective acceptance of the system as it was, and that there was also impotence, either legal or practical, to do anything about it. A striking feature of the Roman system was its durability. This reflects the fact that of all the options available to some of its people the Roman system seemed the least unpalatable.

The Romano-British all had to operate in a system that was determined in the main by the conquering culture. What is impossible for us is to establish the extent of deliberate participation, whether willingly or begrudgingly, and also to track the process of assimilation, especially as it has always been very clear that the experience of Roman domination varied wildly between regions. After all, a Briton might have spent an impecunious lifetime suffering exploitation, and loathing his Romanized oppressors, but been content to use a Roman road when it suited him and accept its inevitable impact on his life. His grandson may have developed into a far more willing participant when money and position came his way as a result. In the end human beings can make very polarized decisions, even within a family, depending on the prospect of immediate advantages or disadvantages of any given situation. Collaboration, cohabitation and compliance are often the consequences of expediency and we can see all of these beginning to occur in some parts of Britain before the Roman invasion.

That conquering Roman culture has remained one of the defining forces of our own era; it includes the expression of identity through Latinate literacy and it is our conduit to Roman Britain because we are able to understand much of it. Yes, it is patently obvious that the record is a self-selecting and unsatisfactory resource because it necessarily preserves evidence of those most inclined to attest to their own lives that way. But it is what we have.

Roman Britain has in fact left us a surprisingly rich and varied record of people for whom this was their home. They include those who were born there, and those who arrived as soldiers or immigrants. Some were merely passing through, while others died and were commemorated in Britain. Some experienced lives of tragic brevity while others witnessed decades of the province's vibrant history and lived to epic old ages to tell the tale. Some had ringside seats to history while others were simply part of the background. The record includes everything from the emperors who came this way to individuals whose lives have left no impact on the grand histories of the human past but whose chance survival in the record gives us the opportunity to witness life as a child, a slave, a mourned wife or husband, a maker of pottery or a truant from the workplace. Some are anonymous, while others have names that have to stand for the untold millions about whom we know nothing at all.

This book cannot be about grand dynasties of Roman villa owners or fiercely proud British families that traced their lineages back to tribal Britain. No doubt these existed. But they are lost to the ages and this is a central issue when it comes to Roman Britain. Our knowledge of this era is handicapped by the restricted visibility. It is sobering to have to acknowledge that we have no records even of the owner of a villa estate, let alone how he and his family earned their living. Archaeology has struggled to fill the gap but it necessarily only provides generalities as explanations. It can almost never recreate the uniquely random circumstances that conspire to determine all sorts of phenomena, decisions and events in the human experience. It may be possible to identify that a villa burned down and was demolished in the late fourth century and ascribe this nebulously to the disorder of the time, but tracing the affiliations of the owner, and the accidents and happenstance that befell him to lead to this terminal outcome for his home, is impossible. Yet we all know that our own lives are determined by such unpredictable events.

Instead this book is about the soldiers and women of Rome's most northerly frontier, slave girls, potters, errant tilers, jewellers, immigrants and others whose claim to fame is often no more than a fleeting glimpse of their lives or the circumstances of their death. Their stories are drawn from four centuries or more of the human experience of the Roman era on the edge of the then known world. Some of them are well known today, such as the freedwoman Regina. Others lurk only in the archives of Romano-British inscriptions or excavation reports. Together these sources provide a rich seam of isolated incidents, personalities and memorials creating a remarkable record of the 360 years of Britain's time as a Roman province.

Our dependence on the visible and literate record for these individual experiences means that we are unavoidably reliant on inscriptions left by those who were inclined to leave them in the first place, and which have survived. Among these revenants, the soldiers of the garrison are by far and away the most prominent, followed a close second by immigrants from across the Roman Empire. Their stories paint an animated picture of a world populated by transient Spaniards, Gauls, Thracians, Greeks and Italians among others. Britons, by comparison, are tantalizingly scarce.

This seems odd, since by definition Britons ought to have monopolized the population, but this takes us back to visibility. Perhaps we should focus far more closely on the relatively enormous native rural population of Roman Britain, and use the better records of the medieval period as a basis for comparison.[3] It is a laudable but relatively futile aspiration. The vast underbelly of the Romano-British population has left little that would help us distinguish individual lives; medieval comparisons might in any case be very misleading or they might not – we cannot judge it either way. The same problem afflicts so many other studies of ancient society. The Mycenaean world of the Greek Bronze Age, for example, is known to us more or less only from the handed-down tales of the warrior elite in Homer's poems, and through the archaeological remnants of that elite in the grave circles at Mycenae or the tholos tombs and the great citadels. Of the untold hundreds of thousands who must have toiled in Greece's stony hills to support that elite caste we know almost nothing.

Moreover, visibility is a two-way process. Those who leave a record can only be accessed by those who understand or can see that record. This of course begs the question – is the record that we have a gross misrepresentation of the reality at the time or is it the case that the Roman cultural dominance was evident then too? We can never answer that question but it remains the case that the so-called 'Celtic' peoples of Britannia are annoyingly elusive in any capacity. It is worth mentioning here that the term 'Celtic' is almost completely inappropriate. Never applied to the peoples of Britain by the Romans it is largely a latter-day fabrication in which antiquarians conceived that there existed a greater 'Celtic' culture across Europe. There did not. The term was applied in antiquity to some peoples of Central Europe and it includes elements who found their way to Britain in the army, but beyond that the word has no relevance. It is even a moot point as to whether a Briton from the south-east could even understand a Briton of the far north. Without any written forms of the ancient British languages it is impossible for us to tell, but it is likely that regional dialects were replete with words and colloquial forms that were quite alien and incomprehensible to tribes located hundreds of miles away.

One of the issues is the Roman paradox. In the Roman world it was possible for an individual to become so subsumed into Roman culture, at least insofar as that person is manifested to us, that his or her origins disappeared, yet by virtue of being Romanized he or she had a far better chance of appearing in the accessible record and of belonging to a broadly similar culture. That record is the gift of literacy, itself being Rome's greatest gift to British history, but not necessarily to the Britons. A man or a woman bearing a completely Roman name on an inscription may have come from almost anywhere in the Roman world unless they tell us precisely otherwise – and most do not. So, a Briton, or half-Briton, who was brought up in a 'Romanized' household or consciously decided to pursue that route might as a result obfuscate his or her origins, deliberately or incidentally, while at the same time become recorded in a way that is recognizable to us. At the time this obscuring of origins might not have been in the least bit misleading to the people around our Briton to whom he or she would have been obviously a Briton from the evidence of accent or appearance. Conversely, in the sense of how such a person is attested in the record it may no longer be possible for us to tell. It is also possible, indeed even likely, that the vast majority of Britons had little or no access to literacy beyond a basic familiarity, even if they acquired some everyday Latin in their speech, a common language being a crucial component in creating a broader cultural identity. This would explain the relative scarcity of inscriptions attesting native Britons in their own right, and the virtual absence of any evidence for the transliteration of native languages into Latin characters in Britain.[4] Britons who did acquire literacy were likely to have promptly concealed much of their native identity beneath a new, Romanized one, either deliberately or accidentally.

Only in those rare instances where a British origin is specified are we on firmer ground, as with Regina the Catuvellaunian freedwoman. Similis, a member of the Cantiaci tribe from Kent, made a dedication at Colchester to the Suleviae goddesses and thus preserved his name in the record. Lossio Veda, who appeared in Colchester between 222 and 235, is an instance of a person from beyond the province's northern frontier who uniquely identifies himself as both a Caledonian and as someone who expresses himself through a Roman conduit. Thereby he becomes visible as an individual to us. Conversely, Apion was an Egyptian who joined the Roman imperial navy at Misenum in Italy. From there he wrote to his father, Epimachus, in Egypt to tell him that he was now named 'Antonius Maximus', an innocuous and completely anodyne Roman name that reveals nothing about his origins.[5] Had the papyrus letter he sent home not survived we would know nothing about where he came from had his name turned up on, say, a Roman military document or a tombstone. How many Britons lie metaphorically buried beneath Roman names in Britain or beyond? Since we know from the acerbic comments made by the fourth-century Gallo-Roman poet Ausonius that Britons were regarded as a kind of underclass, perhaps some of them took steps to disguise their origins. After all, in the late first century BC Virgil had described the Britons as being 'utterly separated from the whole world', an observation reflected in Catullus' description of them a few years earlier in the aftermath of Caesar's invasions as 'terrifying' and 'furthermost'.[6] These clearly positioned the Britons in the Roman mindset as wholly alien and alienated in every way. Ausonius' observations, discussed in chapter 7 of this book, suggest that in some respects little had changed four hundred years later. Given the rarity of demonstrably ethnic Britons in the record of Roman Britain, perhaps Virgil's and Catullus' words were more prescient than either could have imagined.

It is in any case worth asking: what was a 'Briton'? One thing is for certain: the 'Britons', at least prior to the Roman invasion, would have had no concept of themselves as such. Their fealty and identity would have been locked into the tribe each belonged to. Moreover, the cross-Channel contacts between British and Gaulish tribes before the Roman conquest, as well as long-distance contacts with Iberian and Mediterranean traders, mean that many Britons must have had a far more dispersed ancestry than the Britons probably appreciated. Tacitus commented on the physical varieties to be found in Britain and noted that while Gaulish influence was considerable in the south it also seemed that the Caledonians had German ancestry and the Silures in Wales had features which suggested at least some Iberian parentage.[7] Tacitus' information was primarily anecdotal and traditional but there was surely some truth in it. During the Roman period this process probably intensified in every region that was under Roman control. Modern scientific techniques might make it possible to unravel some of these connections but at present little is known beyond occasional individual examples. Instead we must content ourselves with recognizing that being a Catuvellaunian, Trinovantian or Silurian was probably as much a state of mind as was being a 'Roman', with each masking considerable variations and combinations of ethnic origin.

No one now knows how large the population of Roman Britain was. Guesses range from two million to six and anywhere in between. Even then it might have fluctuated considerably during the period, depending on episodes of famine or disease which have gone unrecorded. It is also impossible to know what either the birth or death rate was, though we can assume that the latter was extremely high by our standards. Within that population we can estimate a Roman military population of around 30,000 to 40,000 during the conquest period, multiplied by several times if we assume the existence of associated families, legal or illegal. The rural population will always have been the vast majority of the remainder, blurring into the urban population in areas around the towns. It is certain for reasons already discussed that the ethnicity of these populations will have differed. The military populations will have contained the greatest diversity, followed closely by the urban populations. The rural population, however, will have been less susceptible to influxes, but it is also true that a certain amount of increased mobility, thanks to better communications and higher levels of internal provincial security compared to the pre-Roman era, will have meant that immigrant DNA must have entered there too.

These are all unavoidably vague observations. However, we have firmer evidence for longevity. It is a fact not always appreciated that human beings are little more capable of living to grand old ages now than they ever were. Nutrition, sanitation and the control of disease have vastly increased an individual's chances of a ripe old age but that is all. We are not fundamentally 'different' from the Romano-British, who may in some respects have been far fitter and more resilient than us. The tombstones of the province are our most reliable indicators and they record everything from death in infancy to centenarians, though the evidence is so haphazard and so biased to the immigrant community that it is useless for any statistical measurements. Instead it gives us a sense of what sort of lifespans were possible. Centenarians were very unusual, but then so they were in the 1800s. Claudia Crysis was a woman who died in Lincoln, probably sometime in the second century. We know nothing about her except that her name suggests she had blonde hair and that she died when she was ninety.[8] In reality this may well have been approximate – after all, by the time she expired there would have been very few people around able to testify to the veracity of her claim – and if she had started life on a native farmstead or been enslaved there would be no means of knowing when she was born. But she must have been very, very old when she passed away.

At Caerleon, home from the late first century to the II Legion Augusta, Julius Valens was buried by his wife Julia Secundina and his son Julius Martinus. Julius Valens had reached the epic age of a hundred, a fact which is stated with no elaboration or ceremony as if it was of not the slightest import.[9] Nevertheless, it is unique in our records of Roman Britain, though as such a round figure it is possible it was no more than an approximation. Julius Valens had probably served for twenty-five or more years as a legionary, which means that he must have lived in and around the fortress for another fifty years or more once he retired. One can imagine him as a veritable Chelsea Pensioner of his era, happy to ramble on about his experiences at the edge of the known world in Rome's most volatile and wildest province. Perhaps he spent time building one or other of the Walls. Julia may well have been a second wife. She was to die at the comparatively modest age of seventy-five, and was buried by their son close to her husband. Their tombstones came to light in 1815 in an orchard near the fortress. Close by was another tombstone which is a reminder that each of these tales is unique. Julia Veneria died at the age of thirty-two and was buried by her husband Julius Alesander and their son Julius Belicianus, who cannot have been much more than a teenager.[10] At Cirencester Nemmonius Verecundus died when he was seventy-five, while at nearby Gloucester Titus Lusius Nymphius gave up the ghost when he was only twenty.[11] At York, by another legionary fortress, Quintus Corellius Fortis buried his thirteen-year-old daughter Corellia Optata. 'Optata' means something like 'the desired girl', only adding to the poignancy of her untimely demise. The text her grieving father had carved on her stone described him as 'a pitiable victim of unfair hope'.[12] Premature death was obviously far more commonplace than it is today but it was clearly no more easily accepted.

Inevitably the choice of real lives for this book has meant that all too many have had to be omitted. A choice has been made of a range of people whose lives parallel the history of the province of Britannia. They make for a parade of individuals whose idiosyncrasies and names would not seem out of place in a Roman equivalent of the works of Charles Dickens or Jane Austen. Austalis, the errant tiler of London, is redolent of any of Dickens's affable and picaresque rogues, and the slave girls Regina and Fortunata are as sentimental figures as any of his female heroines. The epistolary friendship of Claudia Severa and Sulpicia Lepidina is as affectionate and heart-warming an episode as any from Jane Austen's novels. Through the miracle of literacy, or through chance actions, they are each immortalized. But their lives are also sobering reminders that all things must pass. The grandiose tomb of Classicianus the procurator must have seemed imposing and appropriate in the time immediately following his death, especially to those who regarded him as a great man. But even within the Roman period he drifted so far into the past that his tomb could be demolished and its blocks used in a bastion attached to London's late Roman defensive walls.

I hope that those who appear in these pages will help us to see Roman Britain as a human drama, and a reflection of our own lives and our own time. In the grand scheme of things the sixteen centuries that have passed since the end of the Roman period is very little time at all. This was their home and in a real sense we still share it with them, their ghosts, their gods, their hopes, their disappointments and their dreams. Like those of us alive today they share the remarkable freak of chance that they were born and lived at all in the face of impossible odds; and their lives helped shape the gene pool from which we are drawn.[13]

I would like to thank a number of people who both wittingly and unwittingly contributed to the inception of this book. Professor David Kennedy of the University of Western Australia allowed me to try out a very early version of the idea on his enthusiastic and well-informed Roman Archaeology Group (RAG) at Perth over Easter 2013. That Australian adventure opened my eyes to the remarkable phenomenon and individual experiences of a land and its indigenous culture when they are impacted upon by an alien imperial culture and all the parallels with Roman Britain that it entailed. RAG's secretary Norah Cooper encouraged the evolution of the idea and directed me to some fascinating anthropology books that took it on a stage further, as well as making some observations on the text as it developed. The journalist and classicist Charlotte Higgins wrote to me when compiling research for her journey through Roman Britain, *Under Another Sky*. She replied to one of my emails to say that I should publish some of what I had written to her about life in Roman Britain and this encouragement contributed more than she realizes to the inception of this book. Dr Martin Henig of the University of Oxford was kind enough to respond to some queries. Dr Miles Russell of Bournemouth University has also shared with me some of his theories and ideas which have proved interesting to consider. Dr Joann Fletcher of the University of York generously read through the whole text at an early stage, making several very valuable comments and assessing the validity of the book as conceived and executed. This was enormously useful. I am also grateful to Joel Holmstrom of the University of Tasmania whose questions and observations led to some very useful refinements of the opening parts of the text.

I will forever be indebted to Catherine Johns, former keeper at the British Museum, whose friendship, imagination and support have been invaluable over now many decades. She also has an unmatched feel for the period which is never more evident than in her elegant and sensitively written reports on the great Romano-British treasures discovered in recent years. Heather McCallum at Yale University Press contacted me about writing for her and in the course of our ensuing discussions the concept for the book took shape and acquired a life of its own. Her enthusiastic reception of the idea, and her assistance with refining it, were essential. Thanks are also due to Ann Bone for her invaluable and meticulous editing work on the text during the production of this book and to Candida Brazil at Yale University Press for seeing the book through to publication. Any errors which remain are, of course, entirely my responsibility.

I should also add that the experience of becoming a History teacher late in life, charged with delivering lessons on everything from the totalitarian regimes of the twentieth century to the slave trade of the eighteenth and nineteenth centuries, as well as teaching Roman history, has been a transformative experience. Only by moving out beyond one's specialist field does the past become an accumulated whole of which each and every period seems to have a parallel and enduring existence. I should therefore thank some of the hundreds of girls who sat through my classes and whose questions and interest broadened my own vision of the Roman era in Britain as part of the larger perspective of the history of these islands and the world.

Guy de la Bédoyère, Welby, Lincolnshire

CHAPTER ONE

COLD CONTACT: THE COMING OF CAESAR, 55 BC–AD 41

The Britain which Julius Caesar invaded was in geographical terms much as it is today though with some variation in the coastline, especially in the east. It would be wrong to dismiss it as some sort of barbarian fringe of the classical world. Britain was home to a complex tribal culture that had developed over millennia and which for the most part we can only access through archaeology. Like most human societies sooner or later, pressure on land and resources eventually generated the physical evidence of tension and conflict. Part of this was the emergence of a warrior elite who invested (or wasted, depending on the point of view) the surplus produce of their tribal communities in strongholds, weaponry and, as the first millennium BC drew to a close, in the products of the Roman world which sat beside armaments as the totemic symbols of success and status. This applied especially to the tribes of the south-east who had the easiest cross-Channel access to Roman influence. These were people whose numbers included exceptionally skilled craftsmen and, no doubt, craftswomen. They were capable of manufacturing high-quality pottery, bronze and precious metal artefacts. They also included men and women whose interests in power were as great as those of any Roman politician or general. But Britain was in other respects a very different place.

The closest we can come to the ordinary Britons of this period is through some of Caesar's observations about the life of the Britons but he drew his comments from very general observations of the tribes of the south-east. Inevitably he contrasted them relatively favourably with those of the interior simply because they were more recognizably 'civilized' by virtue of the similarity of their lifestyles to those of the Gauls. He was most intrigued by the manner in which fertile women were shared between groups of men who were usually brothers, or fathers and sons. These numbered as many as twelve men. Their communities, not surprisingly, centred on productive arable and pastoral agriculture and were successful enough to support what Caesar described as *creberrima aedificia*, 'closely packed homesteads'.[1]

Caesar was by no means the first person to write anything about Britain. Diodorus Siculus wrote around the same time but based some of what he set down on the works of Pytheas, a Greek geographer who explored north-west Europe in the late fourth century BC. Diodorus was particularly interested in the extraction of Cornish tin which played such an important part in the production of bronze in antiquity.[2] The real point is that his account showed how prehistoric Britain was not only home to organized metal extraction industries but also linked into a complex web of trading routes across Europe by land and sea. Inevitably the metal had to be paid for and at the time this must have involved imported manufactured goods and perishables.

Britain was, however, also home to expert craftsmen. These included the people who created the magnificent gold and electrum torcs found at Snettisham in Norfolk. These ceremonial necklets consist of thick bands made up from strands of gold or electrum twisted in the manner that a rope is made. Decorative terminals were fitted to each end, sometimes in the form of fantastic animals. It is easy enough to describe these items but it is worth remembering how much time and trouble it must have taken anyone to get to the point where they could make such things. The torcs are clearly evidence for individuals spending years as apprentices to master craftsmen and then being able to produce such pieces themselves. These skills must have been handed down from father to son across generations and there is every possibility that the Snettisham jeweller's hoard of the second century AD was buried by a descendant of one of these Iron Age masters. We have no names for the makers of the torcs but their workmanship bears witness to their lives.

Strabo, a geographer who wrote during Augustus' time, was impressed by the degree of civilization exhibited by the Britons. Nonetheless, he dismissed them as 'simpler and more barbaric' than the Gauls and regarded them as lacking in any agricultural competence, though he was almost certainly referring to more northerly tribes.[3] His famous description of the Britons he had seen in Rome, presumably at a slave market, was written down a few decades later but makes for an interesting observation. The Britons he saw were 'bow-legged', presumably from some sort of nutritional deficiency, but were still tall enough to tower over the Romans by 'as much as half a foot'. Tall or not, the Britons were soon to find that while their chieftains and chariots could make life painful for the Romans they could not stop them.

Nevertheless, there was no cohesive 'British' culture, an illusion created by our contemporary predilection for labelling the Britons collectively as 'Celtic'. There was no sense of Britain as a whole entity. Although people gathered in nucleated communities, these had little resemblance to towns in the way that we or the Romans would understand them. There was no written record or code of law; without a literate tradition, the whole mindset of the Britons was inevitably different. Into this world Caesar ventured. In the long run what followed was a remarkable convergence of traditions from which so many of the personalities in this book emerged. The invasion of 55 BC was a box-office success but simultaneously militarily inconclusive and perfunctory. Caesar's fleet was memorably damaged by a storm and any idea that he would be able to pursue a war in Britain was put to bed when an uprising kicked off in Gaul. The next year he came back, ostensibly to punish the Britons for failing to hand over hostages in the agreed numbers; Cassius Dio, however, claimed that Caesar 'coveted' Britain and would have used any pretext to try again.[4]

Any invasion necessarily involves two groups of people: those engaged in performing the invasion and those on the receiving end. Whichever group wins tends to write the history not only of the invasion but also of what came before and what came next. Julius Caesar's exploits in Britain are a little more ambivalent. In his case it depends on who you read, or rather would read if there was a choice. There is not. There is Caesar's account and nothing else apart from fleeting mentions by other ancient sources. It would take a remarkably dense historian not to appreciate that Caesar's descriptions of his two expeditions to Britain in 55 and 54 BC are selective and distinctly partisan, despite his overbearing efforts to try and compose a version of events that masquerades as objective.

Caesar's invasions of Britain were sideshows in his conquest of Gaul and his political aspirations. In 59 BC the three most ambitious and important members of Rome's ruling senatorial elite, Pompey (the dominant member), Crassus and Caesar, formed an unofficial alliance now known as the First Triumvirate and carved up the Roman world between them. In 58 BC Caesar was given control of Cisalpine Gaul, and then Transalpine Gaul. Along with these provinces came command of a massive army, giving Caesar enormous potential power which made the triumvirate potentially unstable. In 56 BC the agreement was renewed and Caesar's command consequently extended. Being at the head of his army was essential if he was ever to challenge Pompey. The conquest of Gaul lasted from 58 to 51 BC, during which his two inconclusive forays to Britain took place. Sustaining that conquest not only justified his retention of a military command but also allowed Caesar to build up one of the most effective and efficient armies in the ancient world. Britain was neither essential to Caesar's plan nor even of sustained interest to him as an indulgence but it did provide the opportunity to publicize his prowess and titillate the Roman mob.

The Roman adventures across the Channel in the summers of 55 and 54 BC have no archaeological, epigraphic or numismatic manifestation so we are left exclusively with Caesar's account and passing references by other, much later Roman historians such as Tacitus and Cassius Dio. Tacitus tells us practically nothing and Dio provides mostly a précis of Caesar's more expansive account, though he does confirm that the expeditions greatly impressed the people of Rome.[5] No inscriptions, such as the tombstone of a soldier who had participated in the war across the Channel, have survived either, if indeed they ever even existed. In short, without Caesar's description of his exploits in Britain we would know little more than that they had happened. This leaves us slightly disadvantaged when it comes to the experience of participants and witnesses, even by the standards of the time.

However, there are some glimmers in the dark. Marcus Tullius Cicero was one of Rome's greatest orators and lawyers and would meet his end as a result of the vicious partisan politics in the aftermath of Caesar's assassination in 44 BC. A decade earlier, in happier times, he received a letter from his brother Quintus who was on campaign with Caesar in Gaul, and at one point commanding the XIV Legion. The letters of Quintus do not survive but Cicero's excited responses, written at the end of August 54 BC, do.[6] Cicero was fascinated by the terrifying prospect of the vast unending sea the Romans called the Ocean which it is clear Quintus had graphically described to him, along with the coastline. Clearly part of the appeal of being in Caesar's war was the prospect of writing home with tales of high adventure.

So in 54 BC Quintus Tullius Cicero was in Britain with Caesar's army on the second of the two invasions of Britain. As such he stands for thousands of other Romans travelling over the capricious Channel that summer. Cicero looked forward to news of the landscape, local customs and tribes, the battles and of Caesar himself. Further references make it clear that a letter from Britain took, astonishingly, no more than around four to five weeks to reach Rome. Given that a fortnight for a letter to cross some parts of Europe today is still quite possible, this was a remarkable achievement. On 13 September Cicero heard again from Quintus, whose letter had left Britain on 10 August.[7] Incredibly, Quintus seems to have been more concerned with a composition of his own called *Erigona*, presumably based on the myth of Erigone. Erigone was the daughter of Icarius, who was killed by his shepherds to whom Dionysus had given wine in return for Icarius' kindness. Erigone committed suicide when she found her father's body and Dionysus forced all Athenian girls to commit suicide too. This is a striking comment on what almost seems to have been a gentleman's polite summer campaign fighting the Britons and engaging in refined literary pursuits in the evening; it is reminiscent of some of the young officers in the First World War who had abandoned university careers to take part in what they believed would be the noblest and greatest experience of a lifetime. In Quintus' case this literary indulgence was in spite of confronting an agile mobile enemy who used chariots to enter the Roman columns, only to dismount and fight on foot. The charioteers withdrew to wait in the wings in case the British warriors were forced to retreat and needed transport.[8] Quintus is not mentioned by Caesar as being in Britain in his account of the expeditions of 55 and 54 BC even though he pops up several times when Caesar describes events in Gaul. Without the letters we would not know that Quintus had gone to Britain.

We leave Quintus on 1 September 54 BC – the day Caesar wrote to Cicero himself and said he was down on the British coast, but that Quintus was not with him.[9] Subsequent correspondence that autumn showed that Quintus had probably by then returned to Gaul, his British adventure over. Cicero makes no further reference to the island and its inhabitants, his attention more closely focused on the political situation in Rome. Caesar was no less concerned with Rome – the next decade would see him rise to the climax of his power as dictator for life and just as soon meet his end in 44 BC. In the meantime, though, Caesar realized that prosecuting a war in Britain risked losing Gaul and thereby everything he had fought for. He was right; he returned to Gaul in time to head off uprisings in the winter of 54–53 BC and disappeared from British history.

Caesar came because invading Britain was a show-stealing adventure. He had the time, the army and the opportunity to invade the end of the world. He had a pretext in the form of Mandubracius, a member of the Trinovantian tribe who controlled what is now Essex and part of Suffolk. The Trinovantian king, Mandubracius' father, was killed by Cassivellaunus, presumed to have been king of the Catuvellauni, by far and away the most powerful tribe in Britain.

What of the Britons who witnessed the invading army? Needless to say, we have nothing by them and once more we have to turn to Caesar, who painted a vivid picture of British tribal society. In 55 and 54 BC Cassivellaunus had a power base north of the Thames where Hertfordshire is now. What we know in general about Iron Age tribal chieftains is that their personal prestige could rise or fall with the wind. Cassivellaunus appears in Caesar's account described as a ruler whose hegemony lay north of the Thames but whose prestige was so great that other British rulers placed him in charge of their resistance to Caesar's invasions, even though they had previously been fighting him, as

Mandubracius' experience bore witness. This was a dangerous development because it upset the divide-and-rule process that usually worked so well for the Romans.

Cassivellaunus was a pragmatist. He organized defensive installations on the north bank of the Thames to inhibit a Roman crossing but Caesar found out from prisoners what had been prepared and organized a vigorous and sustained assault on the Britons, who promptly (according to Caesar) ran away. Recognizing that this kind of confrontation was not going to work, Cassivellaunus dispersed his men, apart from a key force of crack charioteers. With this mobile force he withdrew but tracked the Roman advance, drawing them deeper and deeper into Britain. His men ordered villagers to withdraw into woodland with their livestock in order to deny the Romans easy pickings of food and sent his chariots to harry the Roman army. Caesar was forced to keep his column tight and only lay waste to land in the immediate vicinity.

Cassivellaunus, however, was hoist by his own petard. The Trinovantes were the weak link in his power structure. They saw their chance and seized it. Still smarting from the death of their king, Mandubracius' father, at the hands of Cassivellaunus they offered to surrender to the Romans. This sort of short-term tactical self-interest would be the Britons' undoing not only now but also in the future. Mandubracius, who was with Caesar, was sent to oversee the capitulation and handing over of hostages and tribute. Cassivellaunus' power structure began to fragment. Various other tribes gave up the fight and surrendered to Caesar, supplying him with vital intelligence about Cassivellaunus' stronghold for good measure. The last gasp was when Cassivellaunus tried to organize several Kentish tribes to attack Caesar's coastal camp; it went disastrously wrong and the Roman garrison fought them off, even managing to capture one of their leaders, a man called Lugotorix.

Cassivellaunus gave up the fight but it would probably be a mistake to assume that he regarded this as a serious setback. He must have known that Caesar could not stay and that a face-saving treaty would allow Caesar to withdraw and claim a fairly meaningless victory, leaving the Britons to regroup. The peace treaty was arranged with the help of Commius, the Gaulish Atrebatic chieftain who for the moment had fought with Caesar.

In reality though, whatever Cassivellaunus' hopes, things had changed forever. Roman interference in tribal politics was a fact of life and the Britons were as responsible for this as the Romans. The fragmentation of the fragile tribal alliance headed by Cassivellaunus was a portent. The years between Caesar's expeditions and the coming of Claudius in 43 form something of an interlude, though this does not mean there was no contact. Far from it. Britain was drawn more and more into the Roman orbit, but this is only really true of the ruling elite in the tribes of the south-east. Their graves and their dynastic coinage show that prestige, power and wealth were becoming manifested increasingly in a Roman format. This was deliberate on the part of both the Romans and the Britons. Under Augustus a concerted policy was adopted to foster independent frontier regimes that were loyal to Rome – the so-called client-king system. This quasi-feudal arrangement meant that Rome was supposed to be able to count on reliable frontier states which acted as buffer zones around the Empire. Augustus proudly recounted those kings who had sought his protection; these included 'Dumnobellaunus and Tincommius, Kings of the Britons'.[10] Such rulers were usually obliged to contribute diplomatic hostages, known as *obsides* (singular *obses*), to Rome. This was preferable to another British war, which Augustus wished to avoid, preferring to settle affairs in Gaul, but which briefly looked like a distinct possibility in 27 and 26 BC.[11]

The coins of Dubnovellaunus, presumably the same man ('Dumnobellaunus') as the one mentioned by Augustus in his *Res Gestae*, are mostly found in Kent, suggesting he was a ruler of the Cantiaci. He would have had been well placed to make contact with the Roman world. Indeed, he would have had no choice. Tincommius now seems actually to have been called Tincomarus on the evidence of coinage. He was a ruler of the Atrebates tribe in central southern England. Apart from the reference by Augustus we only know about this man from his coins but they tell us a lot. He was the son of a ruler called Commius (or Commios), which is explicitly stated on Tincomarus' coins. This is done in Latin, itself a remarkable development which shows that the tribal elite were beginning to adopt Latin for formal statements about their status and lineage. The coins of Commius feature his name but have no similar Latin phrases or terms. He may be the Commius referred to on numerous occasions by Caesar or a son of the same name (too much time is involved for there definitely to be only one Commius). Caesar's Commius finally turned on Caesar and went to war against him, only to be defeated in or around the year 50 BC. At this point he successfully fled to Britain and founded a dynasty there.

Regardless of whether or not Caesar's Commius had fallen out with him, Rome had made its mark. Quite apart from any Latin phrasing on the coins of Tincomarus, there were also other dramatic iconographic changes. The Commius coins still exhibit the abstract 'Celtic' horses of a longer native tradition, with only tenuous concessions to realism. Some of Tincomarus' coins show similar horses but others substitute horses drawn from classical tradition and were clearly derived from Roman coins. Others feature lions, a boy riding on a dolphin, and even a bust of Medusa. They must have been struck from dies created by immigrant craftsmen. Tincomarus was branding himself in the Roman mould and perhaps had already been a diplomatic hostage sent to Rome. The message was one he sent out to his elite and to Augustus – the silver and gold coins involved were not for general circulation and the images would have been incomprehensible to that general population: these were the means of storing wealth and firmly establishing affiliation in the knowledge that Roman patronage was vital in British power politics.

Linking all this in any precise and individual sense to the archaeological record is almost impossible. Even if some of the British tribal elite were adopting some Roman symbols of power, this never included recording their names in any recognizable form on their monuments or graves. The anonymous occupant of a chieftain's grave at Welwyn Garden City in Hertfordshire in Catuvellaunian territory is about the closest we can come to the actual people involved. Dated to the late first century BC the grave goods were the paraphernalia of (presumably) a man of exalted status in the tribe. It may have been the grave of someone whose name we know, but now there is no means at all of confirming it. One possible candidate is Tasciovanus, a prominent ruler of the Catuvellauni in the late first century BC and early first century AD, or a close associate or family member of his. He was cremated and buried with a substantial collection of high-quality native ceramic, bone and metal products, including some made in Gaul. However, his equipage also included five Roman wine amphorae, which were easily the largest components of the assemblage, and a Roman silver cup.[12] The East Leicestershire Hoard, found between 1999 and 2003, included thousands of Iron Age tribal and Roman Republican coins as well as a Roman gilded silver parade helmet.[13] We cannot now know if the Roman goods in these deposits were received as gifts from a Roman merchant in return for access to trade routes into tribal territory, gifts from the Roman government in return for fealty, or were simply purchases made by the deceased or his family from goods offered them through commercial contacts. It does not matter. The Welwyn grave and the East Leicestershire Hoard are a clear reflection of the tribal elite's habits and tastes attested in the scattered Roman literary and epigraphic record: the trappings of a person of importance in late Iron Age tribal society could include prestige goods manufactured in the Roman world used to support a culture which placed great emphasis on feasting and drinking. Their appeal will also have involved several criteria: they were expensive, exclusive, exotic and rare. The ostentatious display of expensive material such as Roman silver cups or wine amphorae was as important as enjoying them; they served to distinguish some of the British elite from the lesser mortals of their tribes. Lesser mortals had to be content with being bound up into a 'body bundle' and deposited at the bottom of a disused storage pit.[14]

The Mycenaean elite, around 1,500 years or more earlier in Greece, were buried with goods that advertised similar exclusivity and there are many other parallels. Ironically, the Roman world itself was less given to that sort of subterranean posthumous ostentation. Instead, the status of a deceased person of quality was commemorated in pompous funerary inscriptions on conspicuous mausolea in a public place that recounted positions held, privileges awarded, and beneficence distributed to the ordinary people. It was not so in tribal Britain and one of the striking contrasts between this late Iron Age culture and the period of Roman rule is the fading out of the chieftain-style grave.

Meanwhile, two other Atrebatic rulers called Eppillus and Verica claimed also to be sons of Commius. Like Tincomarus they issued coins with Latin legends and a hybrid mix of native and classical symbols.

They all issued coins bearing their claimed lineage COM.F or COMM.F (for *Commii Filius*, 'son of Commius'), recalling coins of Augustus which frequently stated CAESAR.DIVI.F, 'son of the deified Caesar'. One remarkable joint issue of Eppillus and Verica even depicted Augustus' birth sign, the Capricorn. Others show that Eppillus claimed to be 'king of Calleva'.

What are we to make of these? We know so little about the details of tribal politics that we cannot be certain if these three men were competing with one another for Roman support, forming and breaking alliances among themselves as circumstances changed, or whether they were cynically playing Rome at its own game and posing as allies for as long as it suited their own purposes. They operated in a system ultimately overseen by a priestly caste known as the Druids who operated in Gaul but are also known to have existed in Britain. The Druids arbitrated over all disputes and determined anything to do with religion. Their power was vested in their ability to condemn any miscreants to exclusion from participation in sacrificial rituals and to mete out ruthless sanctions. If the interpretation of one human body found at Danebury hill-fort in Hampshire is correct, this could include death by mutilation: a young man had had his pelvis cut out of his body, and legs chopped off at the thighs.[15] There is no guarantee that 'Druids' were responsible but the grisly and gratuitous nature of the dismemberment must surely smack of some sort of ritualized procedure, which might also have included punishment.

Just how far the Druids were directing events in late Iron Age tribal Britain after Caesar's invasions we do not know. At any rate, their interference or manipulation of tribal chieftains is evident from the fact that in AD 59 the then governor of Britain, Suetonius Paulinus, felt the need to go and destroy their British headquarters in Anglesey. What is certain is that half a century before that the game was increasingly being played by Rome's rules. This drew the tribal rulers of south-east Britain closer and closer into the Roman net.

Augustus was succeeded by his stepson Tiberius in AD 14. Tiberius' reign was to last twenty-three years but during that time Britain seems to have been of little concern. The tribes of the south-east continued to issue coins that marked their increasing tendency to brand themselves as rulers in a Roman idiom. Tiberius' death in 37 was followed by the elevation of his highly popular young nephew Gaius, known as 'Caligula'. Caligula was the son of the brilliant, but deceased, general Germanicus. He was also descended directly from Augustus. His magnificent lineage was let down by his consummate lack of political or military experience. Well aware of this, Caligula found other ways to experiment with his almost limitless power, but when an opportunity came along to gain the sort of military prestige his predecessors had enjoyed he decided to seize it.

During Caligula's short reign (37–41) a remarkable incident took place. Adminius, a son of Cunobelinus, king of the Catuvellauni who ruled from Camulodunum (Colchester), was banished by his father. He promptly collected up a small entourage and went over to Caligula who was then on campaign in Germany, allowing the emperor to behave as if the whole of Britain had surrendered to him.[16] Appropriately enough, coins of a man called Amminus, who was probably the same person, are distinctly classical in style. Found in Kent, they are probably evidence for a fiefdom he held from his father until they fell out.

The interesting thing about this episode is that it shows how volatile British tribal politics could be and how scuttling off for Roman help was becoming the solution of choice for any British tribal chieftain or would-be chieftain who was smarting from a slight. Cunobelinus was busily aggrandizing himself at the expense of a number of adjacent tribes and had very possibly been able to do this because he had been over-indulged with Roman support. By the 40s Cunobelinus had expanded his control eastwards and evidently taken over the Trinovantes, whose area of control equated roughly to where Essex is now, and requisitioned their capital at Camulodunum for his own. It is easy enough to think of modern parallels where 'client-king' dictators have been the beneficiaries of ill-conceived support from western states that have then had to turn on their erstwhile tame supporters when the latter developed designs above their station. Certainly the coins of Cunobelinus are as 'Roman' as anything produced by the Atrebatic kings, and in some cases more so, even to the extent of producing monarchical-style portrait coins.

Cunobelinus was not to feature in the story of the Roman invasion since by 43 he was dead, but another ruler, Verica of the Atrebates, did.

Based on coin evidence, Verica seems to have been in control of that tribe since around AD 10. Verica was the catalyst for the invasion of Britain. Cassius Dio, who wrote in Greek, called him Berikos and simply tells us that he had been driven out of Britain after an uprising.[17] This man is almost certainly the same individual who appears on coins struck in central southern Britain and who styled himself 'Verica, son of Commius'. Some of these coins were minted bearing the name Calleva, an Atrebatic stronghold which would later become the Roman regional tribal (civitas) capital of Calleva Atrebatum, known to us as Silchester.[18] *Calleva Atrebatum* means something like 'the town in the woods of the Atrebates tribe'.

One of Verica's silver coins depicts him unequivocally in the guise of a Roman emperor, complete with laurel wreath and clearly copied from imperial Roman silver coins issued by Tiberius (14–37) or Caligula (37–41).[19] Reconstructing Iron Age lineages is far from straightforward, though in this case we have some unusual clues. Around a century earlier a Commius 'the Atrebatian' was defeated by Caesar in Gaul and fled to Britain (see above). It is highly unlikely that Verica could really have been his son so either he was simply symbolically claiming descent from Commius or another man of that name had lived in between. The story is complicated by coins naming Tincomarus and Eppillus.[20] Each called himself 'son of Commius', which may be a factual statement or merely a claim to a fabricated lineage.

What seems certain is that the leaders of this tribe had become beguiled by the Roman trappings and templates of status and power. Augustus recorded in his *Res Gestae* that Tincomarus was one of several kings from Britain and other territories who 'had sought refuge' with him 'as suppliants'.[21] This much was apparent from their coins, which featured Latin legends and classicized imagery, including prancing horses, Medusa, and even a sphinx. The archaeological evidence from Calleva of a town-like settlement with a nascent street grid supports this evolving taste for Roman customs.

This tribal position conflicts slightly with Commius running away from Caesar, but perhaps his descendants were a little more pragmatic. Certainly by Augustus' time the system of engaging client kings was well established, creating convenient frontier buffer zones. However, these tribes often proved unreliable and unstable. By the year 43 Verica had fled to Claudius and sought his assistance in what was probably some sort of internal tribal schism involving a coup. We do not know what precisely had happened, but Verica was evidently extremely pragmatic, and had decided to cash in on his loyalty to Rome. Self-interest was all. The tribal leaders in Britain passed their lives engaged in perpetual petty territorial disputes, wantonly spending the marginal produce of their largely subsistence agricultural communities on importing Roman luxury goods for their own consumption and financing their endless internecine wars. There seems to have been little sense of collective responsibility or even consciousness in the face of the Roman threat. It was a fatal weakness that would be their undoing.

As a result, tribal territorial zones fluctuated in haphazard and unpredictable ways that are impossible to unravel in detail from either archaeology or recorded history. Only the scattered evidence of tribal coinage can give us a hint and even that is demonstrably unreliable in many respects. In any case, rivalry within the Atrebates tribe may have been the problem, or the ambitions of Verica's Catuvellaunian neighbours to the east. Whatever the truth, the Romans had their pretext to invade and tribal politics were about to change forever.

CHAPTER TWO

QUISLINGS AND REBELS, AD 41–61

The men and women who survive in the record of Roman Britain in its first two decades are in the main the ordinary soldiers, cavalry troopers and officers of the imperial Roman army. To this day Marcus Favonius Facilis, a centurion with the XX Legion, stares out from his tombstone effigy found at Colchester where the legion was based between 43 and 47. His is the first face of Roman Britain to survive. But other, vastly more colourful characters, made grander entrances, of whom Caratacus and Boudica are by far and away the best known.

To the Britons of the south-east the influx of Roman soldiers must have been the most conspicuous and challenging part of the invasion of 43. In one sense the Roman army offered a sensational opportunity for a British warrior to flex his muscles and give the ancient world's greatest superpower an exasperating challenge. The potential for tribal prestige in that context was immense. The coming of Rome also provided a decisive opportunity for a tribal leader to annihilate his or her local enemies. The first few years of the Roman era in Britain are filled with tales of evanescent tribal leaders, dramatic personalities who flit across the stage only to disappear, publicized by the Romans who were tantalized, bewildered and titillated by these powerful but unpredictable characters.

Caratacus was one of the sons of Cunobelinus, the king of the Catuvellauni who had died in or around 41. The family had already exhibited dysfunctional tendencies. Of his two other brothers, Adminius had been exiled before 41. We do not know why but it may well have been for excessive obsequiousness to the Romans. Caratacus and his other brother, Togodumnus, fought the Romans as soon as they arrived. They did not do well, but while Togodumnus was soon killed in the Roman war Caratacus proceeded to have a remarkable career by giving the Romans a monumental runaround.

Whereas Caratacus was a fully fledged warrior in 41, Boudica was probably no more than a teenager. Her place on centre stage would not come for another seventeen years. In 41, Marcus Favonius Facilis was a career soldier as yet unaware that his future and his death lay in Britannia. He was far from alone in that prospect. Neither he nor Boudica would survive the next two turbulent decades. Meanwhile the year 41 was a turning point in more ways than one. The murder in Rome of Caligula that year brought to an end a curiously memorable reign in which a critical weakness of the Roman Empire was exposed: the phenomenal amount of real power enjoyed by the emperors was simply too much for someone who lacked either the political or military experience to handle the position. Caligula's abortive efforts to plan an invasion of Britain scarcely helped since abandoning the scheme merely advertised the caprices of his personality further.

The accession of Claudius in 41 brought the most improbable candidate to power. The decisions Claudius made were based on his own political requirements but they would have a staggering impact on the thousands of Romans who were shipped to Britain, and the hundreds of thousands of Britons and their descendants whose lives were reshaped by the invasion. Claudius had never sought power and no one, least of all himself, had ever considered him a prospect. Marginalized by his physical handicaps and hopelessly overshadowed by the celebrated military reputation of his long-dead brother Germanicus, Claudius was nevertheless the only Julio-Claudian candidate available to a Praetorian Guard that faced potential disbandment without an emperor. Claudius had a considerable pedigree, being able to trace his descent from Livia, the wife of Augustus, by her first marriage, and Octavia, Augustus' sister, by her marriage to Mark Antony. He also had the principal virtue of being both alive and an adult male, a qualification which the rest of the surviving imperial royal family lacked. In short, the Praetorian Guard had no choice if they wished to remain employed. Neither had Claudius. Had he said no, he would almost certainly have been killed by any other opportunist who saw a chance for total power and bought the army's flexible loyalty.

Claudius might have been unwilling but in certain respects he was more than equal to his new job. He saw that matching or exceeding the achievements of his exalted predecessors might be the means by which he could assert himself over the Praetorian Guard, impress the mob and consolidate his position. One of the projects he commissioned was the new port at Ostia, where the Tiber was silting up and confounding the grain ship crews as they tried to moor out at sea for lighters to carry off the cargo. Both Caesar and Augustus had failed to deal with the problem. The other project was the invasion of Britain, which Caesar had left unfinished and which Augustus had not touched.

There is no real mystery behind that fateful decision. Claudius needed to show he was made of the same mettle as Germanicus. He needed the publicity of a military triumph. Caligula's aborted invasion meant that the plans and military resources were on hand. Since Britain is an island, a disaster would avoid compromising Roman troops on the continent and thereby destabilizing the Empire. In short, it was a well-calculated risk. It probably did not need a pretext but one was provided anyway, in the obliging form of Verica of the Atrebates. Verica's role in the drama of Roman Britain was to provide Claudius with a pretext for invasion. Verica may only have been interested in negotiating a local intervention. If so, he miscalculated because the result was ultimately the gradual neutralization of all tribal power in most of Britain. History is littered with episodes like this: isolated, petty local feuds that lead to events of epic international significance. Verica's mission to Claudius was a truly decisive one in British history. The other way of interpreting this is asking if Verica was simply a stooge, someone instructed by Claudius to pose as a legitimate monarch who had been toppled by an 'illegal' insurrection. Whoever's agenda Verica was trying to serve, he disappears from the record as soon as he appears. We know nothing about his part in the invasion, even if he had one. He may have stayed in Rome or returned triumphantly in Claudius' train in the late summer of

43 to be reinstalled on his throne and stare smugly at his thwarted rivals while they were carried off in chains. What became of his dynasty we will never know apart from a possible link with Togidubnus, who was to play a more important role in the decades to come.

The invasion itself was led by Aulus Plautius. Plautius came from a family whose members had played the right cards in the reign of Augustus. In AD 9 Claudius, then eighteen, was married to Plautia Urgulanilla, the granddaughter of Urgulania, the close friend of Augustus' wife Livia; though Claudius later divorced her for 'scandalous lewdness and suspicion of murder'.[1] The Plautii had other political and familial connections to Claudius, which inevitably meant that Aulus Plautius was drawn to the emperor's attention. He had some of the right experience, having put down a slave rebellion in Italy under Tiberius and served in some official leadership capacity in the province of Illyricum.[2] He showed appropriate deference to Claudius in that late summer of 43, calling a halt to the advance and allowing the emperor to lead the triumphant march on Camulodunum, then the capital of the Catuvellauni. For his successful leadership Plautius was rewarded with an ovation in Rome that year.

The minor players in the dramatic events of the invasion were, inevitably, soldiers. The Roman army played an enormously important role in everyday life. Soldiers were the state's main tools. They acted as an imperial bodyguard, police force, road and bridge builders, engineers, architects and customs officials, as well as fighting wars, garrisoning frontiers and building fortifications. In the frontier provinces like Britain they were the main driving force of Romanization, not least because as a community soldiers were far more likely to be literate than the general population, which means that they also dominate the accessible record in the form of inscriptions. They were unified by their common allegiance to the emperor but their loyalty was first and foremost to their individual units and commanders. They were 'Roman' but they came from all over the Empire and as a result they injected a significant amount of new blood into Britain. In their wake came traders, wives, mistresses and camp followers of all descriptions. Their combined influence on the process of turning Britain into a Roman province was immeasurably greater than any other factor and consequently they monopolize the record.

Perhaps one of these men was responsible for the hoard of gold coins buried at Bredgar near Sittingbourne in Kent. Found in 1957, the hoard consisted of thirty-seven gold aurei dating from Julius Caesar to issues of Claudius made in AD 41–2.[3] There was no trace of a pot or any other kind of container and instead the coins were found lying stacked together as if they had been rolled up in a piece of cloth. Speculating about the purpose, and abandonment, of any kind of coin hoard is an indulgence at best and futile at worst but in this instance the location, type and date of the coins unavoidably lead one to wonder if the owner was a member of the Claudian army. It is easy to imagine how soldiers advancing along northern Kent and anticipating the battle that did take place against Caratacus and Togodumnus in those first few days, probably on the Medway, might have taken care of their valuables by burying them. However, it is hard to see how they could have had very much confidence about recovering them while on campaign in a fast-moving war. The value was enormous, equivalent to more than four years' worth of a legionary's pay, which alone makes it more likely this hoard belonged to a senior centurion, or an officer. In fact, Claudius struck so little gold and silver after AD 42 that technically speaking the hoard could have been buried easily as late as the end of his reign in 54. But in this case the value of the coins and the location do make for a reasonable case that one soldier, whose destiny was to get no further in the invasion, had decided to bury his savings.

It has long been known that by the time of the Boudican Revolt in the year 60 the garrison of Britain included the II, IX, XIV and XX Legions and an unknown number of auxiliary troops. But there were other units, too, whose members took part in that remarkable war and afterwards went home or were sent to other places. Marcus Vettius Valens was a member of the VIII Cohort of the Praetorian Guard in 43. He went on to have a distinguished career and even rose to the position of procurator of the province of Lusitania. By 66 he was retired and had returned to Italy, being buried at Rimini, which was perhaps his hometown. Vettius Valens is reminiscent of members of the British army whose early career covered the Second World War and went on to live through other conflicts and jobs but who must always have looked back on the remarkable fact that as young men they took part in one of the great epic adventures of the twentieth century. Vettius Valens' tombstone records the fact that he was decorated in the British war, receiving necklets, armlets and medals as his reward – and doubtless also the entitlement to tell his tales for the rest of his days.[4] He was not alone. Gaius Gavius, tribune of the XII Praetorian Cohort, was commemorated by the town councillors at Turin for his part in the British war and the decorations he received.

Others were not so lucky. Marcus Favonius Facilis appears in sculptured form on his tombstone at Colchester. He was probably Italian and served with the XX Legion where he had risen to the position of centurion. All this, and the information that he belonged to the Pollian voting tribe, confirms that Facilis was a Roman citizen. The legions that arrived in 43 were soon dispersed. The II Legion headed into the south Midlands and south-west,[5] the XIV across the Midlands, and the IX went north. For around four years the XX stayed at Colchester where their legionary fortress controlled the former Catuvellaunian stronghold of Camulodunum, which became its fortress. In or around 47 the XX was ordered to hand over the fortress to veterans to establish a colony, and head for the frontier in the west. An unpleasant and forbidding reminder of the early stages of a war of conquest that would last decades, Colchester at this time sported trophies in the form of human heads along its ramparts.

At some point during this time, or perhaps within a decade or so later, Favonius Facilis met his end. There is no suggestion that his death was violent and the tombstone's text tells us nothing about his age, though as a centurion he must have been in his middle years. In some respects the tombstone is entirely conventional for the Roman army but it holds a truly special place in British history. His face is the face of Rome and the very fact that he was depicted in 'realistic' human form makes him a novelty and, perhaps to the Britons, an incomprehensible one. His tombstone has enormous symbolic significance: it represents one of the first instances of classicized sculpture in Britain. This was an entirely alien concept in a place where realistic representations of human beings simply did not, so far as we know, exist other than in occasional depictions on the tribal dynastic coinage that had been influenced by Roman designs. Facilis' funerary monument is thus the first 'realistic' representation of an individual human being in British history.

Modern anthropological studies have shown that cultures which have no tradition of representing the human, or indeed any living form in two-dimensional or sculptural form can find it almost impossible to recognize such depictions as individuals, or even sometimes struggle to see them as generically human.[6] His *cognomen* Facilis means 'easily done'. He may well have inherited it from his father or an earlier forbear and its meaning includes many possibilities. Among those might be the possibility that he or an ancestor was born with ease. Favonius, his family name, was a familiar enough one in the Roman world but it was also applied to the west wind, commemorated by Horace as an optimistic sign of the coming of spring.[7] Although we do not know the details of his career, it is likely that he had participated in the invasion proper and witnessed Claudius' arrival at Colchester. He was well enough off not only to have had his own slaves but also to have freed them and they honoured their obligations to their former master by erecting his tombstone. He was one of the first of the Romans to be buried in Britain, at least that we know of, and his burial was thus a corner of a foreign field which would forever now be Roman.[8] Unusually, the tombstone was found more or less where it was originally erected; nearby was a lead container with cremated bones which must be the mortal remains of Facilis.

A recent revenant of this era is Lucius Valerius Geminus, sometime member of the II Legion Augusta. Like Facilis he too was a member of the Pollian voting tribe, and in his case probably came from north-western Italy. Valerius Geminus died at fifty, by which time he was already a veteran though possibly had not been retired for very long. His tombstone was found at Alchester, where an extremely early fort was built in the mid–40s. The II Legion was at Exeter a little over a decade later but it now seems possible that Alchester was at least one of its early bases, though apart from the tombstone there is no other evidence to substantiate this. Valerius Geminus may have retired while the legion was still there, choosing to live nearby in a civilian settlement outside the fort near his old friends, only to die and be buried there too. Or, he may have died at a later date, requesting in his will that he was buried at his old base. Either way it is very likely that he participated in the invasion as a member of the II Legion.[9]

Perhaps Valerius Geminus had lived in fear of the II Legion's camp prefect Publius Anicius Maximus. A career soldier who rose to the centurionate in the XII Legion he was transferred to the II Legion as *praefectus castrorum*, the apogee of a centurion's career and marking out the fact that he was not only third in command in the legion, but also of equestrian status.[10] As camp prefect he could be left in sole command of the legion if the senatorial legate (commanding officer) and his second, the senatorial tribune, were away. The inscription that records the career of Anicius Maximus states that he had been decorated for his part in the *bellum Britannicum* ('British War') before proceeding to become prefect of the army in Egypt.[11] He must have dined out on tales of his experiences in the wild and unknown areas of south-western Britain.

Many of the most interesting soldiers in early Roman Britain belonged to the auxiliary units. These were raised in provinces around the Empire and provided a career route into being a Roman citizen. Local warriors hired to fight for, say, the Fourth Cohort of Gauls would find themselves stationed elsewhere in the Roman world to avoid any chance that their loyalties to their homes might come into conflict with the state's needs. After twenty-five years such men could hope to receive an honourable discharge and at that point become Roman citizens, thus enfranchising their descendants too. The ethnicity of each of these units became absorbed into the provinces where they were stationed, since the men would often find partners among the womenfolk in the vicinity of their forts, with their sons sometimes enlisting with their fathers' units in due course. In time the original ethnic identity of the units became little more than a nominal title. Moreover, in some cases a man might enlist with an ethnic unit but have no connection at all with the province from which the unit had originally come, as in the case of Sextus Valerius Genialis (see below).

The legionary Favonius Facilis is often spoken of today in the same breath as the Thracian trooper Longinus Sdapeze, son of Matygus, whose tombstone was found nearby.[12] Whereas Facilis' tombstone is passive, civilized, and with the deceased depicted in almost ghostly form, Longinus' tombstone is far more dynamic, violent and barbaric. We have in Longinus our first instance of Rome's multicultural impact on Britain. Longinus was a Thracian from Sardica in south-eastern

Europe (approximately equivalent to southern Bulgaria), who served with the First Cavalry Wing of Thracians. Longinus turns to face us from the saddle as he tramples an enemy under hoof. The representation is stereotypical for a Roman auxiliary cavalry trooper but no less ironic for all that. Not so long before, it would have been a Thracian who was being trampled by a Roman. Now we have a Romanized Thracian who presents himself to us in almost cinematic form as a proud member of the Roman armed forces. Longinus seems to have signed up at around the age of twenty-five, attracted no doubt by the prospect of full citizenship after twenty-five years of service. He never made it. He died at forty after no more than fifteen years in the saddle on Rome's behalf, with the last part of his career spent in Britain.[13] We know that the XX Legion was moved west around 47 and its accompanying auxiliaries presumably went with it, leaving the graves of their deceased comrades behind.

Another of these eyewitnesses to the tumultuous events of 43 must have been the Spaniard Lucius Vitellius Tancinus, a trooper with the Cavalry Wing of Vettones, a unit from Spain. Vitellius Tancinus died at or near Bath on the Fosse Way when he was forty-six after twenty-six years' service, robbed of the chance to enjoy retirement and citizenship.[14] In his case he had already earned this privilege when the whole unit was made Roman citizens. The award was probably made for feats in the invasion war. By the time Tancinus died the Roman army had laid out and constructed a grand transprovince road between Lincoln and Exeter. Exeter was an early legionary base but Lincoln did not become one until after 60.

Perhaps the most interesting of all these early soldiers is Sextus Valerius Genialis, another Thracian auxiliary trooper but this time with a difference. He is similarly depicted in stock heroic mode trampling an enemy under hoof. His tombstone was found at Cirencester, then a fort deep in the heart of the newly conquered part of lowland Britain, and probably belongs to some point in the late 40s or 50s. His unit was apparently the same as the one Longinus served in – perhaps the two men had known each other. What makes Genialis different is that not only was he a Roman citizen, or at least posed as one, but he was also not a Thracian. He is explicitly stated to have been a member of the Frisiavones from the lower Rhine. This helps us enormously for it reminds us not to be too literal about these auxiliary units whose provincial regional labels were probably in many cases no more than nominal or historical, with recruits being picked up along the way as the units were moved about the Empire. Had Genialis' tombstone omitted this crucial piece of information we might very well have concluded that he was another ethnic Thracian. He also sports a relatively banal and innocuous Roman name which on its own tells us nothing about his origins. The most likely explanation is that he joined the Thracians when they were stationed in Lower Germany just before coming to Britain. He probably therefore witnessed the invasion first-hand, surviving to clock up twenty years on the payroll before dying.

It was men like these whom Caratacus and Togodumnus faced in the late summer of 43, fighting for their lives, their royal lineages, their lands and their birthright. Both were defeated, apparently somewhere in Kent, perhaps around the same time as the Bredgar hoarder was busy wrapping up and burying his savings. Togodumnus was killed at some early point in the fighting, leaving the Britons who were most inclined to resist the invasion to coalesce around Caratacus. In some respects the anti-Roman position adopted by Caratacus is odd. Coins bearing his name show Hercules on one side and a distinctly Roman-looking eagle on the other, reflecting a tradition already established by Cunobelinus.

What provoked Caratacus to carry on the fight must have been in part based on the knowledge that some of the tribes that had once been Catuvellaunian vassals were beginning actively to side with the Romans. In short he had no choice apart from fighting other than to surrender and become a lickspittle himself. In British tribal politics, transient loyalties were easily bought (and betrayed) by the Romans. If it is true that Verica represented a faction among the Atrebates who had thought Roman support against the Catuvellauni would help their cause, then the notion that the Romans were exclusively villains and the Britons exclusively victims is exposed for the nonsense it is. All parties were trying to play the situation to their own advantage.

Caratacus was smart enough to see that for the moment at least his cause in the south-east was lost. Perhaps he simply could not count on enough support, or perhaps he could not count on not being betrayed by a faction in his own tribe. He removed himself to south Wales, where his prestige was unconditionally admired. The Silures, a virulently anti-Roman tribe, accepted his leadership and followed him against the new Roman governor Ostorius Scapula who arrived in 47. The war was not easy but Scapula defeated the Britons; Caratacus fled and ran straight into the hands of a quisling in the form of Cartimandua, queen of the Brigantes, the tribe occupying what is now northern England. She calculated that her best prospect lay in handing him over to the Romans and so she did.

The Cartimandua story is one of the most intriguing in the annals of the tribal chiefs of the Britons, not least because of the manner in which it illustrates the self-destructive power politics of endless infighting. The Britons, as Tacitus so memorably observed, were inclined to fight as individual tribes rather than collectively and were easily overcome as a result.[15] Cartimandua does not seem to have been coerced into surrendering Caratacus; instead the story has more in common with how Pompey was executed in Egypt, where he had fled after the Battle of Pharsalus in 48 BC. The execution was on the orders of the pharaoh Ptolemy XIII in the belief that this would please Caesar, or at least make him more likely to return to Rome once he had been presented with Pompey's embalmed head. Cartimandua doubtless calculated that an investment of this kind would pay dividends in the future, as indeed it did. Some seventeen years later in around 68 the Brigantes split between supporters of the queen and those of her husband, Venutius. The story appears to be that Cartimandua had taken up with her husband's aide, Vellocatus, and pushed out Venutius. The tribal war that followed led to the Romans rescuing Cartimandua, at which point she evaporates from the record, presumably ending her days in some sort of Roman bolt-hole in the south.[16]

Meanwhile, back in the year 51, Caratacus had sustained his resistance for nine years, which is in any sense a remarkable record. One wonders whether his journey to Cartimandua was a genuine miscalculation or a deliberate attempt to give up the fight. He was taken to Rome, where his pride and dignity allowed Claudius to pardon him and release his family. It is at this stage a matter of interest that they not only paid homage to Claudius but also to his then wife, Agrippina the Younger, sister of Caligula. Tacitus regarded this as evidence of Agrippina's unprecedented power and influence as a Roman woman, which he interpreted as further evidence of how the days of the emperors marked an era of decadence and decline. Agrippina was playing a dangerous game as she elevated her profile to one of incongruous equality with Claudius. Tacitus, of course, wrote in the full knowledge that Agrippina remained in control when her son Nero succeeded Claudius in 54. In the Roman system there was literally no precedent for such a role or even a formal office for a woman to occupy; women had no political status. But to the Britons Agrippina's role as a co-ruler or even ruler in her own right would have seemed entirely comprehensible. Therefore the other way of interpreting the respect Caratacus and his family showed Agrippina was that as Britons they came from a society where women were able to rise not only to high status but also to even higher status than some men, epitomized by Cartimandua and Boudica. In the meantime Claudius pardoned Caratacus out of respect for his dignified speech in which Caratacus observed that his sustained resistance had enhanced Roman glory once he was finally defeated. His reward was also to be pensioned off, but then he disappeared from the story.[17] However, his speech, albeit in Tacitus' words, is a unique record of a Briton not only abroad but also addressing an emperor at the centre of the Roman world.

The Boudican War has remained without question the most emotive and memorable episode in the history of Roman Britain, told and retold both in books and on television. The warrior queen Boudica is the one person in that period whom almost everyone has heard of, regardless of how inaccurately or inappropriately. This sounds reassuring but for the fact that we really have no reliable knowledge about her at all. The Boudican War comes down to us exclusively through two Roman historians: Tacitus and Dio. Neither had seen her and nor had they been to Britain. Moreover, in neither case do we have the slightest hint of their sources of information. Cassius Dio lived around 150 years after her death. Tacitus lived closer to the time and may even have been born in her lifetime, which means that he could have known men who had fought in that war. But even they had probably never seen Boudica unless they had been able to make her out across the battlefield. Suetonius makes only a fleeting reference to the debacle and no mention of Boudica at all. Given her colourful prominence in other accounts, this omission is perhaps more striking than at first it appears, especially as he also lived close enough to the time to have known aged veterans of the war.

Tacitus and Dio were senators. Both had a cynical view of the emperors who, they believed, had steadily appropriated the birthright of the Roman elite through a systematic erosion of senatorial privileges. They also exulted in evidence that some of the emperors had been susceptible to the machinations of imperial women. Livia, the wife of Augustus, was depicted as a scheming matriarch and arch manipulator determined to make sure her son by her first marriage, Tiberius, succeeded Augustus, as indeed he did in the absence of any other living heir by AD 14. Claudius was a particular target because of his susceptibility to women and his outright public humiliation at being cuckolded by his third wife, Messalina. Messalina had indulged herself not only by a bigamous marriage but had also participated in a competition to outdo Rome's most 'productive' prostitute. Claudius had next married his niece Agrippina whom we have already met.

Both Tacitus and Cassius Dio wrote about Boudica with the knowledge of how Nero's final years from 64 to 68 had seen the Roman world ruled by an odious, narcissistic, murderous and uncontrollable maniac who exhibited none of the personal qualities deemed desirable in any Roman man and certainly not someone of the senatorial class. He had already had his mother, Agrippina, murdered in 59, a move that opened the way for his descent into the abyss. Nero typified the epigonistic decline of the Julio-Claudian line in the eyes of moralizing Roman historians. Nero's behaviour, including debasing himself by appearing in the theatre (a profession normally barred even from voting), was in their eyes the nadir of decadence. In the context of their stories nothing suited their purpose better than a character that could be depicted as a counterpoise; in short, Boudica was a woman who exhibited all the attributes they would have preferred in a Roman emperor.

It is precisely this agenda that complicates our understanding of Boudica. How much is she a Roman construct, and how much is the truth? Even her name conveniently means 'Victoria'. We can never answer that but we have to recognize that she is at best a literary character made up of some elements of truth and other mythologized features that converted her into a box-office turn rather in the manner that William Wallace, the Scottish independence warrior, has been treated since his death in 1305. In the speech attributed to her by Tacitus in the final battle, Boudica is presented as a woman of the people, a victim of Roman oppression like all the others in her army. In that sense the Boudica of Tacitus and Dio outgrew her own place in history and was transformed into a timeless female heroine who embodies a panoply of other British Amazons from Elizabeth I to Christabel Pankhurst.

Boudica's age is unknown but she had two daughters who were old enough to be raped by Roman troops in the year 60, so she was probably somewhere between twenty-five and thirty-five. This means that at least half of her life had been spent during the time of the Roman occupation. Although she is described as the wife of Prasutagus, client king of the Iceni, it is unlikely that she was his only one, though of her kin and origins we know nothing at all. In the world of tribal chieftains her apparent lack of a son would hardly have been an advantage, regardless of the fact that women were able to take on positions of influential and powerful leadership.

The story of the Boudican Revolt has been recounted so many times there is no need to repeat it here in great detail. Prasutagus failed to understand the duplicity of the Romans who occupied Britain. This does not mean the Roman system was universally evil – it patently was not, but history is replete with tales of the utter barbarity of occupying forces of all kinds. Men (and women) sometimes seem to have a special ability to behave with appalling cruelty when outside the immediate confines and regulating influences of their home cultures. The Iceni had not taken kindly to the arrival of the Romans but by 59 Prasutagus had decided that he had to come to some sort of accommodation. His plan to leave half his kingdom to the Romans and thereby ensure the security of the remaining half foundered on the greed of the procurator Catus Decianus and the garrison in the area. Their decision on the death of Prasutagus to carpetbag Icenian territory, flog Boudica and rape her daughters changed everything.

What is more significant is that a small local rising rapidly snowballed into an international crisis that quite literally compromised not only the nascent province of Britannia but also the credibility of the whole Roman state. The obvious question here must be whether the personality of Boudica was the main catalyst in that or whether a more general long-term backdrop of grievances was responsible. The answer is probably both. The October Revolution of 1917 in Russia grew out of a series of cumulative discontents but took the galvanizing catalysts of Lenin and Trotsky to give it form and direction even though the revolution had really already started of its own accord. Boudica must have known that she had the potential to whip up a firestorm. The Trinovantes had had enough by 60 too. Already crushed and humiliated by the warmongering Catuvellauni under Cunobelinus before the Roman invasion, they simply progressed after 43 to finding themselves under the heel of the Romans. The establishment of Camulodunum (Colchester) as a Roman military colony led to the confiscation of tribal lands which were then granted to the retired legionaries. The Trinovantes were also confronted by the Romans' predilection to act as loan sharks. Encouraged, or forced, to Romanize themselves and participate in all sorts of acts of compulsory allegiance, including the cult of the deified Claudius at the new temple in Camulodunum, they soon found that this cost money. The Romans, such as Nero's tutor Seneca, were only too happy to loan them the necessary funds but no doubt by 60 were beginning to doubt the good sense of lending large amounts of cash to unreliable and barely civilized provincial barbarians. The loans were called in but the Britons could not pay them back. Faced with the prospect of ruinous confiscations or outright rebellion, the Trinovantes chose the latter.

Into this came the volatile character of Boudica but what we cannot know is whether she chose to lead the rebellion because she already knew that the Trinovantes were in meltdown or whether it was a lucky coincidence. Moreover, she can hardly have failed to know, or at any rate soon find out, that the governor Suetonius Paulinus was at that very moment busily wiping out the Druids in Mona (Anglesey). Blamed for fomenting opposition to the Roman occupation, the Druids were an elitist sect of priests given to human sacrifice whose overwhelming prestige invested in them the only unifying power the Britons had. In this context it is perhaps easier to see Boudica herself initially as almost a sideshow to a rebellion that might very well have broken out anyway when word arrived from the Druids about what was going on in Anglesey.

Boudica's role was to give the diffuse rebellion a focus and a figurehead, at least in the story told by the Roman historians. In the idiom of their historical writing it was as essential to build their tale around the juxtaposition of key personalities as it is for the screenwriters of our own time. Although it goes unsaid by either Tacitus or Dio, the fact remains that the Iceni may also have had in mind the prospect of fighting any of the other British tribes that had already capitulated to the Romans. Claudius, after all, explicitly acknowledged on a triumphal arch in Rome that eleven such British rulers had done so. In that respect the Icenian and Trinovantian rising of the year 60 may have been no more than a variation, albeit an almost unbelievably brutal one, on the intertribal warfare that had characterized Britain before 42.

In the end, though, Boudica had no workable plan and she had nothing obvious to offer the rebels beyond chaos, destruction and, ultimately, hunger since nothing was done to plan for the harvest. If she had won she would have been presented with thousands of starving followers and almost certainly fomented a destructive civil war in Britain, fighting off the tribes who had thrown in their lot with the Romans. In a real sense she was a dinosaur. The unfortunate fact was that too many of the Britons had either resigned themselves to the Roman occupation or, like Togidubnus (see below), taken advantage of it. The unavoidable fact is that the collapse of the rebellion, when it came, was total. The reality is that people join rebellions for many different reasons and, if Tacitus can be believed, many of the Boudican hordes had encumbered themselves with too much loot, which presumably had been their main focus rather than any political ideals. When the Boudican rebels finally met Suetonius Paulinus with the XIV and part of the XX Legions somewhere in the Midlands, they allowed him to choose the spot. Their tactics were chaotic and compromised by their numbers, and the presence of their family followers and baggage train. The Roman tactics were typically measured and disciplined. Boudica in the end showed that she lacked any of the practical skills necessary to lead an army.

Boudica was said by Tacitus to have poisoned herself. In Dio's account she grew ill and died. The fact that these accounts are both specific but incompatible shows how troublesome it is to take too seriously the precise references to Boudica's character and appearance, the latter appearing only in Dio, as well as her role in the rebellion. Perhaps it does not matter. Like all the best literary constructs, the personality of Boudica will remain just that – a creation of two Roman historians who saw in her a device that served their own purposes. It made no difference in the end.

There is one postscript to this devastating episode. The II Legion, based at Exeter during the revolt, seems to have been in an interregnum at this stage. Neither the legionary commander nor his senatorial tribune second was with the legion. Instead it was under the command of Poenius Postumus, the camp prefect. We do not know when he succeeded Anicius Maximus, whom we met earlier, but like his predecessor he will have been a career soldier who rose through the centurionate to one of the most distinguished positions in the Roman army. He may well have participated in the invasion seventeen years before, though it is equally possible that he was promoted to the post from a legion based elsewhere in the Empire. His promotion to camp prefect, whenever it came and however it was earned, was a fateful moment. Suetonius Paulinus had sent word to the II Legion to join him. The IX Legion had been devastated by an encounter with the rebels early in the war and was effectively knocked out. The II Legion's participation was essential but Poenius Postumus refused to join the governor. His decision is not difficult to understand. Had he been right, he would have been celebrated as a hero, the saviour of the II Legion, the only British-based legion to escape the Boudican War. He may well have believed the province was lost already, but by keeping the II Legion in its fortress he condemned it, and himself, to ignominy once Boudica's army was beaten. He had no option but to commit suicide. The II Legion was denied the battle honours given to the XIV and XX and Poenius Postumus was immortalized as a coward.

The XIV and XX Legions emerged covered with glory, being awarded the names *Martia Victrix* ('warlike and glorious') and *Valeria Victrix* ('powerful and victorious') respectively. We might spare a thought for Marcus Petronius, an Italian from Vicenza and a standard-bearer with the XIV Legion, who had served for eighteen years when he died some time between about 50 and 65.[18] His tombstone, found at the legion's base at Wroxeter, lacks the crucial *Martia Victrix* titles so he probably expired in the 50s and was cheated of the chance to fight in the legion's greatest hour. However, he had perhaps already seen enough of war since his service probably began before 43, which means he must have seen almost continuous fighting in Britain since the invasion.

Boudica illustrated the downside to the client-king system. But it could work well (depending on your point of view). The Romans preferred to rule through men like Togidubnus. If controlling Cartimandua and Boudica was like trying to herd wildcats, Togidubnus was like nurturing a docile puppy. This curious individual is known only to us from a reference in Tacitus and an inscription found in Chichester.[19] Tacitus says in the *Agricola* that 'he remained completely loyal down to our own times', or at least that is how it is usually translated and much ink has been expended on speculating about that passage's precise meaning. Togidubnus was thus a client king, essentially a tame local ruler who reigned under Rome's supervision. Tacitus says that 'certain states' (*quaedam civitates*) were given to Togidubnus; evidently, therefore, he ruled over more than one tribal area under Roman supervision. The *Agricola* was composed in around the mid–90s which means that Togidubnus must have been fairly old if he had survived to that point and still been of an age to be useful to the Romans in the 40s and early 50s. This is unnecessarily complicated. The key phrase is *nostram usque memoriam*, which more accurately means 'continuously [to] our period of recollection' – this is not quite the same as saying that he was still alive in the 90s. It is perhaps better read in colloquial English as meaning that his loyalty had lasted into 'living memory'. Juba II, client king of Mauretania in North Africa, ruled from 25 BC to AD 23, a period of around forty-eight years. He was only around twenty when he was made king of Mauretania. If we speculate that Togidubnus was in a similar situation, then he was perhaps around twenty in 44. If he lived as long as Juba another forty-eight years takes him to the year 92, well within a period that Tacitus would have referred to as one that he recalled. Since this is an entirely plausible scenario there is no need to refute it out of hand because there is no more evidence either way. It is also worth noting that Juba II is known to have been a diplomatic hostage, an *obses*; it is therefore possible that Togidubnus had been one, too, prior to his installation as king in Britain.[20]

Unlike Caratacus, we have little idea of Togidubnus' personality. He is presented to us by Tacitus as a pro-Roman puppet, which he probably was, and appears on the Chichester inscription in much the same light, called 'great king in Britain' and bearing the forenames Tiberius Claudius. These suggest that he was made a Roman citizen under Claudius. An obvious parallel scenario is Judaea where Agrippa I ruled. He was granted the kingdom of Judaea by Claudius but died in 44, whereupon Claudius annexed the kingdom, fearing a Jewish nationalist revival. Agrippa I's brother Herod was given the subsidiary kingdom of Chalcis in 41 and on his death in 48 Agrippa's son, Agrippa II, was given Chalcis and subsequently additional territories by Claudius. Until 48, Agrippa II had lived at Claudius' court (as his father had done a generation before) and had clearly been cultivated as a Roman ally, which indeed he proved to be until his death around the year 95, even issuing coins with the legend *Agrippa Philocaisaros*, 'Agrippa, Caesar-beloved'.[21] His longevity in this respect only goes to show further that the idea that Togidubnus remained actively loyal until a time Tacitus could recall is completely plausible.

Tacitus called him 'King Cogidumnus' or 'King Togidumnus', the latter having 'equal textual authority'; in any case 'Tog-' is far more plausible as a native name than 'Cog-'.[22] As so often it is hard to be definitive because the Chichester inscription is damaged at the exact points that would have specified both the first part of his name and his title. Togidubnus gave permission for a temple to Neptune and Minerva 'for the welfare of the [imperial] divine house' to be erected in Chichester, which must therefore have been one of his tribal capitals. Chichester's formal name was Noviomagus Reginorum, 'The New Market of the Regini', but this can only have been one of the several 'states' which he ruled over. No evidence has been found from anywhere else to prove which others he controlled, but the archaeological evidence from Silchester of a nascent Roman-type town emerging prior to the year 43 suggests that the Atrebates tribe is another prime candidate. Moreover, tile stamps bearing the name of Nero show that imperial-sponsored building was going on at Silchester.

Irritatingly, the Chichester inscription carries no date, while another inscription, now lost, from Chichester is a dedication to Nero in 59 in the name of the local senate but carries no reference to Togidubnus.[23] This leads us back to speculation. Was he, perhaps, a scion of the house of Verica, perhaps sent to Rome as an *obses*, returning as a suitably pro-Roman and compliant youth to avenge his forbear's flight? If so, how was he regarded by the rest of his tribe? Unfortunately, there is absolutely nothing in the record to link Togidubnus to Verica apart from circumstance. Togidubnus never issued any coinage in his own name, though other Roman client kings were able to do this such as Agrippa II did, so we are none the wiser. If the lack of local coinage was a consequence of Togidubnus being specifically prohibited from doing so then this suggests that he was perhaps a lesser form of client king. No British tribal leader appears to have issued any coinage after 43. This fact is even more interesting given the chronic shortage of coinage under Claudius and Nero which resulted in the mass production of degenerate copies of official Roman coins by the Roman army for use in Britain until 64, when Nero's coinage started to be manufactured in large amounts.

Much has been made of the palace at Fishbourne, a few miles west of Chichester, as a possible home for Togidubnus. Its resemblance to the great country villas of Italy and the decorative features including mosaics, wall-paintings and stucco make it a possible showcase for the rewards of loyalty to Rome. Recent work on some of the sculpture found there has suggested that a small marble bust depicts Nero.[24] But it remains no less possible that Fishbourne was occupied by the governors of the province of Britannia. Here they would be safe in the knowledge that they were safely resident in a canton where the local tribal elite could be counted on not to rock the boat, either in the long winters between campaigns or in the summer when the governor was away fighting or progressing round the province dealing with government and justice. Whatever the truth, Togidubnus is to all intents and purposes the last of the southern British tribal leaders to feature in the story of Roman Britain at all. If he had descendants they are lost to the ages, though the interesting case of Sallustius Lucullus, a governor of Britain under Domitian, has provoked a controversial suggestion.[25]

However, Togidubnus was not the only one to bear the names of Claudius. A gold ring found nearby, bearing the name Tiberius Claudius

Catuarus, perhaps belonged to a wealthy tribal kinsman of his, enfranchised at the same time and also elevated to a status equivalent to the Roman equestrian aristocracy, thus entitling him to wear such a ring.[26] However, although this is distinctly possible, it is a lot to read into a ring and we should be careful. Whatever the rules about such privileges, the Roman world was prone to ignoring them. Petronius' *Satyricon*, written about the same time as Togidubnus was client king, makes it clear that his vulgar freedman character Trimalchio had no qualms about wearing rings to which he was not entitled.[27] If this was not a familiar abuse there would have been no joke. Moreover, the name 'Tiberius Claudius' was by no means unique to the first century and could easily be carried by descendants well into the future, so it is quite possible that Tiberius Claudius Catuarus, even if he was connected to Togidubnus (and that is not certain at all), had lived somewhat later.[28]

The Roman system depended on inculcating a suitable array of acolytes who owed their positions to the new regime. At Barkway in Hertfordshire was the site of a shrine to Mars conflated variously with the native deities Alator and Toutatis. One of the votive plaques left here was punched with the name of Tiberius Claudius Primus, the freedman of someone called Attius.[29] Attius, we can probably assume, was called Tiberius Claudius Attius and had either been enfranchised by Claudius or Nero, or was descended from someone who had been. Barkway was well within Catuvellaunian territory, a tribe that had presented the greatest threat to the Roman conquest in its earliest years. Building up a reliable support base in Britain was essential for the Roman authorities, as was rewarding loyal servants. Rewards could come in the form of lucrative concessions. Britain was rich in minerals and the lead deposits in the Mendips, Derbyshire and Wales were especially attractive prospects, not least because these lead ores also yielded silver. By the time of Vespasian (69–79) one of the lessees was Tiberius Claudius Triferna, another individual who had received citizenship under Claudius or Nero and may well have taken up his concession under one of them. Now he found himself smelting lead pigs which were stamped with his name, that of Vespasian and the provenance 'British [lead] from the lead-silver works' in the Mendips. He may very well also be the man whose name was abbreviated to TI.CL.TR on lead pigs from Derbyshire.[30]

Triferna is a Latin name, probably derived from *trifer* which means a plant that bears fruit three times a year. Therefore, he is likely also to have come from Italy or Gaul to take up the mining work on behalf of the state in return for a profitable cut. Other such men are known, for example Gaius Julius Protus and Publius Rubrius Abascantus, both of whom worked in Derbyshire out of the main mining centre, Lutudarum, a place that has yet to be located. Transliterated from Greek into Latin, Abascantus means 'unenvied' and is found across the Roman Empire but especially in Italy, Gaul and Spain. The Rubrii were a well-established Roman line, featuring in a number of references by Cicero in the first century BC. Abascantus was perhaps one of their freedmen or a descendant of one and made his living in the new province of Britain. Some of these men, though we do not know who, decided to combine their efforts and form cooperative ventures; thereafter they called themselves the 'Lutudarensian Partners'.[31]

With the passing of Togidubnus the Romans abandoned their client-king system. It had proved dramatically, and intolerably, unreliable. His death, however, was not to come until long after the catastrophic events of the years 60–1. The inscription from Chichester which records a vow of loyalty to Nero in 59 was a strangely prescient one. Why then? Was it a nervously subservient gesture by a tribe that feared unrest elsewhere? Or was it to do with the fact that Nero had killed his mother, Agrippina, that year and was beginning to assert himself more conspicuously? Under such circumstances a judicious acolyte might see good sense in a conspicuous display of loyalty. Or was it simply a routine gesture and is it merely a chance survival of what were once many standard declarations of loyalty? Either way, the events of the next two years and their outcome meant that a display of loyalty might very well prove to have been an opportune decision.

Of ordinary individual civilians we have little or no trace at this early stage of Roman Britain's history, but there is a rare glimpse at the fort at Templeborough, near Rotherham, in Yorkshire. The fort was a long-lived installation and has produced a small clutch of tombstones which probably belong to the second half of the first century AD. They provide no precise dating clues beyond the fact that the funerary invocation *Dis*

Manibus ('To the Spirits of the Departed') is not abbreviated at all on one stone and on the other is only reduced to 'DIS M'. This formula was new at the time of the invasion and does not appear on any tombstones in Britain of known date until the 60s; as its familiarity grew so it was more likely to be compressed to 'DM'.[32]

Templeborough was garrisoned at the time by the Fourth Cohort of Gauls. One of their number was Crotus, who died there at the age of forty apparently as a veteran (*emeritus*) of the unit and was buried by his wife Flavia Peregrina.[33] Flavia's name means literally 'Flavia the Provincial' and was simply a Latinized statement of fact which had become a name. Her husband was probably a native Gaul and he had perhaps brought her with him or married her in Britain. His age does not square with the information that he was a military veteran since this meant he ought to have served at least twenty-five years and thus had signed up at fifteen. However, the word *emeritus*, abbreviated on the tombstone to EM, can also mean 'unfit for service'. If so, then Crotus might have been invalided out of the army early, which would explain why he does not appear to have been awarded Roman citizenship on discharge.

Much more interesting than this pair though is the remarkable tombstone of Verecunda, daughter of Rufus, and 'Dobunnian citizen'. She died at the age of thirty-five and was buried by her husband Excingus at his own expense.[34] The Dobunni were the British tribe that occupied an area in the Cotswolds. By the late 40s a Roman fort had been established at a crossroads close to the native stronghold of Bagendon where Sextus Valerius Genialis, mentioned earlier, had been based. Within around twenty-five years at the most it had been given up and the civitas capital of Corinium Dobunnorum established on the site, now known to us as Cirencester. It is tempting to imagine that Excingus, serving with the army, arrived at Cirencester where he found Verecunda and married her, taking her with him when his unit was moved north.

In one sense it is remarkable that a British woman could have abandoned her own people so easily, but in another it is worth remembering that if Excingus was a native Gaul fighting with an auxiliary unit in the Roman army (and his name suggests he was), then he probably did not seem so very different from the men of the Dobunni. He will probably have offered Verecunda security and some status. However, Excingus tells us nothing about himself, which means we do not know if he was even a soldier, though his inclination to memorialize his wife this way makes it very likely that he was. It has been suggested that the pair were both British but this seems unlikely; if they were then we would probably have far more examples of inscriptions recording similar matches. Another who may have made a life as an army wife or was employed in some capacity was a woman whose name survives only as Ved(.)ic(. .), who died aged thirty at the fort of Ilkley in the same general era and area as Verecunda.[35] She was a member of the Cornovii tribe whose territory was in the West Midlands. The XIV Legion was based at Wroxeter, close to the old tribal centre at the Wrekin, during the mid-first century. This means that her unknown husband (if indeed she had one) had probably met her while stationed with the XIV Legion there or one of its attendant auxiliary units. As with Verecunda, the plain fact is that being commemorated with a stereotypical Roman tombstone with inscription in a frontier context makes it almost inevitable that she was buried by a soldier or someone with close military connections and who came from a place other than Britain.

One death from this period makes for an exceptionally grim record. Some time in the late first century AD or the first two decades of the second century, a man was seriously injured by being deliberately struck violently in the head. Next he was garrotted in order to break his neck and finally he had his throat cut. These were all in addition to other injuries. He was about twenty-five years of age and had not led a hard life, as evidenced by his manicured nails and trimmed facial hair. It is not now possible to know why he was then thrown into the peat bog at Lindow in Cheshire which preserved his remains. He is one of a number of ancient bodies known from that bog. He may have been a criminal or murderer, and therefore sentenced to death, or someone selected to be killed as part of a macabre ritual. The Romans were revolted by human sacrifice, despite their inordinately violent society, so this rules out the Roman authorities from being responsible if the purpose was religious. But it is possible that he might have been sacrificed by tribal Britons of the area who wished to propitiate the gods once they were faced with the Roman invasion. It is worth noting that this seems to have happened in

Latin America when the Conquistadores arrived in the fifteenth century and presented the vulnerable indigenous peoples with an unprecedented crisis and threat. Moreover, this is entirely in keeping with classical descriptions of the Druids and their predilection for human sacrifice.[36] However, it is no less possible that he was done to death by his fellow tribesmen, or by the Roman authorities, for committing a crime about which we know nothing.

These had been a tumultuous few years. Britain had changed forever. In an age of relatively short lifespans for most people, there would have been very few in the late first century AD who could have had any recollection of what it had been like to live in Britain without a Roman presence. This all-pervading force had a dramatic effect on the nature of the surviving record, which was now increasingly characterized by unequivocally Roman aspects.

CHAPTER THREE

ROMAN BRITAIN'S BOOM YEARS, AD 61–161

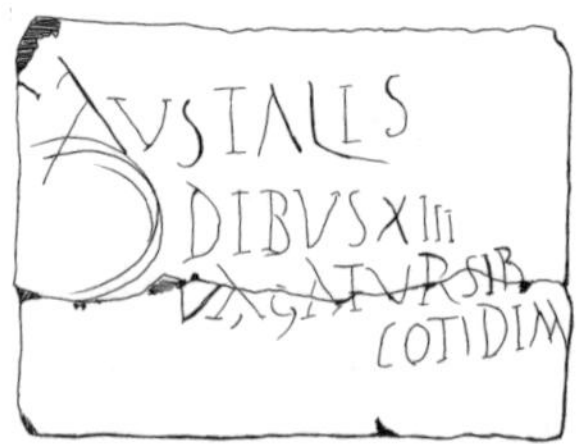

One of the most interesting comments made by a Roman historian comes from the *Annals* of Tacitus when describing the Boudican War. He tells us that London already existed as a thriving mercantile centre and was packed with traders and goods.[1] The description is instantly redolent of London as we see it today and as it has been for centuries. This port town had grown up around the Roman river crossing but it was wiped out by the Boudican hordes in 60–1 and burned to the ground. Incredibly, within only a few years the boom town of Roman Britain was in business again but this time the evidence comes predominantly from the vast quantities of material excavated from the Roman wharfs buried deep beneath the modern City of London. Clearly, by the late 60s London's wharfs once more teemed with the crews of ships, traders, soldiers, immigrants and officials. Warehouses clustered along the docks, filled with imported goods which arrived from across the Empire, no doubt priced accordingly to reflect the vast cost of shipping from the Mediterranean. Along the riverbanks and beyond, public buildings were being erected on a grand scale. The street frontages were cluttered with businesses of all kinds housed in flimsy buildings and the streets themselves were congested with carts, draught animals and men and women from all over the Roman Empire. Considering that a generation before the north bank of the Thames had simply been a rural river valley with occasional farmsteads dotted among fields, woods and marshes, the transformation of an area little more than a square mile into an international classical city was remarkable.

Today it is not easy to imagine the impact of this kind of activity in a place that had seen nothing like it before. However, the development in San Francisco or Melbourne as ports and the dramatic Victorian civic architecture built in both during the mid- to late 1800s is perhaps a useful way of imagining what happened in London in the 70s and 80s as an imperial culture imposed itself on a land that had seen nothing like it before. Such projects can be seen as exciting, audacious and stimulating, or as oppressive, presumptuous and exploitative. The Roman world was built around the concept of the city. Rome was the hub but Rome was far more than that. Rome was the very conscious essence of Roman civilization. It was as if there was no other way in which the Romans could define themselves or others. So it was that all existing cities absorbed into the Roman world came eventually to mimic Rome in their social and political systems. In provinces like Britain where towns did not yet really exist they were laid out and operated by the Romans in that idiom from the start. The process of urban development in Britain had begun soon after the conquest with the establishment of Camulodunum as a Roman colony, an explicit advertisement of Roman urban life. The Boudican Revolt nearly strangled the process at birth, but after 61 the development of the towns was restarted (plates 2 and 3).

The impact must have been considerable and out of the archaeological discoveries has come a huge amount of evidence for Britain's first Londoners. This was the first age of Britain's cities. The years AD 61–161 were some of the most remarkable in Roman Britain's history. The bodies on the battlefield where the Boudican dream came to an end were gathered up and the army was sent to quash any residual traces of rebellion. The brutality of their behaviour was soon replaced with a more constructive and positive approach. At any rate, the simple fact is that rebellion ceased in most of what we call England. Either the Britons had given up the fight and accepted Roman exploitation and oppression or they had decided that perhaps what the Romans had to offer was preferable to the instability of tribal politics.

Britain developed in two ways. In the centre and south the towns started to take shape, hubs in a network of roads across which Roman communications and commodities started to proliferate. These roads also led to Wales and to the north to where the bulk of the army was now stationed. During the next century their building works would produce the greatest physical legacy of the Roman era, principally in the Hadrian's Wall system, which by the early 160s was finally confirmed as the northern border of the province of Britannia. It is during this period of a hundred years that the people of Roman Britain really start to emerge. Nonetheless, for all the conspicuous manifestations of Roman life, the truth must be that for the vast majority of the population any real sense of change was minimal. Life remained short and hard, with endless toil in the countryside.

Into the wreckage of London in the year 61 the emperor Nero sent a new procurator to administer the province's finances. Tacitus describes how in the aftermath of the Revolt a more sympathetic procurator was appointed to Britain.[2] The rebellion had been provoked in part by the callous treatment meted out to the Iceni by Catus Decianus, the previous incumbent. Britain was governed by an imperial legate of consular rank, a senator who had worked his way up through a series of magistracies and jobs to be elected a consul. Such men had usually served as commanders of legions and probably also governed other, less or equally challenging, provinces before being sent to Britain. Governing Britain was onerous and arduous and at this time still involved annual campaigning. Not only was it impossible for the governor to handle all the administration, but it was also undesirable that any one man be given so much power – after all, with four legions and their attendant auxiliary units Britain had an enormous garrison. It made sense to hive off financial administration to a lesser official, in this case the procurator, a man of equestrian rank, the next aristocratic tier below the senators. Moreover, under normal circumstances an equestrian could not automatically assume that he or his family could be promoted to senatorial status, though this could and did sometimes happen.

Tacitus disapproved of the new procurator he referred to as 'Julius Classicianus' because he believed Classicianus was more interested in appeasement than serving Rome's interests. He therefore alleged that the procurator played a role in recommending that the governor Suetonius Paulinus be removed. Paulinus was thought by Classicianus to have been over-harsh in the revenge he sought for the rebellion. Classicianus' tombstone has survived, with parts found in 1852 and 1935 (plate 3).[3] They go a long way to explaining why Tacitus took the position he did. Classicianus must have arrived in Britain soon after the final battle with Boudica. As an equestrian he was of lesser status than both Paulinus and Tacitus. Tacitus was an elitist and believed in the dignity, tradition and superiority of the senators.

Moreover, Classicianus was almost certainly of Gaulish origin. His full name was '[Gaius Julius] Alpinus Classicianus of the Fabian voting tribe'. 'Alpinus' is a name most commonly found in Gaul. The process of enfranchising suitable Gauls began under Caesar, and Classicianus' full name suggests an ancestor of his was one of the beneficiaries. The process continued under Claudius, who in 48 even admitted leading Gauls to the Senate in Rome.[4] The name 'Classicianus' is probably simply derived from the Latin word *classicus*, which simply means 'superior' or 'of the highest rank', in other words 'Gaius Julius Alpinus, the High-Class One'. However, before the discovery of more of the tomb in 1935, the name led the Romano-British expert R.G. Collingwood to reject the idea that the man named on the tombstone was the same one mentioned by Tacitus, which was what the nineteenth-century antiquarian Charles Roach Smith had suggested. Collingwood argued in 1928 with unswerving confidence that the name must come from *classis* ('fleet') and that Classicianus had some connection with the Roman navy. Collingwood translated the name as 'Fabius Alpinus, formerly of the navy' and stated sagely that 'Roach Smith was obviously wrong to think of connecting him with Julius Classicianus in Tacitus'.[5] It was an argument that reflected a curiously two-dimensional perspective in those days in which a military connection, however abstruse, was always preferred to common sense and was also regarded as exclusive of any other possibilities. The 1935 discovery ended any further doubt by producing a further section of the text which confirmed Classicianus, regardless of the origin of his name, to be the procurator of the province of Britannia at London and thus indeed the man referred to with such disdain by Tacitus. The case of Classicianus is a sobering reminder of how tenuous our links can be to the people of Roman Britain when they come down to us through such a fragmentary record. When the information is not definitive it is often better to recognize more than one possible interpretation. In any case, at least two further lines of the inscription still remain to be found; if they ever are, we will learn a great deal more for certain about Classicianus' career.[6]

In the meantime, thanks to what we have of the text, it is now certain that Classicianus' wife, who erected his tomb, was a woman called Julia Pacata Indiana or Induta, the daughter of a pro-Roman Gaulish leader of the Treveri tribe called Julius Indus. Although the last part of her name is incomplete on the tomb, part of the surviving text specifies that she was *Indi filia*, 'daughter of Indus'. The union of the couple and their elevation had their origin in the complex tribal politics of Gaul. It had been Roman practice to reward Gaulish tribal leaders for loyalty and valour with Roman citizenship, though it remained a relatively rare privilege. One of the beneficiaries was a member of the Treveri tribe called Julius Florus, but by AD 21 he was already busy leading a rebellion. Disaffection had set in as a result of Roman taxes, while among those tribesmen who had joined the Roman army as auxiliaries the death of Germanicus, the highly popular general and intended successor of Tiberius, in AD 19 had severely damaged their sense of loyalty. Florus decided to entice a Treveri auxiliary cavalry wing to murder Roman merchants. In the event, though, and anticipating aspects of the Boudican Revolt forty years later, most of those who took up arms were those who owed money to the Romans. At that point in the story another of the Treveri nobility, Julius Indus, Julia's father, saw his chance to pursue his own feud with Florus. He used force to disperse the rising, with the result that Florus committed suicide.[7] As so often in the Roman story it was the willingness of Rome's enemies to fight among one another for the sake of their own ambitions that thwarted opposition to Roman rule.

If Indus was an active warrior in 21 then he must by then have been at least twenty years old. He could easily have already been a father, which means that in 61 Julia could have been forty or older. No children are mentioned on the tombstone, though that of itself is not significant because they would only have been named if they were also buried there or had participated in setting up their father's tomb; or, they might have been named on separate markers set up around the tomb. Apart from the indigenous rulers Cartimandua and Boudica, Julia Pacata Indiana is the first securely dated and attested named woman in British history. She symbolizes the remarkable ability of the Roman world to create a hybridized society. Had she been born a century earlier her destiny would have been to produce children for the Gaulish tribal elite. As it was, she was the wife of a Gallo-Roman member of the Roman equestrian class and had entered the prestigious ranks of Roman provincial administration. Apart from her name there is nothing about the monument she erected for her husband that would indicate that it was anything other than the tomb of a Roman official of high status.

The couple must have had an acute understanding of the futility of continuing a confrontational, punitive and exploitative administration, even if this would later annoy Tacitus, and presumably others of the senatorial class. Whether they adopted this position out of a genuine sense of empathy or a more cynical belief that clemency would ultimately prove more profitable we can but guess. That the Roman imperial authorities had appointed Classicianus to the job suggests that they recognized it would be more expedient to soften Roman control of Britain, hold on to the province and thereby avoid losing more face and perhaps encouraging other rebellions elsewhere. The immediate result was animosity between Classicianus and the governor Suetonius Paulinus. Tacitus accused Classicianus of advising the Britons to wait it out until a new and more moderate governor arrived. Classicianus sent word to Rome that the aftermath of the Boudican Revolt would remain unsettled until a new governor arrived.

Nero's initial response, in fact probably on the advice of his tutor Seneca, was to dispatch an imperial freedman called Polyclitus with an enormous entourage to effect a reconciliation between Paulinus and Classicianus. The most revealing part of that development was that the Britons were left completely incredulous at the idea that senior Roman officials would have to defer to an ex-slave.[8] Paulinus was left in post for another year to save face and then a pretext to withdraw him was found when he was responsible for a few ships being lost.

Tacitus' acerbic judgment of Classicianus missed an essential point. The appointment of Classicianus and his personality reflected the Roman world's occasional capacity to operate with a sense of enlightened collective responsibility. It is easy to become obsessed with the mercurial personalities of the emperors and forget that the reason the Roman Empire generally continued to function, rather than constantly fragment into factional disputes, was because there was a system of institutions, law and order that was widely accepted by the population across the Empire. This was operated by officials, the vast majority of whom were provincial in origin, who for the most part had at least some sense of being part of something that was more than exclusively a source of personal gain. This system continued to operate in the background and held the Roman world together.

Classicianus came from a province that had itself been under Roman control for little more than a century. The remarkable thing about Roman Britain is that no one from Britain, so far as we know, ever achieved equestrian status, let alone the position of a provincial procurator or senatorial status. This was in spite of the very close links between some British tribes and those of northern Gaul. This might be due to the fragmentary record, but the total absence of any such individual tends to suggest that the indigenous Romano-British really were deliberately marginalized from mainstream elite Roman society. Alternatively, it might suggest that the indigenous population also struggled to empathize with the Roman sense of collective responsibility, even though some of their Gaulish counterparts seem to have had no such difficulties. In 68, in Gaul, Gaius Julius Vindex, a Gaulish senator from Gallia Aquitainia, led a rebellion against Nero, not because he wanted to turn on the Roman world but rather because he was affronted at Nero's abuses of power and debasement of the post of emperor after such forbears as Augustus.[9]

Classicianus must have died in post by the mid-60s since the text of his tomb makes it plain he was still procurator at the time and he is unlikely to have held the job for more than three to four years. Classicianus also died before his policy of tolerance and accommodation bore fruit. Indeed, he can barely have started; it is hard to see how the post-Boudican restoration of the province can have been expected to take less than a decade or more. However, the archaeology of Roman London shows that the town was not only rapidly reconstructed but also that within fifteen to twenty years there had been explosive commercial development which continued for years to come.

The fact that Classicianus was buried in London is very good evidence that the city had become the de facto capital of the province, though we have as yet to find any evidence of its official incorporation in any formal status, such as being made a colony, at any time. A recent find is the remarkable eagle carved from Cotswold limestone which emerged from a Roman cemetery area to the east of the settlement in a street now known as the Minories, near the Tower of London, in late 2013. The tomb from which it probably came is unknown and thus we have no idea of its owner either, but the nature of the sculpture, which represents an eagle with its wings raised and consuming a snake, is the kind of device usually associated with a tomb of high status. It possibly came from the funerary monument of a man who served in the provincial administration in the late first or second century, though it could equally well have come from the tomb of an affluent and aspirational freedman trader. Remarkably, an almost identical eagle is shown on an altar in a painting in the House of the Vettii, the home of a pair of wealthy freedmen brothers, at Pompeii. The painting, executed not long before the city's destruction in AD 79, shows a large altar and before it the infant Heracles strangling the snakes sent by Hera to kill him out of rage at Zeus' infidelity with Alcmene, Heracles' mother. It was a typical example of the pretensions to learning and culture so often exhibited by Pompeian freedmen and there is no good reason to assume that London's freedmen merchants (of whom there must have been very many) were any different. The Pompeian eagle only differs in not devouring a snake but it is conspicuously eyeing up the snakes being strangled by Heracles and is perhaps alluding to some sort of private Vettii family joke or reference, the significance of which is now lost. The arrival in Britain of this sort of typically Roman material vastly accelerated during the late first century. The elegant bronze patera from a grave in Kent with its magnificent Medusa head would have passed muster in any affluent Roman home in the Western Empire (plates 4 and 5).

London, like most of the towns of Roman Britain in the late first century, was a building site. All the major towns of the province had a forum and basilica government building installed at some point between the 70s and the 130s. London had two; a smaller, early version was operational by the 70s but by Hadrian's time it had been surrounded by a vast replacement and was then demolished. The new Hadrianic basilica of London was cathedral-sized but was never finished. The demands for building materials were enormous and involved the establishment of industries to provide the raw materials.

One small fragment of tile found in a wharfside dump at Billingsgate in London bears a graffito that seems to be all that is left of a roster of names, perhaps at a tilery since the graffito was written while the clay was still wet some time in the late first or early second century. One of the names was the distinctly native (perhaps Gaulish) Boduacus, and below it either Titus or Potitus, each of which was an old Roman name. This was the new world of Roman Britain where men whose names harked back to quite separate traditions could find themselves recorded together.[10]

Augustalis seems to have been another worker involved in London's growth. His name is preserved in a tantalizing text on a tile which was also inscribed before the clay had dried. In a pair of rhyming iambic dimeters, written in Roman cursive script, are the words *Austalis dibus tredecim, vagatur sib cotidim*. Literally translated it means, 'Au(gu)stalis, for thirteen days, wanders off by himself every day'.[11] Augustalis was apparently absenting himself from work. Since the tile was wet when written on, it follows that his fellow workers were employed (or enslaved) at a tilery, a business whose products would have been in massive demand in the Roman London of the late first century. They seem to have been remarkably well-versed for members of such a prosaic occupation; the couplet was composed and written by someone who was not only literate but also modestly educated in the structures of Latin poetry, and who neatly compressed his subject's name to make sure it scanned. This of course raises the possibility that this is not a literal reference to a colleague but perhaps a rendition of a part of a popular song or poem of the time, reproduced as a writing exercise or simply in fun, perhaps composed by a London-based poet (*musicus*).[12] But the temptation to see Augustalis as an actual person whose habit of bunking off from work had become the subject of a ribald comic verse is too attractive to abandon completely.

Augustalis and his colleagues were far from alone. Demand for tiles was massive and other entrepreneurs saw opportunities. One was Cabriabanus, a tiler who probably worked in west Kent where most of his products turn up. He used a roller die to create a flamboyant relief pattern of his name on his hypocaust box-flue tiles even though, once they were cemented into place, it would no longer be visible (plate 6). The relief pattern assisted the tiles' adhesion to the wall so that they could carry hot air around the building. One of his relief patterns even goes as far as to say 'I, Cabriabanus, manufactured this wall tile'.[13] The purpose was perhaps also to identify the tiles when in shared kilns, or in store, as well as to create a branded product.

It is something of an enigma that Roman Britain exhibits little or nothing in the way of a phenomenon known as competitive munificence. In Italian, Gaulish and other Roman towns across the Empire, the local elite queued up to spend their wealth on lavish endowments for their home cities. The gifts bought votes and status for them and their families and a form of immortality in statues and inscriptions erected by the grateful communities. At Herculaneum, Marcus Nonius Balbus, a little-known senator of Augustus' time, became the principal benefactor, erecting the basilica and endowing the town with other facilities. More than a century later, when the town was destroyed by Vesuvius, his statue still overlooked a mezzanine square outside one of the town's baths on the road down to the shore of the Bay of Naples. Balbus was not from Herculaneum by birth but he came from not far away and adopted Herculaneum as his new home. He was essentially a 'local' and his self-serving generosity was typical of the Roman elite. Pliny the Younger, a senator born in the early 60s, lived on into the second century AD and despite a far-ranging career climaxing in the governorship of Bithynia and Pontus never forgot his home town of Como. It was part of the social quid pro quo. In return for these acts of philanthropy the Nonii and the Plinii expected to be recognized by the townsfolk as local worthies in perpetuity. At the theatre, honorific double seats, the *bisellia*, were set aside for such men long after their passing.

In Britain civic magistrates like Pliny and Balbus are almost absent from the record in spite of the evident and sustained programme of public building. The position of *aedile* was the entry-level post to civic magistracies so it was particularly important, but precisely one Romano-British *aedile* has come down to us. This one lurks behind the nebulous anonymity of a Roman name that is remarkable mostly for being so commonplace that it tells us next to nothing about its owner. Marcus Ulpius Januarius paid for a theatre stage which he donated to the town at Petuaria, somewhere near or in Brough-on-Humber, during the reign of Antoninus Pius almost exactly a century after the Roman invasion of AD 43. Worthy of no more than the classification *vicus* (settlement), and not in any sense a formal administrative town, Petuaria was a place of little consequence. However, it lay not far from York and its location on the Humber made it at least a bystander to a great deal of maritime traffic, which included the ferry across the Humber to Ermine Street and the way south via the colony at Lincoln (Lindum).

Januarius regrettably tells us nothing about his origins or provincial affiliations. He also tells us nothing about his past. He does, however, tell us that he was an *aedile* at Petuaria and had paid for the *proscaenium* ('stage') at the town from his own resources.[14] A missing section of text suggests he had paid for even more than that, perhaps additional seating or other architectural embellishments. His position ought to suggest that he was little more than twenty years old and had paid for the facility either as part of his pre-election campaign or as part of his obligations in office; however, there is every possibility that he was somewhat older if his civic career followed a military one. Paying for the privilege of election was simply the way the system worked. Public office could cost a small fortune but there were rewards, not least of which was the status earned for the family and which would be enjoyed by one's descendants for generations to come. The inscription was an important advertisement.

A young man who was elected *aedile* was automatically admitted to the council as a *decurion* (councillor) thereafter, giving him a finger in the pie for life and the more or less automatic election as a *duumvir* (the senior magistracy, plural *duoviri*) in subsequent years. Magistrates always served in pairs to ensure some sort of check and balance so Januarius would have had a colleague who is unknown to us. The inscription dates to no earlier than somewhere between AD 139 and 144, shortly after the time of the accession of Antoninus Pius so Januarius must have been born no later than around the year 120. We can, incidentally, see a town council in action at Caerwent in the early third century when the *decuriones* voted to erect a statue to the then commander of the II Legion Augusta based nearby at Caerleon.[15]

That Januarius had the three-part name (*tria nomina*) of a Roman citizen ought to be fairly certain evidence that he was one, though even that can never be entirely definite. 'Marcus Ulpius' almost certainly only came from having been made a citizen during the reign of Marcus Ulpius Trajanus, emperor between 98 and 117. If our Januarius was too young for that then the next best guess is that he was the son or grandson of someone elevated to that status. The most likely candidate for anyone to have been made a citizen that way, that time, and in a place like Britain is a member of the auxiliary Roman army. In return for loyal service an auxiliary was awarded citizenship on retirement, though in fact this could take place earlier had his unit shown special valour. At that point he might have sought a career in civic administration in the town where he settled.

We can therefore speculate endlessly on the precise route Marcus Ulpius Januarius' name came down to him. Januarius, or his forbear, was probably born in the month of January. He might conceivably have been the son of a freedman who had been awarded his citizenship in Trajan's time. Or he might have been the son of a freedman who had been freed by a soldier who had himself been made a citizen under Trajan. This rather complex web of possibilities illustrates the problem with Roman names unaccompanied by any more expansive information.

Unfortunately, regardless of any of these theoretical routes the fact remains that we have absolutely no idea where Januarius came from. That he was a full Briton seems distinctly unlikely. Petuaria was firmly in the military zone of northern Britain, and not far from the VI Legion's headquarters at York (Eboracum), totally dominated by the Roman army and especially so in the extant record. If Januarius was not an ex-soldier then it is almost inevitable that his father was in the army, or had been a soldier's slave. If so, his father's origins were somewhere on the continent, but it is entirely plausible that his mother was British.

Duoviri, the senior civic magistrates, are also not well known in Britain. None is recorded on an inscription from a building or other civic project but some turn up on the undated stamped tiles produced by the town government of the colony at Gloucester (Glevum). One, for example, was stamped for the 'Commonwealth of the Gloucester people (in the year) of the *duoviri* Perpetuus and Aprilis', others for the '(year of) Optatus and Saturninus' and '(year of) Decimus Sennius Vitalis and

Gaius Valerius An(. . .)', and one in the sole name of 'Publius Aelius Finitus', perhaps produced after his co-*duumvir* had died.[16] A couple of other examples have the partial names of *duoviri* serving as *quinquennales*. Every five years the elected *duoviri* were called by this title because they had the duty of drawing up a census list of town citizens entitled to vote. The names we have from Gloucester include Julius Flo(rus?) and Cornelius Sim(ilis?).[17] There is little we can tell from these about what such men did and where they came from but they do reassure us that individuals were serving in the capacity of Roman civic magistracies in Britain. Their names are all conventionally Roman but that might be expected in a town populated by legionary veterans and their families. Publius Aelius Finitus, for example, must have been enfranchised under (Publius Aelius) Hadrian or descended from someone who had been.

We are on no less uncertain ground with the town councillors of Roman Britain but the instantly striking fact is that yet again the *decuriones* known to us almost all come down to us from the military zone. The only one who does not is a man whose name is lost and who served on the council at Gloucester and that of course was a military colony anyway. Of the other five, three served at the colony of York and one at the colony of Lincoln, with the fifth turning up at Vindolanda where he was probably in transit. The place in which this man, known only as Lucius, was a councillor is unknown. Of the names we have, like Aurelius Senecio of Lincoln, there is nothing to help us identify any ethnic Britons for certain. Moreover, none of them tells us anything about their activities, benefactions or privileges. Senecio's name is recorded on the tombstone he erected for his wife, a woman called Volusia Faustina who died at Lincoln aged twenty-six years and twenty-six days and is stated to have been a 'citizen of Lincoln'. Their names, together with the tombstone's style, place them in the mid to late second century. Faustina was the name of the wife of Antoninus Pius (138–61), a woman also related to the empresses of the emperors Trajan and Hadrian. She died in 140 but her daughter, also Faustina, was the wife of the next emperor, Marcus Aurelius (161–80). Volusia was an old Roman name and recalls Volusius Maecianus who was the young Marcus Aurelius' tutor. Volusia Faustina's thoroughly loyal name suggests she was the daughter of a veteran at the colony, rather than a Briton. Flavius Bellator was a councillor at York. 'Bellator' means 'warrior' and so it is likely he was an ex-soldier, which, given the fact that the military colony at York also lay adjacent to the legionary fortress of the VI Legion, is hardly surprising. Claudius Florentinus, who dedicated the coffin of a deceased father-in-law and camp prefect called Ant[onius?] Gargilianus, was probably an ex-soldier too.[18]

The collective picture of all these examples is of a world in which immigrant communities, mainly in the form of Roman military veterans, replicated the Roman towns of the continent. Their councils and magistracies were modelled on conventional Roman forms and would have been familiar to anyone arriving there from Gaul, Italy or Spain. Nothing similar survives from any of the other Roman towns, and nothing to suggest that ethnic Britons were integrated into the system. This simply could be a question of surviving evidence: civitas capitals like Silchester and Canterbury have little in the way of usable local stone. Titus Tammonius Victor buried his wife Flavia Victorina at Silchester, recorded on a very rare example of a tombstone from the town, and he seems to have been a Roman citizen.[19] His name is a Romanized version of a native one and he was also presumably someone of suitably high status to serve on the council. But he makes no mention of such a fact. So it remains a real possibility that the civic organizations of some Romano-British towns were little more than shams.

The development of Roman Britain's infrastructure was inevitably directed by the governors of the province. About this we know remarkably little, largely thanks to the fact that Tacitus was much more interested in their military campaigns and how these compared or led up to the exploits of his father-in-law, Gnaeus Julius Agricola, who governed Britain for around six to seven years between 78 and 84. This was an unusually long term, nearly double the normal length, and it would see the Roman army reach far into what we call Scotland. This side to his governorship will be covered later; for the moment it is Tacitus' famous observations on Agricola's policy of encouraging the Britons into town life believing they were civilizing themselves, when in fact they were merely enslaving themselves, that is of interest.[20]

As ever with Tacitus the subtext is his feelings about the Roman people and how their plunge into the indulgences and lazy comforts of city life had all but annihilated what had made Rome great. It is a familiar enough complaint and one which in today's world has many echoes. Nevertheless, Tacitus specifically claimed that Agricola really had actively promoted urban development and a Romanized way of life in Britain with some success. Agricola had seen the Boudican Revolt at first hand since as a young man he had served with the XX Legion in those dark days. Of course the purpose must have been to transfer British perceptions and measurements of status into a Roman idiom; in other words it was to create British versions of Classicianus, his wife and her father, Julius Indus. The archaeological evidence, remarkably, supports the idea that he certainly tried. The inscription from the forum at Verulamium (St Albans) clearly refers to Agricola. What is less clear is whether he succeeded because in reality not a single person demonstrably of British descent ever reached any sort of high status in Britain.

What we do have is a rich seam of more ordinary individuals, often demonstrably immigrants, for whom life in the new towns defined their experience of Britannia. Into the cavalcade of activity that was Londinium in the late first or early second century came a Gaulish slave woman called Fortunata. In the Roman world it was common for slaves to have names that seem strangely inappropriate, given their lowly status. It is difficult now to understand how she could ever have been called 'fortunate', but at least her position in the slave hierarchy was not at the bottom of the pile. Fortunata's story survives on a writing tablet found at No. 1 Poultry in London, the site of extensive recent excavations.[21] It was a congested and busy part of the Roman city, where street frontages were lined by businesses and trades all jammed up close to one another.

Fortunata had been owned by someone called Albicianus and was a member of the Diablintes tribe who seem to have lived not far from present-day Le Mans in Gaul. In fact the writing tablet provides the first example of the tribal name in full, reflecting the tenuous and haphazard nature of the record. A milestone with a highly abbreviated text found at Anvers-le-Hamon is the only clue to their geographical location.

Fortunata was probably born to a slave woman and therefore grew up in slavery. By the time Albicianus decided to sell her she was worth 600 denarii, a sum roughly equivalent to double the annual salary of a legionary soldier. It is difficult now to understand what a sum like that meant, but it probably felt equivalent to something like £20,000 to £40,000 today. In other words, it was a considerable sum. Fortunata must have had potential and that suggests she was likely to have been of child-bearing age. She was said to have been healthy and could be guaranteed not to be likely to try and run away. We do not know where the transaction occurred but it was likely to have been in a public place such as the forum on an occasion set aside specifically for slave sales and which had been promoted.[22]

Another writing tablet was written by a man called Rufus, son of Callisunus, to 'Epillicus and all his fellows' in London. The few surviving lines refer rather vaguely to affairs, including the instruction 'carefully look after everything' which might suggest that Epillicus is Rufus' bailiff or household-manager slave in charge of all Rufus' other slaves. The last extant line gets down to business proper: 'see that you do everything diligently so that you convert that girl into cash . . .'[23] 'That girl' was presumably another unfortunate slave. However, in addition to being summarily sold on, there were other risks slaves faced. They might be captured by opportunistic thieves for resale.[24]

Albicianus is trickier. It has been suggested that a garbled, incomplete and barely legible word reading *leg-* between his name and the sum of money indicates that there was some sort of military connection to a legion. That is not impossible. A short distance from the find spot of the tablet is the Roman fort of London where legionaries were on secondment to the governor's staff. But much more likely is that *leg-* is all that is left of *legitime* which would have meant that the price was the 'due' or 'appropriate' one. The buyer was Vegetus, himself a slave but on the staff of an imperial slave called Montanus. The two men were significant individuals in the imperial hierarchy, even if they were slaves. Montanus, who had succeeded another called Iucundus, was almost certainly involved in administering the emperor's interests in Britain, which will have involved managing imperial estates. Fortunata would therefore have become the property of the emperor even if in practice she was actually the slave of Vegetus; this was merely a legal nicety – as a slave himself, Vegetus could not own another slave.

It comes as something of a surprise to discover that in the Roman world, despite the apparent equality of being at the bottom of Roman society, some slaves were more equal than others. Fortunata may well have turned out to be fortunate. Being on the staff of an important member of the imperial staff almost certainly meant a more convivial existence than a short, hard and brutal existence as a slave on some remote mining or farming settlement, even if she was presumably expected to produce for her master children who could in turn be sold on.[25] However, Vegetus may have had more personal motives. Around the same time in London a 'slave of the province' called Anencletus buried his nineteen-year-old wife, Claudia Martina. He was able to afford not only a well-carved tombstone but also to have it designed to support a statue of his wife.[26] They self-evidently cannot have been married for many years and there is every possibility that Anencletus had bought Claudia Martina and married her. It is no less likely that Vegetus had similar plans for Fortunata. These scenarios are a reminder that, unedifying though slavery was, it did not have the same racial connotations as it has in more modern times. In the Roman world, slavery could be (and often was) a temporary phase in a family's life that could be left behind. Fortunata, or her descendants, may very well one day have been freed.

The find spot of the document suggests that Fortunata's purchase took place in London, though she need not necessarily have worked for Vegetus there. She may not even have stayed in Britain since there is every possibility that at some point Vegetus was transferred to another province. This kind of mobility was routine in the Roman world so it is no great surprise to find other people in Roman London whose time there was only a part of their lives. London's role as one of Roman Britain's greatest ports meant a continuous throughput of persons and commodities. Fortunata, who as a slave was counted as both a person and a commodity, must have arrived by ship at some point, perhaps as part of a consignment brought over by Albicianus. Either way, a ship had to be found.

Tiberinius Celerianus was another Londoner from northern Gaul, although he probably lived rather later in the second century. His dedication to the Spirits of the Emperors and to the god Mars Camulos was found in a pit between two temples in Southwark (plate 7).[27] Tiberinius proudly stated himself to be a 'citizen of the Bellovaci' and, the first to do so in any extant record, a 'Londoner'. He usefully tells us also that he was a 'moritix'. An extremely rare word, *moritex* or *moritix* does not exist in Latin and is instead of 'Celtic' origin. However, the word shares its remoter roots with the Latin word *mare* ('sea') and it is now generally believed the term was a local and vernacular term for a seafarer. Tiberinius was thus a shipper, a man who plied his trade across the English Channel and probably maintained property and interests on either side of the water. Other such men are known. Verecundius Diogenes, despite his elaborately Roman and Greek name, was proclaimed to be a *moritex* on his coffin found at York and to have come originally from Bourges in Gallia Aquitainia. He was almost certainly a freedman, serving as a priest of the imperial cult at York as a mark of his status in the colony's commercial community.[28]

It was a dangerous business and men like Verecundius and Tiberinius must have known it. Placating the gods was an important gesture. The wreckage of the Blackfriars Roman cargo boat, found in the anaerobic Thames silt, included a bronze *as* of the emperor Domitian struck in Rome between 88 and 89; it had been placed carefully in the mast step before the mast was raised over it. It was a common enough coin and one which would not have attracted the slightest attention in everyday small change, but it had clearly been placed there deliberately by one of the superstitious crewmen who knew that any protection was better than none on the high seas. On its reverse was the goddess Fortuna, holding the oar with which she steered men's lives. Appropriately enough the coin had been placed with Fortuna on the upper side.[29] The ship had had a mundane life, plying Britain's coastal trade and perhaps occasionally further afield. When it sank it was still laden with Kentish ragstone brought up from the Maidstone area of Kent so it must have made its way down the Medway before heading up the Thames to the provincial capital. That it also still had an unfinished millstone of Yorkshire stone on board suggests a previous voyage had been to northern Britain. Since it sank only around 100 metres from the riverbank it is likely that some who were on board escaped. If Fortuna let the boat down, the survivors might have taken some consolation from the fact they had escaped with their lives.

Tiberinius Celerianus' choice of god, Mars Camulus (or Camulos), was a conflation of a classical and a Gaulish deity, and is called today with questionable appropriateness 'Romano-Celtic'. Probably associated with healing, the deity would have been a familiar enough sight, or at least a familiar enough variant, to have excited little attention. Colchester (Camulodunum) may have been named after him and it is interesting to see also that a man with the thoroughly Roman name of Romulus, and who was the son of Camulogenos, donated a silver skillet to the cult of Mars and the Spirits of the Emperors.[30] The conflation of traditions seems to have been just as evident in the everyday names of such ordinary people in ordinary families whose origins are obscured by this catholic approach.

At or near Lincoln three men came to a deal. Bruccius Colasunus and Caratius Colasunus, presumably brothers, decided to invest in a dedication to Mars and the Spirits of the Emperors. It was a thoroughly conventional dedication which might have been made anywhere in the Empire by people loyal to the state. Even Mars was not in this case conflated with some local variant. In order to make this dedication the Colasuni decided to contribute 100 sesterces between them, a sum which was the equivalent of a single gold coin. The money paid for a statuette of the god about 272 millimetres high on a plinth which was made for them by a man called Celatus, an *aerarius* (coppersmith), who threw in a pound of bronze worth three silver coins (denarii), which were equivalent to 12 sesterces. The product of Celatus' work was a lethargically muscular nude figure of Mars topped with an enormous helmet and plume, his arms held out to hold, presumably, weapons, which are now lost (plate 8). The details of the financial arrangements are recounted on the plinth.[31] The statue was then taken to Torksey on the Foss Dike, a canal which linked the colony at Lincoln to the River Trent, and thrown in, doubtless to the sound of appropriate invocations. There is no indication that the gift fulfilled a vow, though presumably it did, and nor do we learn anything about the Colasuni brothers' business. There is an echo here of the famous freedmen brothers of Pompeii, the Vettii, and their ostentatious house with its vulgar displays. Of course we know nothing about the Colasuni but their names are most likely to be Latinized native ones, suggesting they were of British or Gaulish origin. Their choice of dedication would fit with a pair of provincial freedmen for whom life had brought some success. The coppersmith Celatus' name is clearly derived from *celatum*, a 'secret', which tells us nothing really except that whoever named him probably had a personal reason for such an unusual choice; this might be consistent also with the name given to a slave. Perhaps he too was a freedman and was known to the Colasuni through their web of commercial contacts.

Another flamboyant metalworker was a man with the unequivocally native name Boduogenus. He was responsible for manufacturing a peculiarly elegant bronze skillet (known as a *trulla*) which proudly bears his name on the handle and is decorated with a winged genius and dolphins (plate 9). It was found in 1841 or before at Prickwillow in the Isle of Ely, Cambridgeshire, which unfortunately means we know nothing about the context in which it was deposited. This type of decorated vessel belonged to a southern Italian tradition but the maker's name belongs to Britain or Gaul; obviously, this does not guarantee he was a Briton or a Gaul but it must be a serious possibility. Either way, he was an accomplished artisan servicing a thoroughly Romanized end of the market and perhaps learned his skills as an apprentice in the workshop of an immigrant craftsman. The bronze is inlaid with niello, a compound of sulphur and a metal such as silver or copper used to create a black inlay to highlight decorative features. It is, of course, inconceivable that this was the only piece Boduogenus made but it is the only one to survive known to have been his work. Far too ostentatious to have been a piece of mundane kitchenware, the piece was either a prestigious display item subsequently chosen to be an offering or was specially selected by Boduogenus himself to seek divine protection and support for his livelihood. A record of activities before the fourth century AD at the shrine of the Oak of Mamre at Terebinthus near Hebron in Palestine provides a context. Here it was said that 'each man created some beautiful product of his labour . . . [and] offered it according to his vow, as provision for that feast, both for himself and his dependants'.[32] Of course, not all craftsmen were as accomplished as Boduogenus, or those that were may have been less inclined to dispose of their best work this way. Several notably less impressive examples were found in the sacred spring at Bath.

The remarkable reach of Rome's commercial routes meant that already by the late first century Britain found itself home to an exotic goddess who presided over her ecstatic mystery cult. Isis had reached Italy by the third century BC. Her temple at Pompeii, destroyed in 79, is the best known centre of the cult in the Roman world. It drew on Isis' ancient Egyptian tradition as the giver of life to her murdered brother Osiris, becoming in a classicized idiom a kind of mother goddess who promised an afterlife to her initiates. London apparently also had an Iseum by around this date. None of the initiates or priests is known, but one anonymous individual placed an address on a flagon of the late first century which reads, 'London, at the temple of Isis'.[33] This may simply be a convenient address for an adjacent house, or it may mean the flagon was once temple property.

The availability of exotic cults must have appealed to those who came from further afield than Celerianus' northern Gaul. We do not know Aulus Alfidius Olussa's profession, but someone conveniently added to his tombstone the afterthought that he was 'born at Athens'.[34] He died at the age of seventy, another reminder that people have always been able to live to respectable ages; it is merely the fact that until modern times fewer had a decent chance of doing so. Aulus Alfidius Olussa was apparently a Roman citizen. His *tria nomina* makes that likely enough but the additional information that he was a member of the Pomptine voting tribe might confirm it. Roman citizens outside Rome were all allocated to one of the thirty-one rural tribes, regardless of where they actually lived. Membership of the tribe awarded a citizen nominal voting rights, though practical circumstances meant it was almost impossible for these to be exercised. However, another theory is that the letters POMP are simply short for another part of his name. The form of the inscription dates his death to the late first century, making him a man who must have lived through the invasion of Britain, even if he had not witnessed it personally, perhaps coming to London to make his fortune in the aftermath of the Boudican Revolt.

Nevertheless London's population, like that of anywhere else in Roman Britain or the Empire, would inevitably have tended to a far younger average age than today. In that respect the teeming population of Londinium's streets would have resembled more closely those of a Third World city of the present age. Despite the preponderance of younger people, the premature death of someone like Claudia Martina would have been all too common an experience. The vast majority of tombstones record deaths of people (mainly men) in their twenties, thirties or forties. Children rarely feature on tombstones, which were much more likely to be set up by wives or husbands to each other, by freedmen to their master, or to a soldier by his friends. Occasional family tragedies do filter their way through the fog of time.

Just as with Alfidius Olussa, we may know the names of many others but not how they earned a living. Conversely, the 'Aldgate-Pulborough Potter' is known to us only through his products but even that is enough to establish something of his personality. Samian pottery was a Western Empire version of red-slipped pottery that was produced in a number of places in the Roman world. It served as a higher-quality ceramic product. Samian ware was used almost everywhere in Roman Britain from the time of the invasion until the early third century, when the industry fell into decline and disappeared. Manufacturing samian pottery took great skill, though in fact many of the products exhibit a surprising amount of carelessness. The samian potteries that serviced Britain were almost all in Gaul. A complex web of potters, traders, shippers and retailers kept the industry going, with vast quantities arriving in London and other ports of Roman Britain from the mid-first century to the early third. If Tiberinius Celerianus had no involvement in the trade, he would have known plenty of people who did have.

It would be a great mistake to assume this pottery was high-status material. High status wares were made of glass, silver or gold. Samian pottery was simply a cheap substitute. Far better than ordinary kitchenwares, it was still much cheaper than anything made of glass or bullion and its abundance shows it was accessible to many people. These people included Britons, or so it would seem. One small samian dish of the late first century in date and found in Bedfordshire has a series of names inscribed on the base: Esico, Litullus, Commico and Lousico.[35] They are all native names though they could possibly have originated in Gaul. Why several names should have been inscribed is unclear unless it was a shared dish, perhaps representing several members of the same family, who either used the dish on a daily basis or had shared it at a funeral. And indeed another samian dish found in a Roman cemetery in

Ospringe in Kent has several Roman names around it: Lucius, Lucianus, Iulius, Diantus, Victor, Victoricus and Victorina, with the phrase *vas communis*, 'common dish'.[36]

Samian dishes were also used in cremations as lids for urns containing cremated remains, and turn up in all sorts of quite mundane domestic contexts in modest settlements. In short, samian cannot have been particularly expensive. Today it remains one of the most distinctive of all Roman artefacts found in Britain. Samian ware was almost invariably a rich orange-red colour and was produced in a vast array of forms from small cups to elaborately decorated bowls and dishes. The decoration was often individual to specific factories and many potters added their names to the decorative schemes, or stamped their names in the plain ware cups, dishes and bowls. They are of enormous importance to the dating of Roman sites, especially when collections can be associated with absolute dates. The most important of these is the crate of new samian found at Pompeii which cannot therefore be dated after August 79. Samian from the primary levels on Hadrian's Wall, which cannot have been deposited before about 120–2, is also extremely important. The output of the Gaulish samian factories was on a truly industrial scale, comparable with that of the Victorian potteries of the British Midlands.

Nevertheless, some time in the early second century, probably between 120 and 150, the 'Aldgate-Pulborough Potter' was certain he could break into the samian market. The main drawback to his entrepreneurial scheme was that he seems to have been one of the most incompetent potters ever to try his hand with the wheel. Whether this was a monumental lack of talent, or simply a failure to recognize that training and experience counted for everything, we cannot know. His wares were so triumphantly awful that the only possible explanation for their dispersal into the market at all is that they were bought as curiosities. Found at Aldgate in London and at Pulborough in Sussex (among a few other places), the fragments of bowls were clearly made by the same person. His trademarks were to create chaotic decorated scenes with casually distributed decorative features, and then to cover his bowls with fingerprints, scuff marks and scratches. He finished off his handiwork by over-firing them so badly that the clay blistered and caused the slip to burn and flake off.[37] It is no great surprise to learn that the Aldgate-Pulborough Potter is known only to history from little more than a dozen potsherds. Having said that, his work was not perhaps as conspicuously badly made as it might be today in our world of machine-made products. The Roman world was a handmade world and that went hand in hand with enormous variation in quality. In fact almost all samian ware exhibits surprising levels of poor handiwork, from uneven rims, offset bands of decoration, smudges, the use of worn moulds, to fingerprints and gouges. Even so, the Aldgate-Pulborough Potter did well to stand out, though remarkably the distribution of his products suggests that he enjoyed some modest success with his business.[38]

The Aldgate-Pulborough Potter was not the only one to try his hand at producing local samian for the British market. A rather more organized business, but not necessarily much more successful, was set up at Colchester towards the end of the second century. In 1933, during the excavation of a series of Roman kilns located around 500 metres west of the Roman colony's walls, one kiln turned out to be unique in the archaeology of Roman Britain and still is.[39] That kiln was used for firing samian ware. Large and circular, it was a highly sophisticated piece of apparatus which had clearly been constructed by or on the directions of a master potter. It was fitted with special tubes designed to transmit the heat through the kiln but without allowing fumes or flames to come into direct contact with any of the vessels and thereby wreck the shiny red finish so characteristic of samian ware. The complex joints between the separate sections of the tubes, designed to prevent any gas leakage, were reminiscent of the seals in the joints of the American Space Shuttle's booster rockets. This design feature is never found in ordinary Roman pottery kilns. The excavation also produced the remains of samian pottery moulds, as well as examples of bowls made from them. It was quite clear that two different potters were involved but sadly neither of them signed his work. Known now only as Potter A and Potter B, the former produced pots that were inclined to discolour and which do not seem to have been very durable, while the latter's work had a better surface and colour. Whatever happened, the business does not seem to have lasted long. It may have been an attempt to cash in on the decline of the Gaulish samian potteries, perhaps even by Gaulish potters who moved into Britain to save on overheads by manufacturing locally. Evidently it came to nothing for the kiln was abandoned and Potter A and Potter B simply disappear from history with little or no trace of their products ever making the slightest inroad into the British market.

Brockley Hill (Sulloniacis) lies on the road north-west from London which led to the town of St Albans, known in Roman times as Verulamium. It was a busy thoroughfare, not only because of the proximity of two major towns but also because of the traffic it carried on into the heart of Britain and the Welsh Marches. It was an ideal location for a commercial enterprise and, with the ready availability of clay, it attracted a community of specialist potters. They manufactured, among other things, that peculiarly distinctive type of Roman pottery, the *mortarium*, though in fact production took place in quite a wide area in what is now known as the 'Verulamium Region'. If *mortarium* sounds like a mortar, that is exactly what a *mortarium* was, a heavy-duty shallow bowl with gritted interior and a thick flange which helped the user grip it while food was ground up. The *mortarium* was an essential component of the Roman kitchen and only started to appear in any significant quantities after 43. Initially most of those used in Britain were made by Gaulish potters such as Quintus Valerius Veranus, whose products were shipped over to Britain and began to spread northwards, carried there by the army. But *mortaria* are heavy and it obviously made sense to make them closer to the new markets; this seems to have stimulated a British industry.

Mortarium potters often had the gratifying tendency in the first and second centuries to stamp their work over the flange with dies bearing their names. This was not at all usual for manufacturers of practical everyday wares, which were scarcely ever marked like this. The case of the *mortaria* suggests a very particular kind of branded specialist pride, though there may also have been a practical need to identify their products in shared kilns. The Verulamium Region *mortaria* potters are among the best known because of their stamps, with over fifty having been identified.[40] They include an interesting mix of men with distinctly Roman or Romanized names, such as the citizen Gaius Attius Marinus, active around 95–130, Saturninus, active around 105–40, and Doinus, who was at work earlier between 70 and 110.

The meaning of the name 'Doinus' is not known; it is not a Latin word though it has been Latinized. He was perhaps a man of Gaulish or British origin who acquired the necessary potting skills to make specialist wares. Marinus, whose name simply means 'belonging to the sea' similar to our word 'mariner', may have been the freedman of someone called Gaius Attius (. . .) and would thus have been set up in business by his former master. This was a typical route into commercial activity in the Roman world. He may have been a Briton but it is also possible that he was Gaulish. Gaius Attius Marinus seems to have been particularly entrepreneurial. He made *mortaria* at Brockley Hill and Colchester to begin with, moving on to Radlett in Hertfordshire before reaching Hartshill-Mancetter in the Midlands by around 110. Here he seems to have stayed until he either died or retired around 130. It is possible to track his career from the different ceramic fabrics, literally the individual clays used, of his name-stamped products, which confirm that they were all made by him or his staff. He was joined at Hartshill-Mancetter by other Verulamium Region potters called Doccas and Nidus, perhaps his own freedmen, who had perhaps decided that they could sell to the northern frontier more effectively if they were a little bit closer. It is quite clear from finds of *mortaria* on some northern frontier forts that most were supplied from Hartshill-Mancetter at this time. Sulloniacus was a *mortaria* potter who worked at the Roman military frontier town of Corbridge. His name was linked to the ancient name for Brockley Hill so perhaps he had originally come from there. Indeed, he may have even belonged to the family who had once owned the land at Brockley Hill. Its name, Sulloniacis, is thought to derive from a personal name which would have been 'Sullonios'.[41]

Some of the name stamps show that the *mortarium* business was a trade that could be passed from father to son, a custom which belongs to all cultures at all times. Matugenus, active between 80 and 125 and whose name is very decidedly native (*Matu-* means 'bear'), tells us on his *mortaria* that he was the son of the distinctly Latin-named potter Albinus. We seem here to have what was probably a community of people whose identities were becoming blurred as Roman and native were merged through a mixture of marriage and cultural traditions, such as freely using either Roman or native names. Some of them, Albinus included, and another citizen named Quintus Rutilius Ripanus, tell us that they worked at a place called Lugdunum, thought to be Bricket Wood in Hertfordshire. The products were successful and ended up being scattered all over the area, turning up in London and other towns and rural and military sites across central and northern Britain. Further north at Rossington Bridge near the fort at Doncaster another local *mortarium* dynasty seems to have sprung up when a potter called Sarrius left Hartshill-Mancetter and headed off, presumably to chase after the military market. He stamped his work, sometimes with one or other of a pair of potters called Setibogius and Secundua, perhaps his sons or apprentices. They did well, with their products turning up on both Hadrian's Wall and the Antonine Wall, the short-lived northernmost frontier in the mid-second century that ran roughly between where Edinburgh and Glasgow are now.

In a few cases the potters turned their hands to other products. Dares was a *mortarium* potter in the Verulamium Region who also seems to have manufactured amphorae, which he stamped – even using the same die.[42] His name was especially unusual. One of Aeneas' Trojan warrior companions in Virgil's *Aeneid* was called Dares and another turns up in the *Iliad* as a priest of Hephaistos.[43] It has been suggested that he perhaps arrived in Britain as a slave from the Eastern Empire, though there is no reason why he need not have been born and named in Britain either; as an aside it is worth noting that American slaves were not infrequently named by their owners after characters taken from classical mythology, perpetuating an ancient tradition.

The Verulamium Region potters were by no means the only ones who stamped their work but they are the most conspicuous group of all the Romano-British *mortaria* production centres. By the mid-second century their industry had faded away, to be supplanted by new ones but with potters who were far less inclined to record their names. Britain developed a number of major pottery industries in the third and fourth centuries, capturing large regional markets, but the men and women who made these wares did so in almost total anonymity. The case of Sennianus is an exception (see chapter 6 below).

One of the most significant changes to life in Britain was the arrival of the codified legal system of Roman law, its enforcement through the

Roman administrative system and the appearance of legal documents. Around the same time that the Aldgate-Pulborough Potter was busy putting himself out of business, and Gaius Attius Marinus was establishing himself, some sort of legal hearing involving property resulted in Lucius Julius Bellicus, or his agent, coming to London. The exact nature of the case is unknown but Bellicus asserted his ownership of a wood in the territory of the Cantiaci (Kent). The wood was known as Verlucionum and had cost him 40 denarii when buying it from one Titus Valerius Silvinus. Managed woodland was an essential part of the Roman economy; it was used for fuel, buildings and all sorts of everyday utensils and tools. Indeed, so ubiquitous was wood that the Latin for timber, *materia*, has entered our language as a generic term for any substance used to make something. So a piece of woodland was an important resource.

The name Verlucionum was not unique; a settlement in Wiltshire was called Verlucio, which is believed to mean 'very bright place' based on the Latinized British components.[44] Bellicus' *cognomen* is simply an unaltered Latin word meaning 'pertaining to war', with Lucius Julius being entirely standard and innocuous Roman names. Bellicus might easily have been an ex-soldier, or the son of one, who was awarded the name for his military achievements, but it is no less likely that he was a Briton who had been given a Latin name that reflected his tribal warrior forbears. The reason the case was brought is unknown to us, and so is its resolution, but Bellicus must have been one of thousands who came to London annually to have their cases heard by the provincial governor. Remarkably, the wooden writing tablet document is precisely dated to the 14 March 118 in the reign of Trajan.[45] This places the hearing under the governorship of Marcus Atilius Metilius Bradua or Quintus Pompeius Falco who succeeded him in 118. A startling survival, the tablet must stand in the record now for hundreds of thousands of similar documents that have not survived. It also symbolizes an aspect of the Roman world that we can surely understand: the right to have recourse to the law, and a place to go where that could happen. Forty years later on 3 December 158 a man called Tittius borrowed from another man called Aprilis a sum of money which he agreed were coins of good quality. He also agreed to pay it back with interest at some point in the future (the part of the text which would have specified this is lost). All this was set out in a deed, part of which survived to be excavated in Throgmorton Avenue in London in 2006.[46] It was a trivial enough arrangement, but it demonstrates how the Roman world operated according to a code of legally binding agreements. The agreement was made at a place called Lara, which is sadly now completely unknown. It was probably in Britain, but not necessarily so. At any rate it must be assumed at least that Tittius or Aprilis were in Britain when the deed was lost.

The Roman world was in large part defined by its legal codes. With law went order and in a civilization that prided itself on urban organization there was inevitably going to be an antisocial element of the type so familiar to us today. Gaius Severius Emeritus was a centurion placed, as so many centurions were, in charge of civilian policing. His 'beat' was the region around the religious centre and spa town of Bath, Aquae Sulis, which probably means that he was detached from the II Legion Augusta, which by the late first century was based at Caerleon in South Wales in the old territory of the Silures. Centurions played a vital role in all sorts of everyday supervisory jobs in a world that had no civilian police force. While presumably many of the pilgrims to Bath were ordinary harmless individuals, Severius Emeritus comes across to us like a careworn copper well into middle age frustrated by the endless stupidity of vandalism committed by gangs of oafs in Bath. So, he set up an inscription to record the fact that 'this holy place' had been 'wrecked by the insolent' and that he had restored it (plate 10).[47] One can imagine his exasperation and resignation at what had presumably been only one in a series of annoying incidents and which he was glad to leave behind him when he finally retired.

CHAPTER FOUR

LIFE ON THE FRONTIER

The comings and goings in the towns of the developing province will have been viewed with a distant curiosity by the troops stationed on the northern frontier. Many will have passed through London or been stationed there at some point in their careers. Far away from London's congested wharfs and elaborate public buildings, a mundane incident took place in the fort at Carlisle on 7 November 83. It was the last winter of several years of campaigning on the northern frontier by the governor Gnaeus Julius Agricola, who had been charged with completing the conquest of Britain. That war had now been going on for forty years. Two soldiers participating in the fighting had business to settle. Quintus Cassius Secundus, a soldier of the XX Legion, confirmed in writing that he had borrowed 100 silver denarii from one of his compatriots, Gaius Geminius Mansuetus. The sum was considerable and was at least equivalent to four months' pay before deductions. It is on the one hand remarkable that Cassius Secundus was prepared to indebt himself to that extent, and on the other remarkable that Geminius Mansuetus had it to lend. The transaction was recorded on a writing tablet which ended up in silt that had filled a recess between cobbles laid over a military ditch at Carlisle.[1] Fascinatingly, a Cassius Secundus who was a veteran of the XX Legion died at the age of eighty and was buried at the legion's base at Chester some time in the second century after an honourable discharge.[2] If this is the same man then he clearly survived Agricola's war and lived on through to the time when his legion was sent north once more, this time to build Hadrian's Wall.

We do not where either man came from originally, but Gaul, Italy or Spain are the most likely candidates. We can only hope that Cassius Secundus paid his debt to Geminius Mansuetus, who disappears from the record after 83. One who certainly never came back from the war was Ammonius, son of Damio, a centurion with the auxiliary infantry unit, the First Cohort of Hispanians.[3] His name suggests that he originated in the eastern part of the Empire; wherever he joined up he went on to serve twenty-seven years but never lived to enjoy the fruits of retirement. His tombstone bears the full legend *Dis Manibus*, 'to the spirits of the departed', which is normally taken to be typical of the first century – later inscriptions abbreviate this to DM. The stone was reused in a medieval chapel at Ardoch in Perthshire, close to the site of a Roman fort first occupied in the early 80s when a series of forts along the Gask Ridge was established by Agricola.

The most protracted campaigns took place in the late 70s and early 80s when Agricola embarked on a war to conquer the whole of northern Britain. His tenure began in or around 78, just eighteen years after the Boudican Revolt. His war would have been unthinkable had the province in the south not been comprehensively secured, and since he had been with the XX Legion during the Boudican Revolt he knew better than most how nearly Britain had been lost.

Agricola's campaigns involved the XX Legion and part of the IX. Thanks to the fact that his son-in-law was the historian Tacitus we know a remarkable amount about the progress deep into the north, despite the inevitable bias. Archaeology and aerial photography have gone a long way to support some of the detail and there is no question that Agricola conducted an astonishingly efficient and sustained campaign which resulted in a huge development of the province's infrastructure. In the summer of 83 the war reached its climax in the Battle of Mons Graupius, somewhere in eastern or north-eastern Scotland, where the Caledonian tribal leader Calgacus was defeated.

Demetrius was a Greek academic who must have served on Agricola's staff and turns up on some strange inscriptions found at the legionary fortress of York, by then home to the IX Legion. York is no surprise – Agricola must have based himself in this new fortress which would evolve into the military capital of the northern frontier zone and later the political capital of the northern part of Britannia. Demetrius deposited two silvered bronze plaques. One is dedicated to the gods of the governor's residence, and the other to Oceanus and Tethys. It was a very esoteric gesture. In 325 BC Alexander the Great had left a similar dedication at the mouth of the Indus on the other side of the known world. Demetrius must be one and the same with a Demetrius of Tarsus who told the historian Plutarch about taking part in an expedition to 'remote and desolate islands' off the coast of Britain some time just before the year 83; he must have meant the Hebrides. He visited one and found it to have only a few 'holy men' for inhabitants whom the Romans regarded as sacrosanct and would not harm, itself an interesting anticipation of the Christian hermits who would live in these places in future centuries. The dedication left by Demetrius now recorded his own visit to the opposite end of the world from the one Alexander had reached more than four centuries earlier.[4]

Unlike Tacitus these three men perhaps personally witnessed the final battle in the Agricolan campaign at Mons Graupius. Tacitus provides a detailed account of the speech given by the tribal leader Calgacus.[5] It is of course almost completely implausible that Tacitus had the slightest idea of what Calgacus really said, if he said anything at all, or even if indeed he really existed. The name Calgacus means 'swordsman' which suggests a generic warrior figure; he is unmentioned at earlier points in the campaign or subsequently, making it likely that he was created by Tacitus in order for him to juxtapose the tribal position against Agricola's, whose speech as quoted by Tacitus has more chance of at least being loosely based on what the governor delivered that day. Since his Agricolan narrative was built around the career of a specific personality, it made dramatic sense for Tacitus' hero to fight a warrior of equivalent prestige among his own people.

This literary device was one that ancient historians tended to employ when they wanted to dramatize a confrontation and provide a context in which they could set what they perceived to be opposing points of view. Nevertheless, Tacitus may have had access to an agglomeration of evidence that gave him a good idea of how some Britons viewed the Roman presence half a century after Claudius arrived. Calgacus was therefore utilized as a noble-savage mouthpiece for a litany of grievances that Tacitus could use as evidence for the decay of Roman society, Agricola of course being an exception. Calgacus' fictitious speech included a stinging criticism of his own people whose internecine quarrels had given the Roman army a cycle of victories, compounded by the willingness of Gauls, Germans and now Britons to fight for the Romans. Calgacus is depicted unwittingly by Tacitus as a proto-Trotsky advocate for world revolution: if the Caledonians stand firm now, then the rest of the Britons, and the Gauls and Germans will surely rise up too and throw off the yoke of servitude in the form of taxation or labour in the mines. The speech allowed Tacitus to put into Calgacus' mouth an excoriating critique of the decadent state of the Roman world; this was really his purpose. The Romans are depicted as merciless and indiscriminate plunderers who 'create desolation and call it peace'. Tacitus refers to the Britons sold into slavery, itself an interesting echo of the fate of Fortunata, the Gaulish slave, or, more than a century later, Regina, the British tribeswoman, slave and freedwoman wife of Barates. Calgacus' speech and the man himself might be a work of fiction but even so they probably enshrine aspects of the experience of some Britons under Roman dominion in the late first century.

In the aftermath of the Agricolan war the northern frontier in Britain settled down to rather more than thirty years of inconclusive garrisoning. Vindolanda was one fort of dozens of new installations in northern Britain. The Ninth Cohort of Batavians was one unit of dozens of auxiliary units stationed across northern and western Britain, along with three citizen legions, the II, IX and XX. Thanks to a freak set of circumstances some of the Batavians' archives have survived in the form of wooden writing tablets. The tablets represent therefore only one very small moment in a complex and extensive world. We know little about the state of Britain at the end of the first century at the time the tablets ended up being buried and preserved beyond the fact that Agricola's conquests in Scotland had been abandoned. Roman Britain thereafter equated to what is now England and Wales, with a kind of frontier stretching between the Tyne and the Solway Firth. The spine of the frontier was a road, now known as the Stanegate, with forts along it, such as Vindolanda, and others to the rear and forward.

One of the greatest paradoxes in Romano-British history is the historical silence after 84, in spite of it having been an obsession of Roman historians up to that date. The only reference from now until the accession of Hadrian more than thirty years later is to a governor of Britain during the reign of Domitian (81–96), one of the three or four who must have succeeded Agricola. Domitian ordered the execution of Sallustius Lucullus, governor of Britain, for renaming a new design of spear the 'Lucullan'; he had perhaps designed it himself, and quite conceivably as a result of his experiences in Britain.[6]

There is a curious postscript to this story which in an ideal world would have turned out to be one of the most interesting biographical vignettes from the whole period. Lucullus seems to have stimulated a great deal of latter-day speculation, which centres on a stone inscription purporting to be by him found at Chichester, though it is now long lost.[7] The text was apparently a 'dedication' to Domitian. Another, genuine, stone inscription from Chichester also names a Lucullus, son of Amminus, who made a dedication to the Genius of the Place. Since 'Amminus' appears to be a Romanized form of a British name, it has been suggested this Lucullus was a descendant of Togidubnus, known to have been resident as a client king in the area in the late first century.[8] This led to a more recent suggestion that the Luculli of the two stones were one and the same, and that therefore Sallustius Lucullus was a man of British tribal descent who uniquely rose to the senatorial order and was made a governor of Britain.[9] The story would be fascinating if true but in reality there is no means of verifying the authenticity of a long-lost inscription.[10] Sallustius Lucullus must be content with a single known reference about the spear that brought his demise during the rule of a paranoid emperor.

Nevertheless, it is worth saying that the inscription, also from Chichester, which names Togidubnus, himself only otherwise verified in a single reference by Tacitus, would almost certainly have been rejected by some scholars as a fake had its text survived only as an antiquarian record of a stone now lost. This would have been on the grounds that it was 'too good to be true' – just as the Classicianus tombstone was rejected by Collingwood as being that of the procurator, and the principal reason now given by some for refuting the idea that Sallustius Lucullus and the Lucullus of the Chichester inscriptions are one and the same man.

Instead we are left for these decades with one of the most astonishing archives from anywhere in the Empire at all. Agricola was withdrawn and Tacitus' attention went with him. It is left to the Vindolanda letters to fill the void, which they do in such an unusually idiosyncratic manner that it is hard to believe the chance circumstances that led to their survival. Devoid almost entirely of history in the true sense of the word, instead they record everyday life in a very colourful way, though the translations of their texts must be used with caution (see the Note on Sources at the end of this book).

One tablet refers to the Britons in general rather than individuals but it goes some way to helping us understand where Britons existed in the social hierarchy. It should be said that Vindolanda was not in any sense manned by 'Romans' in the pure sense. The principal unit based at Vindolanda at this time was an infantry auxiliary unit, the First Cohort of Tungrians. The Tungri were a tribe from Gallia Belgica, originally regarded by the Romans and the Gauls as part of the Germanic peoples.[11] One of the other units stationed at Vindolanda around this time was the Ninth Cohort of Batavians. The Batavians came originally from the part of the world we now call Holland. A unit like either of these was commanded by an equestrian prefect, almost certainly of provincial origin himself. The writing tablet concerned is fragmentary and tells us no more than that the Britons did not use armour, many were mounted but did not use swords while mounted, and they did not throw javelins from horseback. It is not clear whether the writer is referring to Britons serving as irregular auxiliaries or Britons as enemies. He may be discussing would-be recruits who insisted on being mounted, which was better paid, but could not fight the Roman way while on horseback. Either way the writer used the key term *Brittunculi* to describe them.[12] The word is pejorative – it denotes in disparaging terms that the Britons were a lesser, inferior group of people; in our terms this would be racist. In Roman terms it is interesting that the writer who was almost certainly a provincial recruit himself perceived himself to be superior to the

Britons, regardless of whether he was talking about native recruits or the enemy. Indeed, in this respect he was actively seeking to assert his own Roman-ness by compensation through denigration of another ethnic group.

As so often with Roman Britain the Britons are otherwise more or less absent. Instead we have the records of those stationed at Vindolanda, those who traded with the fort, and those who were their correspondents elsewhere. Chrauttius seems to have been a soldier at the fort who wrote to his friend and former comrade Veldedeius at London. Veldedeius had evidently been detached to serve on the governor's bodyguard in the provincial capital as a groom (*equisio*). The letter concerns trivial business including Chrauttius' hopes that a pair of shears he wanted from a veterinary doctor called Virilis can be sent to him.[13] He also wants his greetings sent to his sister Thuttena. This is especially interesting. Thuttena must have lived in London, which one might not have expected had Chrauttius been a recruit who had signed up with the Roman army on the continent, leaving his family behind when he was posted to Britain. Instead it looks more as if he came with his family in tow, perhaps not even joining the army until he was in Britain. This is reminiscent of the family memorial of Tadius Exuperatus from Caerleon which dates from a century later.[14] Why the letter was at Vindolanda, if it was sent to London originally, can only be explained if Veldedeius was subsequently restored to his old unit and returned to Vindolanda bringing the letter back among his effects, unless it was a copy.

One of the most famous of the Vindolanda tablets is the letter from Octavius to Candidus. Octavius was involved in some way with the trading of commodities, though it is not clear whether he was acquiring these in the capacity of a military official or whether he was a private trader hoping to sell them on to the army, in this case through Candidus, who was at Vindolanda. His main concern is that Candidus sends him money so that he can pay for goods on which he had already laid out a deposit. These included grain and hides. A lack of stock had already caused Octavius a problem – someone called Frontinus had turned up to buy hides, saying he would return for them on 13 January. Unfortunately, Octavius could not supply them till 1 March, the upshot of which was that Frontinus got his hides from elsewhere. Part of the problem seems to have been the roads – Octavius had been reluctant to send his wagons down 'while the roads are bad'. This is not in any sense a paraphrase – the Latin (*dum viae male sunt*) says exactly and unequivocally that. The letter is a fleeting glimpse of the ad hoc manner in which the army was supplied and a small indication of the people involved in servicing its colossal needs.[15] Some of the goods which were shipped up to Vindolanda proudly bore their manufacturers' name stamps and trademarks, such as the leather shoes made by Lucius Aebutius Thales, son of Titus, stamped with his name, vine leaves and cornucopiae.[16] His name alone is a matter of some interest. Aebutius was a well-known old Roman family name, but Thales was a Greek philosopher from Miletus, which perhaps means that the shoemaker was by origin a Greek or was named by someone who enjoyed such esoteric connections, rather as if someone today named a child after Bertrand Russell or Proust. It is possible he worked on the northern frontier but London or York is probably more likely.

Thuttena, the sister of Chrauttius, is a reminder that women were just as much a part of the soldiers' world. While she might have stayed in London, other women accompanied their menfolk to the frontier. This was a well-established part of the Roman army's life. In the year AD 9 during the reign of Augustus, Quinctilius Varus was governor of Germany. Over-confident and oppressive in his style, Varus soon faced an uprising designed to attract him out on campaign. This he did, accompanied by a substantial wagontrain and 'not a few women and children'.[17] This slowed the march down and contributed to the ensuing disaster in which Varus and three legions were completely wiped out.

Almost a century later women and children were still part of the dangerous world on the edge of the Roman Empire. This may represent sustained complacency or it may represent the realization that frontier life was much more palatable if a sense of normal life could be sustained, whatever the risks. In 1837 the British soldier and explorer Henry Rawlinson, then in Persia and thus very far from home, friends and family, just as the Roman frontier garrisons were remote from theirs, recorded in his diary how the acquisition of a woman companion 'enlivens my solitude'.[18]

The most famous letter of all from Vindolanda is the one written by Claudia Severa to her friend Sulpicia Lepidina. Both women were the wives of commanding officers. Claudia was the wife of a man called Aelius Brocchus who commanded an unknown unit at an unknown place called Briga, presumably somewhere not too far from Vindolanda. Sulpicia was the wife of Flavius Cerealis, the commanding officer of the Ninth Cohort of Batavians at Vindolanda, whom we know from one of the other documents to have been in post in the year 104, during the reign of Trajan (98–117). Claudia wanted Sulpicia to attend her birthday party and sent greetings from herself, her husband and her son. The letter is brief and appears to have been written by a scribe apart from a postscript in another hand, probably Claudia's own. If so, this is the earliest known Latin inscription by a woman (plate 11).[19] The letter is instantly redolent of the world of the British army in India or Afghanistan, or the US army in the American West, in the nineteenth century where officers and their families in particular tried to maintain some semblance of civilized life. The impression is reinforced by the discovery at Vindolanda of a tablet bearing a writing exercise which reproduces a line from Virgil's *Aeneid*.[20] The method of teaching was commonplace in antiquity and of course continued to be so for centuries afterwards. It is reasonable to suggest that the Vindolanda examples were being used by the children of the commanding officer. At Silchester, the capital of the tribal region of the Atrebates, there is another Virgilian tag, in this case *conticuere omnes*, 'all fell silent', and attached to a list of names inscribed on a tile while the clay was still wet.[21]

We have here at Vindolanda an effort to sustain polite society among the families of the officer class. For women the experience must have been challenging, with the endless problems caused by being at the end of the supply chain in one of the remotest parts of their known world and with, presumably, the constant risk of death or serious injury afflicting their husbands. It also shows that Claudia was entirely comfortable with the idea that Sulpicia would have set out, chaperoned and guarded of course, in a carriage across the wild uplands of northern Britain to attend a birthday party. We can only guess at their ages but since Claudia had 'a little son' (*filiolus*), she is likely to have been no more than twenty to twenty-five at the oldest. She may have been still a teenager. For such women life was fraught with all sorts of potential disasters, from the death of their children to the unexpected death of their husbands at the hands of the enemy or from natural causes.[22] We might remember here the death of the Dobunnian tribeswoman Verecunda at Templeborough at the age of thirty-five mentioned earlier.

Nonetheless, it is clear even from the lists of household goods and clothing that there was time enough for relaxation and enjoyment of a reasonable standard of living. One document lists 'tunics for dining', while others mention a range of foodstuffs from chicken to grain, beans to cumin, and nuts to ham. If Claudia and Severa were friends so, too, were their husbands. Cerealis wrote to Brocchus to ask for some hunting nets to be sent as a favour, though he added a request that they be strongly repaired first.[23] A century or more later, little had changed for officers commanding these units in the far north as they idled away their spare time hunting.[24]

Some found other ways to pass the time. Around 150 years earlier, Quintus Tullius Cicero had used his spare moments on campaign in Britain to indulge in literary composition. Now a Roman poet found his way to the northern frontier. A Junius Juvenalis is known to have commanded the First Cohort of Dalmatians, an auxiliary infantry unit which was certainly in Britain by the year 122 and based at the fort of Maryport on the Cumbrian coast by 138.[25] This could very well be the poet Decimus Junius Juvenalis, known to us as Juvenal. The identification is not only because of the name. The inscription recording his command was found at Aquinum (modern Aquino) in Italy, Juvenal's birthplace. In his second *Satire* Juvenal referred to how Roman arms had conquered the 'Orcades [Orkneys] and short-nighted Britons', which sounds very much like a personal anecdote; the shortness of nights would only have been apparent in the summer, the principal campaigning season.[26] Various references in Juvenal's poetry suggest that he wrote during the reigns of Trajan and Hadrian, by which time he was already of advancing years. If he was therefore born some time between AD 60 and 70 then his position as the commanding officer of an auxiliary unit must belong probably to the 90s, or around the same time as the Vindolanda letters.

If Juvenal was based at Maryport (Alauna) it is a pity that no inscription has survived from the fort there to confirm that. The coastal fort has produced a large number of dedications to Jupiter Optimus Maximus in the name of the resident unit and a succession of commanding officers. All these men were equestrian officers and would have expected to serve with a number of different units as they worked their way up the career ladder. Of their origins we normally know nothing. Their names usually give nothing away either, though a rare instance from Maryport is one of the Jupiter dedications of a later date. Lucius Antistius Lupus Verianus came from Sicca Veneria, a colony in North Africa (in present-day Tunisia), to serve as the prefect commanding the First Cohort of Spaniards.[27] By the late first century AD their equestrian rank was of no great significance. They could have come from almost any established part of the Roman world where a provincial aristocracy had had time to emerge. Their forbears from a century before may have been tribal warriors, as were those of Classicianus and his wife Julia Pacata Indiana, or they may have come from Italy or another long-settled part of the Roman world. Their respective appointments in northern Britain were probably for two to three years, after which they would have been transferred to another unit, assuming of course that they had done their jobs well and also stayed alive, doubtless taking their wives and children with them. At this stage they were probably still young men by our standards and were likely to have been in their twenties or, at most, their thirties.[28]

The commanders of auxiliary units also periodically saw their troops come to the end of their service. The reward for good service was an honourable discharge and Roman citizenship. The soldiers concerned could receive or commission copies of the official record of their new status which had been set up in Rome on a wall close to the temple of the divine Augustus. These are called today *diplomata*, though their Roman name is unknown. Engraved on bronze tablets these personal copies have a good chance of surviving and many have been found, though they are often badly damaged and fragmentary. They are invaluable for providing an exact date and a list of the units involved, which therefore provide us with certain knowledge about some units being stationed in Britain at that time. On 19 January 103, for example, citizenship was granted to a Spaniard called Reburrus, son of Severus, a non-commissioned officer serving in the First Cavalry Wing of Tampian Pannonians in Britain under the governorship of Lucius Neratius Marcellus.[29] His children and descendants received the same privilege and he could now legally marry any existing wife that he might have. The tablet was found in 1812 at Malpas in Cheshire, a location that has no apparent connection whatsoever with Reburrus and his unit, which was probably based at a fort on the northern frontier somewhere.

The disparate findspots of these *diplomata* raise the interesting possibility that they were quite liable to end up in Roman-period collections of militaria, much as medals, military apparel and weapons still are today; this cannot be proved, but it would explain why so many turn up in strangely non-military locations such as Sydenham in Kent. Alternatively they may have been lost by the retired old soldiers' families in the locations to which they moved after military service. Tantalizingly, very few British examples survive in good enough states of preservation for the name of the owner to be read. Sometimes the metal has been shamelessly reused, proving that *diplomata* could fall into the hands of people who had no interest in their former importance. One found in Cirencester, and dated to the reign of Antoninus Pius, had been cut down into a disc, apparently to make part of a mirror, a rather undignified (if pragmatic) end for the record of a soldier's pride.[30]

While the Batavian garrison at Vindolanda was busy policing its part of northern Britain at the end of the first century, some Britons were busy policing other Roman frontiers. Lucco was a member of the Dobunnian tribe from the area around Cirencester but in the year 105, during the reign of Trajan, he retired from the Roman army after twenty-five years' service with the First thousand-strong Cohort of Britons, made Roman citizens, in the province of Pannonia (roughly equivalent to parts of Austria, Hungary, Croatia, Serbia and others), where he had married a local woman of the Azali tribe called Tutula and had a son called Similis and two daughters called Lucca and Pacata.[31] This means that he had been recruited into the army around the year 80 and apparently never returned to his homeland. It was not always the case that members of these ethnic auxiliary units all came from the same place. However, it is likely that many of them did so – at least to begin with. For young men from the more southerly tribes of Britain in search of adventure the prospect of fighting for the Roman army may have made up for being deprived by Roman rule of the chance to live up to the British tribal ancestral tradition of internecine heroic warfare.

Given Britain's maritime tradition it is only appropriate that at least one seafaring Briton pops up somewhere else. Aemilius was a member of the Dumnonii, the tribe whose area was centred on Exeter (Isca Dumnoniorum) and Devon, which has had a maritime tradition throughout British history.[32] Aemilius served with the *classis Germanica* (the imperial Roman fleet of the German provinces), which presumably means he sailed imperial warships and transports up and down the Rhine and into the North Sea, though we know that fleet servicemen could be deployed to erect fort buildings and fortifications and even supervise metal extraction. In terms of pay and conditions, though, members of the fleet did not do as well as soldiers in the army. Aemilius never returned home. He died and was buried at Cologne.

Lucco and Aemilius were not alone in leaving Britain behind them. 'Novantico of Ratae', presumably a member of the Corieltauvi tribe because he came from Leicester (Ratae Corieltauvorum), served until 106 with the First Ulpian Cohort of Britons, decorated for valour and made Roman citizens, which had served under Trajan in the Second Dacian War.[33] Novantico's father was a man called Adcoprovatus. One wonders how this old tribesman of the British Midlands felt about his son going off to fight for the invaders and ending up as a Roman citizen called Marcus Ulpius Novantico. These are not the only examples but there are very few such Britons known to us now; however, they go some way to illustrate how the mobility of fighting-age males in the Roman world contributed to the ethnic blur of the period. As Pannonians and Dacians fathered children by British women, so British men fathered children by Pannonian and Dacian women and these children became the source of subsequent recruits. Moreover, these ethnic 'British' cohorts were not exclusively manned by Britons. Some of the soldiers attested in these units are demonstrably not Britons, showing that unless a soldier's personal origin is explicitly stated on his tombstone or other source nothing can be taken for granted about where he came from just by virtue of his membership of any particular auxiliary unit.[34] This applies to any ethnic auxiliary unit at any time or any place.

By the time Hadrian came to Britain in or around the year 121 or 122, Sulpicia Lepidina and her husband Flavius Cerealis were probably either dead or were enjoying the income and privileges of Cerealis' promotion, perhaps even to a prestigious post as a procurator or prefect after several successive periods of commanding auxiliary units. Unfortunately, as so often, we know about these individuals from only one or two references, but we can be sure that for this couple, and Claudia and Brocchus, Roman Britain was just one brief phase in their lives. One fact is as good as certain: like most people we know about from the Roman era in Britain, they will have come from somewhere else in the Empire.

Hadrian's arrival came after more than a generation's worth of steady ossification on the northern frontier. With no evidence that there was any kind of grand strategy to conquer Britain, for decades the soldiers in the north had grown accustomed to the enervating world of a static garrison army. Hadrian was a stickler for military discipline. He came to Britain from Germany where he had been disgusted by the comfortable living enjoyed by the garrison there. He had banned dining rooms, among other luxuries, and dealt with corruption in the quartermasters' stores as well as in general provincial administration.[35] When he arrived in Britain he is said to have 'corrected many [things]', which suggests that he had uncovered similar problems there too.[36] Presumably the successors of Cerealis and Brocchus had to hang up their hunting nets.

Rome's perception of Britain was also more widely disseminated in the form of the first coin to depict Britannia, issued in around 119. On the obverse is a portrait of Hadrian and on the reverse a female figure sits atop a pile of rocks. She holds her head with one hand and a spear with the other. Beside her is a shield. It is not clear whether she is supposed to represent the native Britannia crushed and cowed by Rome or whether she is a representation of the militarized province under duress. Either way it is plain that Britain was perceived as a wild and warlike place. This is in marked contrast to other provincial coins issued by Hadrian that depict the more peaceable, luxuriant or fruitful attributes of places like Spain, Africa and Egypt. The design would go through several Roman manifestations before being revived in the triumphant form first found on Charles II's farthings, which continued in use on Britain's circulating coinage until recently.

For the whole army in Roman Britain the world was about to change with the orders to build the new wall across the northern frontier. Hadrian's policy was simple: he recognized that the Empire was over-stretched. The territories conquered by his predecessor Trajan proved to be unstable and maintaining the existing provinces in a peaceful state was proving difficult enough. Egypt, Libya and Palestine were showing signs of rebellion and the Britons 'were not able to be held under Roman dominion'.[37] This was important, though it is unlikely the author meant the Britons of the settled southern part of the province. Hadrian had expressed the opinion, which he had borrowed from a speech made by Cato in 167 BC, that the Macedonians were ungovernable and therefore should be made free and allowed to rule themselves independently. If the Britons were exhibiting a similar resistance to Roman government then giving up Britain must have been considered at this stage in the proceedings, almost eighty years since the island was invaded.

In the event a compromise was reached. The Wall would, in the words of Hadrian's Roman biographer, 'force apart' the Romans and Britons.[38] Northern Britain would effectively become an imperial hinterland, an independent zone only tenuously supervised and policed by a garrison that based itself along and behind a new mural frontier. The man charged with the new wall's construction was the governor Aulus Platorius Nepos, who arrived in Britain in 122, perhaps with Hadrian.[39] He brought with him the VI Legion, evidently to replace the IX Legion, a unit that had been in Britain from the beginning but whose disappearance by this date has remained an enduring enigma. It is probable that it was either destroyed or so badly mauled in northern Britain in the years just before Hadrian became emperor in 117 that it was given up. An expedition was sent to Britain to bolster the garrison either at the very end of Trajan's reign or just after Hadrian became emperor, perhaps because of the trouble at the time. Consisting of a 3,000-strong detachment of legionaries from the VII, VIII and XX Legions, then based on the continent, one of its commanders was a centurion called Titus Pontius Sabinus from Ferentinum in Italy.[40] Junius Dubitatus was a soldier in the VIII Legion.

He had a rather elegant shield plate made of bronze. An eagle decorated the central boss and around it eight panels depicted a pair of legionary standards, the four seasons, Mars and a bull. Dubitatus had punched his name in tiny dots on the plate and added the information that he was in the century commanded by the centurion Julius Magnus.[41] He may have thrown the shield into the River Tyne, which was where the plate was found, or dropped it when the detachment of his legion arrived from its base at Strasbourg. It was either an unfortunate accident or a very deliberate offering to whatever divine forces lurked in the river. Either way the shield, made of wood and hide, would have rotted away leaving only the plate to commemorate one of the VIII's troops.

Britain's frontier zone was not in any sense restricted to the north or the Walls. Britain is an island and it also needed to be protected, and its military personnel serviced, by a naval force. The force in question was the *classis Britannica*, 'the Britannic Fleet', based at Dover. The fleet was simply another branch of the Roman army, but on inferior conditions of service. Despite their lesser status, fleet troops were dispatched to Hadrian's Wall to labour alongside the legionaries constructing it during the reign of Hadrian. One unit built a granary at the new fort of Benwell (Condercum), though in practice the fleet must also have been charged with transporting men and goods to the Wall zone. Junius Dubitatus may very well have dropped his shield boss into the Tyne from a fleet ship.[42] The members of the fleet are largely anonymous but Lucius Aufidius Pantera was the equestrian commanding officer in the late 130s. Appropriately enough he erected an altar to Neptune at another fort used by the fleet, at Lympne (Lemanis) in Kent.[43] The fleet is the most prominently recorded military unit in south-eastern Roman Britain. Not only must it have played an enormously important role in cross-Channel traffic as a police force and official transportation system, but it also had control of the ironworks in the Weald of Kent, an indispensable resource for the Roman military.[44] Pantera's duties and responsibilities were considerable. His name means, literally, 'panther', a popular animal for wild beast bouts in the circus but it can also mean a mass simultaneous capture.

The new frontier, now the most famous of all Britain's Roman monuments and probably also in antiquity, emerged over the next ten to fifteen years. A curious piece of apparatus, Hadrian's Wall was much more than just a wall. Pierced by fortified gateways, now known as mile-castles, around every Roman mile, and embellished with lookout towers every third of a mile in between, the Wall was reinforced with a forward ditch. The eastern half was made of stone, the west from turf and timber. Later developments saw the Wall reduced in width from the planned 10 feet to 8 feet, the addition of a series of auxiliary forts attached to or crossing the Wall, and a rearward ditch and bank system known today as the Vallum (a misuse of the Latin word *vallum* which actually means the frontier proper), and the rebuilding of the turf stretch in stone. The Wall is now known to have been called probably the Vallum Aelii ('the Aelian Frontier'), and the territory beyond *trans vallum* (see below).

Perhaps one of the auxiliary solders ordered to garrison the new installation was Mansuetus, son of Lucius. On 14 April in the year 135 Mansuetus reached the end of his nominal twenty-five years' service with the Second Cohort of Dalmatians.[45] The fort he was based at is unknown but in the 300s his unit was at Carvoran, a Stanegate fort just south of Hadrian's Wall, making it quite possible it had been stationed in the area since the time the frontier was built, if not before.

It is clear from the monumental amount of archaeology that has been carried out along the Wall over the last two centuries that the 76-mile frontier was subject to endless modifications, abandonment, repairs and rebuilding throughout its history. It has also been, without parallel, the greatest single source of all our evidence about those who lived in Roman Britain from its earliest phases and right through to the end, when working parties from the towns in the south were sent north to patch it up in the final years of the province's history.

For Aulus Platorius Nepos the task of administration and delegation must have been gigantic. Fortunately, he brought plenty of experience from a prestigious senatorial career. His career had begun with the curatorship of roads in Italy such as the Via Cassia. He rose to become the commander of a legion before governing Thrace, Lower Germany and then Britain. His name appears on the earliest inscriptions found in the milecastles along the wall. They are also the earliest stone inscriptions from Britain actually to name any of the governors. As such they record a strangely incongruous element to the job. Nepos had served as consul in 119, as it happens alongside Hadrian. This meant he was now of proconsular rank, technically the same as the emperor. It was considered inappropriate for anyone to be of equivalent rank to the emperor, at least on a formal basis, even though it was essential for a challenging place like Britain to be governed only by men of the greatest experience. So Nepos' inscriptions record him as having been of propraetorian rank (the next rung below) to avoid such a breach of protocol, whereas he was, like all of Britain's other governors, of proconsular rank. The Vindolanda letters, which are mostly concerned with everyday concerns, include only a few references to the governor, but when they do he is described as someone who has served as consul.[46]

Apart from inspecting the works, Nepos is unlikely to have got his hands dirty. Needless to say that job fell to the poor bloody infantry, in this case mostly detachments from all three legions then stationed in Britain: the II Augusta, serving out its eternal shame for not participating in the Boudican War, the XX Valeria Victrix, proudly bearing its titles for the exact reverse, and VI Victrix, which Nepos had brought. The men involved emerge from the sands of time through the quality control inscriptions inserted into the Wall and the occasional graffiti. Now known as centurial stones, the quality control slabs seem to have been designed to record which band of brothers had built which stretch, presumably so that any poor work could result in appropriately targeted punishments. This policy of accountability, so beloved of our own era, must also have been presented as an incentive-based scheme, a sort of performance-related system in which the best stretches were rewarded. They tell us little beyond the names, such as the centurion Peregrinus from the fort at Benwell.[47] One of the more productive work gangs was the century of Cassius Priscus; four stones recording his men's work have turned up from several locations along the Wall.[48] Perhaps he was an especially inspiring (or punitive) leader, or simply lucky – many such stones have been reused in field walls and farmhouses and turn up entirely by chance. Flavius Carantinus was one of the men at work in the quarries. He found time one day to carve into the living rock about half a mile south of Turret 25b the words *Petra Flavi Carantini*, 'the rock of Flavius Carantinus'.[49] In 1934 his inscription was removed from the rock face and taken to Chesters Museum, where it remains. Perhaps he was as exasperated as the men charged with digging out the ditch at Limestone Corner. By the time they had cut several lewis holes into vast blocks which they had laboriously hacked out with tools, wedges and water, they decided the job was beyond them and abandoned it. Their blocks remain to this day exactly where they left them.

One of the more memorable names from the Wall's building stones is the centurion Hortensius Proculus of the XX Legion found at the fort of Haltonchesters.[50] The name derives from *hortensis*, 'of a garden', but he was perhaps named after, or descended from a freedman or relative of the orator Quintus Hortensius Hortalus, a rival of Cicero's in the mid-first century BC. Cicero records the legendary figure of Proculus from Rome's earliest days, who had been greeted by the ghost of the murdered Romulus.[51] There may be no connection at all other than family pretensions but it is still a striking comment that in this corner of the Roman world was a centurion with a name that had echoes of a classical world entirely beyond the comprehension either of the Britons or, probably, most of the soldiers in the Roman frontier army. On the other hand, the population of the Roman world was, by our standards, extremely small and its tentacles of kinship extensive, cherished, attested and verifiable. This makes it entirely possible that some sort of familial connection with the family Hortensius Hortalus existed, however tenuous.

There has not been an army in history that has not expended vast amounts of effort on projects or initiatives only to see them abandoned before the cement or paint has dried. And so it was with Hadrian's Wall. The XX Legion's relatively new fortress at Chester (Deva) seems to have become part mothballed, with building work suspended while at least half the legion was away for what must have seemed like a lifetime. It is not even clear if the Wall itself was finished by the end of Hadrian's reign in 138. The legions had built the Wall and its systems but it would be the auxiliaries who made this their home. Their personal records provide some of the most colourful records of life in Roman Britain and will be looked at in more detail in later chapters.

Not all the legions or all the auxiliaries found themselves on the northern frontier. The centurial stones from the Wall show that only selected detachments had been sent from each legion. The XX Legion, for example, remained in control of northern Wales along with the assistance of auxiliary units such as the First Cohort of Sunici from Germany, who were based at Caernarfon. The XX Legion had a works depot at Holt in Clwyd and one day in the second century it seems a soldier from Caernarfon went to Holt, perhaps to collect a consignment of tiles. He recorded himself on a roof tile bearing the XX Legion's stamp while it was still wet in a stylish graffito reading 'Julius Aventinus, soldier of the First Cohort of Sunici'.[52] For some reason the tile was later built into one of the kilns at Holt rather than being taken away by Aventinus, hence its preservation. The soldier's name is superficially Roman but Aventinus, the name of one of seven hills of Rome, is found most often in Britain and Gaul. Moreover, Aventinus could not spell his Latin. He wrote *milis* instead of *miles* ('soldier'), and *cortis prima* instead of *cohortis primae* ('of the First Cohort'). He spoke Latin and was literate but he was clearly not particularly well educated. His spellings perhaps indicate how he heard and pronounced Latin words and therefore might preserve something of his regional accent. His origins lay in a frontier province but he had acquired a clumsy though indisputably Roman veneer and identity which he was keen to memorialize; as such, Julius Aventinus symbolizes the Romanized provincial.

Hadrian was succeeded by Antoninus Pius (138–61), a man considered to be of remarkable honour and integrity. Whatever problems the Wall had been designed to solve, it failed, apart from keeping the soldiers busy. How it functioned and impacted on both the Romans and the Britons is far from clear. The existence of the milecastles shows that the Wall was never designed to be an impenetrable frontier; the most plausible interpretation is that it was designed to discourage massed assaults but also to facilitate supervised crossings of the Wall by limiting numbers and scrutinizing or forcibly dispersing those who came through. It was also evidently a base for operations into the territory beyond. Lucius Junius Victorinus Flavius Caelianus was the commanding officer of the VI Legion. Either around now, or later in the second century, he decided to make a dedication to an unknown god to commemorate what he proudly called his 'successful deeds' *trans vallum* ('beyond the frontier').[53]

Soon the territory known as *trans vallum* would be behind the frontier. Antoninus Pius was confronted with renewed warfare in Britain. The new governor, Quintus Lollius Urbicus, defeated the Britons and was ordered to build a new wall, this time of turf.[54] It was an important time. In 143 the province of Roman Britain was a century old. Claudius' triumph had been a little premature. After a hundred years, despite settlement of the south, the north remained dangerous, unpredictable and undesirable. In that year Antoninus Pius issued a great series of coins depicting Britannia, evidently in some sort of commemoration of Rome's tenuous ownership of the province, while continuing to acknowledge Britannia's warlike nature. The new wall was to be built between the Clyde and the Forth, a far narrower neck of land.

The soldiers who built the new frontier were drawn from the same units as those that had built Hadrian's Wall. However, a generation younger and belonging to a different artistic era they seem to have had more extravagant tastes when it came to commemorating their work. The inscriptions they set up to mark key points along the wall are flamboyantly carved, but record only the unit and the emperor. Their new wall would be in use for little more than a generation, meaning that almost all the known inscriptions must have been set up by the early 160s. Occasionally, individuals emerge. At Croy Hill, Dunbarton, a detachment of the VI Legion worked under the command of a man called Fabius Liberalis. His rank is unknown and his name innocuously Roman. They set up an altar to the nymphs, water goddesses they had perhaps concluded resided in a stream, pool or lake in the vicinity.[55] It was typical of the Roman world that a spiritual presence was readily identified in almost any inanimate context. Fearful of the consequences of failing to acknowledge a god, Romanized peoples often moved swiftly to propitiate any potential divine forces in a conspicuous manner.

Remote though it was, the Antonine Wall was still part of an Empire that stretched for thousands of miles. It was serviced by trade routes that stretched to the other end of the Mediterranean. At Auchendavy a boy called Salmanes died aged fifteen and was buried by his father, a man with the same name. Salmanes is a Semitic name. Perhaps father and son arrived in Britain in the wake of one of the units stationed on the new wall. The First Cohort of Hamian archers from Syria, then based not far away at Bar Hill, has been suggested as the most likely.[56]

Roman soldiers seem to have been very superstitious. A II Legion centurion called Marcus Cocceius Firmus was especially vigilant in this respect. Also at Auchendavy, he set up at least four altars, elegantly carved by the same hand. Two are fairly restrained, one dedicated to Diana and Apollo, and the other to Jupiter and the imperial family. If that seems rather broad, Cocceius Firmus was far from finished. Recognizing the importance of fending off any vengeful local deities, he dedicated another to the Genius of the Land of Britannica, and a fourth to an array of spirits: Mars, Minerva, the goddesses of the parade ground, Hercules, Epona and Victory. Evidently, he wished to leave nothing to chance. It is fairly astonishing to have four inscriptions naming the same person but amazingly he turns up in another source too, in this case a legal record. A slave woman was condemned for some unknown crime to penal servitude in the saltworks (salt was extracted in a number of locations in Britain), from which she was captured by pirates or foreign raiders. They sold her on, but she was then ransomed, apparently being bought back by one Cocceius Firmus who had to be reimbursed for the expense by the public purse. This remarkable story survives in the sixth-century emperor Justinian's legal *Digest* where this Cocceius Firmus is specified as a centurion; it is very likely that he and the one responsible for the inscriptions are the same man, though we can have no idea if the transaction took place along the Antonine Wall or belonged to a different time and place in this man's career.[57]

Women are virtually absent from the record along the Antonine Wall. One called Verecunda was buried at Auchendavy but her tombstone adds no other information whatsoever.[58] Perhaps the most interesting is Tullia Tacita. Tullia seems to have been a businesswoman, perhaps trading in food or drink which she stamped with a small bronze die reading '(Product) of Tullia Tacita' which was found at the village of Carrington around 20 miles south-east of the eastern end of the Antonine Wall. This would have been unusual but not unprecedented, especially if Tullia had been widowed. The letters were raised and reversed, showing that the stamp was designed to leave her name the right way round pressed into either soft foods like bread or perhaps the bungs inserted into amphorae.[59] Tullia's name is distinctly Roman. Tullia is the feminine version of the family name (*gens*) of the celebrated Roman statesman Marcus Tullius Cicero and the much earlier sixth king of Rome, Servius Tullius. Tacita is the feminine version of the Roman *cognomen* Tacitus which means 'the silent one'. The most likely explanation is that Tullia or a forbear had been freed and that any provincial identity had been buried beneath the alliterative and rhythmic appeal of those old Latin names. It is tempting to imagine that Tullia Tacita made her living supplying the soldiers on the Antonine Wall with foodstuffs.

Despite the construction of the Antonine Wall and the best efforts of Tullia's customers, Britain's northern frontier remained troublesome. An extensive issue of coins in 154 depicted the so-called 'mourning Britannia'. This cryptic image tells us really very little but Pausanias recorded a war in Britain against the Brigantes for this period.[60] In 161, at the beginning of the reign of Marcus Aurelius, a war 'was threatening in Britain'.[61] Against this backdrop the legions in Britain needed bolstering. Interestingly, the garrison along this turf wall included some native Britons. At or near Falkirk a man called Nectovelius, son of Vindex, was serving with the Second Cohort of Thracians, an infantry unit nominally manned by men from Thrace.[62] In fact Nectovelius was a Brigantian tribesman, which means he came from what we call northern England. He died when he was only twenty-nine, after just nine years' service, and must have been recruited by the unit in Britain, perhaps to make up the necessary numbers to man the wall's fortifications. He would not have been the only such Briton hired, and indeed we know of at least one other. Saturninus (if the restoration is correct) came from Gloucester, which was a military colony by the late first century. Saturninus was serving with the First Loyal Cohort of Vardullians when he retired in the 150s so may have been the son of a Gloucester veteran or a veteran's freedman. The Vardullians were at Castlecary, a little further down the new wall from Nectovelius' barracks.

The northern frontier's answer to the Aldgate-Pulborough Potter settled down some time in the late 150s to carve an inscription.[63] We do not know his name but we know that he was careless. The occasion was the arrival of reinforcements for all three of Britain's legions, the II, VI, and XX, during the governorship of Julius Verus around 155–8. The lettering has a certain amount of flamboyance about it but he set out to carve each character without first thinking the job through (plate 12). Things started to go wrong from the outset. He was clearly right-handed, for the lettering slopes down to the right immediately. He made no attempt to draw out the letters first but the stock abbreviations available to him resolved problems in the first and third lines, which included a misspelled 'VEXIL(L)ATO'. By the end of the fourth the inscription had started to go seriously awry. He had already carved LEG.II.AVG.ET for 'the II Legion Augusta and . . .', and had started on the VI Legion's name. He then realized that there was no room for 'LEG', even though he had carved the 'L', and resorted to a ligatured 'LE' with a miniaturized 'G' jammed in at the end of the line. In fact, such a device would have been perfectly normal but it looks extremely strange in an inscription where the other two instances of 'LEG' are written out in full.

The carving improved for the next two lines but then a crisis of space started to loom once more. Presumably, by this point the prospects of having to start all over again were too awful so our hapless sculptor continued remorselessly to the bitter end, drastically over-reducing the font size for the penultimate line. This made more space available for the last line which is incongruously larger than its predecessor. To round off his problems the mason appears not to have known his Latin grammar either, unless he was given a draft text by an ignorant officer; the reinforcements had come from the two German provinces – Germania is feminine but the sculptor carved the masculine *duobus* instead of *duabus*. The finished piece of work has survived in almost perfect condition, immortalizing the consequences of an ill-planned piece which ended up in the River Tyne. It had presumably been erected nearby to commemorate the arrival of these troops, who must have sailed up the Tyne after crossing the North Sea.

This inscription is a fascinating example of the Roman world's ability to break its own rules. Had the slab survived only in fragments or incomplete, any attempt to restore it today with the text that it actually had on it would be automatically refuted on the grounds of implausibility. Here we have the cast-iron proof that the Roman army was quite capable of producing badly laid-out and inaccurate inscriptions, probably because no one at the time either cared very much or even noticed – unless, of course, the reason it ended up in the Tyne was because it was thrown in there by a disgusted legionary legate or aggrieved centurion who kicked the hapless chiseller in after it.

It is very unusual to find an inscription in its original location. The one from the Tyne just described can hardly have been originally intended as something to throw into the river. Altars, tombstones, and building inscriptions were all liable to be reused or discarded, sometimes with what seems quite insulting disregard for their original purpose, but this has often preserved them. A recent find in a recess in the changing room of the baths at the fort of Binchester is an unusual example of an altar still apparently in its original setting. It was dedicated to Fortuna Redux ('Fortuna, the Home-Bringer') by a retired military engineer, 'ex arc(h)itectus', called Eltaominus who had formerly served with the Cavalry Wing of Vettones from Spain. His name has proved something of a mystery, apart from -minus, because there is no direct parallel and the 'tao' element is all but unknown. It is also very unusual for a military engineer, who would normally have been with a legion, to have been attached to an auxiliary unit. Another possible reading is El(ius) Taominus, and indeed some very rare personal names starting Tao- are known in Roman Egypt.[64] This man, who was lost to the ages until 2014, epitomizes the role luck plays in determining the record available to us and the challenges each new find brings.

CHAPTER FIVE

GODS AND GODDESSES

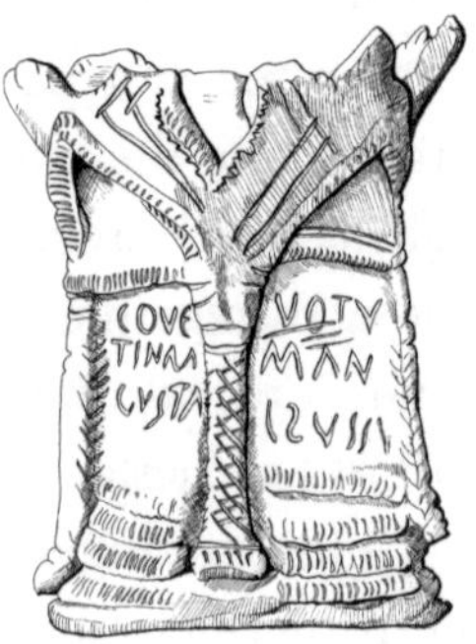

At Chester, base of the XX Legion, a centurion called Sextius (or Sextilius) Marcianus had a vision, by which he presumably meant some sort of hallucination or a dream. As a result he set up a small altar to the goddess of fate, Nemesis, in the amphitheatre where perhaps he had participated in bouts or other contests.[1] It was a relatively trivial dedication but it is the only reason we know about Marcianus during his time in Britain. The text epitomizes the fact that the late second and early third centuries in Britain provide us with our greatest body of evidence for real lives in Roman Britain because of the prolific quantity of inscriptions that were produced, by far and away the majority being from the military zone. And, by far and away the majority of those are concerned in some way or other with gods and goddesses. Soldiers and civilians alike lived in an unreliable world. They sought some sort of security and spiritual sustenance in the vast and endless parade of deities. One source of relief was to be found in the cults that had sprung up around the forts. Soldiers had to endure a more or less continuous litany of official cult observances, usually involving dedications to Jupiter Optimus Maximus or the Imperial House. To this they added innumerable gods, which included those they had brought with them from their home provinces, local British gods whose cults they came across, synthesized British and Roman deities such as Mars-Cocidius, and exotic eastern cults which the Roman Empire had absorbed. It was not just the soldiers who indulged in this limitless pantheon. Religious cults in a Roman idiom proliferated throughout Britain, from towns to the remotest rural locations. Evidence for cult activity appears in just about every context possible.

For the men of the Roman army in Britain in the 160s, such as Marcianus, the townsfolk of the cities and the millions of rural civilians, the Claudian invasion had long since retreated from living memory. The year 43 was as long ago as the Boer War is to us today. For the Britons, especially those in the centre and south, the old days of internecine tribal warfare had become the subject of folk memory and, doubtless, grandiloquent legends and myth. That would have been in spite of the fact that the vast majority still lived little differently from the pre-Roman Iron Age farming communities. The towns were well-established communities, and had been around for the best part of a century or more, though they were lived in by a tiny proportion of the provincial population.

Britannia was still, however, a frontier province and it would remain so to the end. The withdrawal from the Antonine Wall in the 160s marked something of a watershed. Although the Romans would try on more than one further occasion to take control of Scotland, there was no subsequent serious attempt to garrison it permanently. The army moved back to Hadrian's Wall, recommissioned it and settled down for the long haul. Holding on to the north at all proved extremely challenging for much of the rest of the second century and on into the third, but they found plenty of time to worship whatever gods they chose. A new war threatened almost as soon as Marcus Aurelius came to the throne in 161 but yet another generation would pass before the tribes beyond Hadrian's Wall crossed it and ran riot in the north until a new governor, Ulpius Marcellus, defeated them in 184.

The garrisons that occupied the Wall by this date had had time to become established, acquire wives and father children. One poignant instance of a child who never grew up to follow his father was Decibalus, a boy who died and was buried later in the second century at Birdoswald, a fort on the Wall, along with his brother Blaesus.[2] Birdoswald was by then home to the First Aelian Cohort of Dacians, and Decibalus was the name of the Dacian ruler defeated by Trajan in 106 after two major wars. Decibalus may well have had a British mother and a Dacian father who named him after his own national hero. If so, he was not the only one on the Wall given the name. Another Decibalus inscribed his name on the base of a samian bowl in his possession, which was found at Chesters or thereabouts to the east along the Wall.[3]

By 180 Marcus Aurelius had died and been succeeded by his son Commodus, who evolved into a dangerously unstable and self-indulgent ruler. Commodus had soon abrogated almost all responsibility for running the Empire to his praetorian prefect Perennis. Perennis rapidly became the scapegoat for any disaffection in the army, and disaffected soldiers formed a large part of the garrison in Britain. They placed their trust in one of the three legionary legates in Britain, a man called Priscus (though we do not know which legion he commanded), and declared him emperor. It was an exceptionally prescient moment. Priscus was the first of a number of men in the history of Roman Britain who found themselves elevated this way, but he had the wit to recognize that it was an extremely dangerous moment and refused. Frustrated, 1,500 of the troops marched themselves off to Rome and accused Perennis of plotting against Commodus. Commodus believed them and handed over Perennis to be murdered by his own troops.

If the soldiers from Britain believed they had done themselves a favour, they had not. Commodus appointed Helvius Pertinax to be governor of Britain. A rigid stickler for discipline, Pertinax soon found himself facing a mutinous legion and asked to be relieved of his post. In a supremely ironic twist, Pertinax was made emperor himself after the murder of Commodus on the last day of 192. Pertinax's time as governor in Britain is attested only in a couple of ancient sources. Nothing from Britain itself marks out his tenure. However, the well-known villa at Lullingstone in Kent had a long and curious history. At some point in the third century two marble busts of Mediterranean stone and style were deposited in the so-called 'Deep Room' and sealed there (plates 13 and 14). It has long been speculated that new owners of the house had arrived to find traces of previous occupants which included ancestral busts, a common accessory in any Roman family and especially one able to afford such items. The busts are battered, one rather more so than the other. The more damaged one had clearly been cut down at some point. Both represent bearded men of mature years in the style of the late second century who were probably related, though neither is identified. It is possible that the one in worse condition actually depicts Pertinax, whom it certainly resembles. If so, this raises the very interesting possibility that the house at Lullingstone belonged to him. It would certainly have been convenient. Lullingstone lies not far from Watling Street, the main arterial Roman road across northern Kent from the Channel ports to London, along the Darenth Valley. Lullingstone could have been reached in a day from the governor's palace in London. The setting remains rural and secluded to this day so it is easy to see why Pertinax might have found it a pleasant bolt-hole from the tribulations of governing a province, if indeed he ever did own or rent the house. Nevertheless, anyone visiting the house today should bear in mind that the mosaic floor and remains of painted wall plaster belong to the fourth century and a very different time in the house's life. The busts themselves now reside in the British Museum.

Pertinax went the way of so many emperors in those increasingly unstable years. He was killed by the Praetorian Guard, who then auctioned off the Empire. Didius Julianus, a wealthy senator, bid the most and won, but by 193 there were three military commanders with their eyes on the job. One of these was the new governor of Britain, Clodius Albinus. Albinus was clever enough to see that governing a province with a vast garrison gave him a huge amount of bargaining power and a very good chance of winning. Unfortunately, he was also stupid enough not to appreciate that Septimius Severus, with an army in Central Europe, was in the best position to knock him out along with the other contender, Pescennius Niger in Syria. Severus was not only clever but also duplicitous. He persuaded Albinus to side with him as his co-emperor while he, Severus, marched east and defeated Niger. Albinus bought the line and waited for Severus. As soon as Severus had dealt with Niger he turned on Albinus, who had by then finally smelled a rat and rebelled. The horrific climax came in 197 when the two fought it out in an epic battle in Gaul at Lyons which denuded Britain's garrison. Albinus had made a monumental miscalculation and, unlike Priscus a few years before, had risked everything on an ill-conceived gamble.

Severus became emperor and ruled until 211 (see chapter 6). To prevent any future governor of Britain getting the same idea as Clodius Albinus, Severus split Britain into two. The north became Britannia Inferior and the south Britannia Superior. This way the garrison was divided between the overall commands of two governors.

To the south the towns are sometimes regarded as having entered a protracted phase of atrophy, but this may be an illusion. Public building on any grand scale ceased, apart from town defences, but then most towns had what they needed. The work now would be repair and maintenance, not necessarily new building. In the countryside countless rural estates and farmsteads proliferated but apart from occasional improvements amounted to much the same places they had always been. Few were embellished in any way; the grand country villas were still the best part of two centuries in the future. Nevertheless, they were important legal entities with all the attendant niceties of associated documentation. Practically nothing of this has survived beyond a wooden writing tablet found at the bottom of a well at the villa of Chew Stoke in Avon. The handwriting on it has been dated to the late second or third century. The text seems to record the protection of a buyer of property who for some reason has been evicted. Sadly, no names survive on it but we can safely assume that anyone seeking to buy or sell a rural estate would have been involved in similar procedures.[4]

London was steadily taking on all the aspects of an international Roman port. The archetype is Ostia, the celebrated port of Rome whose elegant ruins are today a popular day trip by train from Rome. In antiquity Ostia was home to great public buildings, fine houses, shambolic apartment blocks, and myriad temples, among which were several mithraea (see below). During the late 160s a plague spread throughout the Roman world, facilitated in large part by the movement of immigrants to cities where the concentrated populations enabled widespread infection. The disease seems to have recurred. It cannot now be identified but smallpox and measles are perhaps the most likely.[5] Perhaps a fear of this horror was responsible for a magical spell composed by a likely Greek immigrant called Demetrios who found himself in London. He invoked mysterious deities called Iao, Saboath and Abrasax, as well as

Apollo, to protect him from the 'raging plague' and its horrific 'flesh-wasting' and 'infiltrating pain'. Demetrios had all this scrawled for him in Greek on a pewter sheet which he rolled up to carry round with him in an amulet and which somehow ended up in the Thames at London. Some mistakes in the Greek might be evidence that the person who transcribed the invocation, perhaps at a temple, could read and write Greek but perhaps only as a second language.[6] Of course Demetrios may have had it written somewhere else entirely but there is no reason why the plague should not have reached Britain. Many years later the fourth-century historian Ammianus Marcellinus said that it had infiltrated as far as Gaul and the Rhine, from where of course an endless stream of maritime traffic crossed to Britain.[7]

Demetrios sought his security with an intriguing mix of gods, reflecting the polytheistic nature of the ancient world. But there were already signs of monotheism. The exact time at which Ulpius Silvanus, a veteran of the II Legion, lived is unknown. His name suggests that a forbear had become a citizen during the reign of Trajan. He seems to have joined the legion at its colony at Orange in Gaul but therefore will have spent his career in Britain, where the II Legion was permanently stationed after the invasion of 43. Ulpius Silvanus had joined the cult of Mithras. Soldiers were particularly prone to taking an interest in the exotic cults that were proliferating throughout the Empire at that time. By far and away the most popular among men was Mithraism, a religion that emphasized valour and fortitude in the face of adversity and centred on the killing by Mithras of the sacred bull and release of the life force within for the good of all mankind (depicted in the 'tauroctony'). A saviour cult that also promised an afterlife, and open only to men, Mithraism was of particular appeal to soldiers for its emphasis on bravery, endurance and mystical reverence for progression through a cycle of initiation rites as the faithful advanced through the ranks of the cult's hierarchy. Mithraea are well known throughout the Roman Empire, with forts and ports being the most favoured locations.

Silvanus paid for a small but elegantly carved marble depiction of the tauroctony, the central event in the cult, as central as the crucifixion is to Christianity and to which it bears some conceptual resemblance; both events are re-enacted or commemorated in the principal cult ceremony.

The carving of the tauroctony was found in 1889 near the site of what would later be recognized as the London mithraeum, a remarkable building with an eclectic collection of religious sculptures; it is now one of the Museum of London's greatest treasures. The stone itself is thought to have come from the Luna quarries in Italy and will have been an expensive investment. The mithraeum's structure lurked on the dank and waterlogged banks of the Walbrook Stream, which is a now subterranean tributary of the Thames and which has turned out to be one of the most productive repositories of Roman finds in the whole of Britain, in spite of being in the middle of the modern city of London. We do not know if Silvanus lived in London, if perhaps he had been a member of the governor's bodyguard, whether he was simply passing through, or even whether the sculpture was acquired by a third party and brought to Britain. Certainly, the style of the lettering is more appropriate to an earlier date than the mithraeum, perhaps in the late second century. Either way we can be sure that the mithraeum, which was built around the middle of the third century, would have been frequented by soldiers, both because it was open only to men and also because of its proximity to the fort of the governor's garrison in London.

London was inevitably home to more exotic cults than just that of Mithras. The worship of Isis at London attested in the late first century had apparently endured throughout all this time – she had, after all, evolved into the supreme mother goddess of the Roman world. The London Iseum remains lost but we know that by the third century the building had 'collapsed from old age'. We are told that Marcus Martiannius Pulcher arranged for the building's restoration and set up an altar which must once have sat in the temple's precinct.[8] Pulcher was governor of Britannia Superior so the work must have postdated Severus' division of Britain. Pulcher perhaps was an Isis initiate himself and used his position and resources to organize the repairs. He is very unlikely to have been a Briton and instead probably came to Britain from a series of military and administrative posts he had held earlier in his career in other provinces, where he had acquired a taste for the cult of the Egyptian goddess. If so, he was in tune with many people of his era who looked increasingly for spiritual nourishment in the mystery cults of the East and their promises of redemption and rebirth. At some later date his altar was broken in two and used as rubble fill in London's fourth-century riverside wall. Nearby in the same fill was another temple restoration dedication, this time to Jupiter, but instead of being dedicated by the governor it was by an imperial freedman called Aquilinus, together with three others called Mercator, Audax and Graecus, who were probably slaves. The temples may once have occupied the same precinct only to be summarily cleared away in the fourth century as Christianity took hold.

The intermittent warfare and the imperial ructions across the known world only occasionally intruded on the everyday life of the frontier garrisons. The soldiers who manned Hadrian's Wall in the late second century found themselves on a frontier that had steadily become part of the landscape. The turf section of the Wall was certainly finished in stone, if indeed the curtain was itself ever really finished. Its whitewashed facade confronted, taunted and defied the north. For many men life here was an endless regimen of garrison duties. The vast majority were provincial auxiliaries, stationed in the forts along the Wall. Their entertainment lay only in the civilian settlements that started to cluster around the forts and in the fleshpots of Carlisle and Corbridge. For some, secondment to duties elsewhere in the north or the governor's staff in London must have come as a welcome relief. It is very easy to paint a picture of Roman Britain that makes it sound like a place where fighting was endless. In reality decades might drag by before the aimless daily routine was punctuated with another sporadic raid led by tribal bands of opportunists, or a full-scale war broke out.

Amandus was a military architect, which in reality meant something more akin to what we would call an engineer, who was based at the northern outpost fort of Birrens. His name is Latin but derives from a word meaning to dismiss or send away someone with contempt; in other words he was called 'the Contemptuously Dismissed', which seems both curious and insulting but the name in reality was a very old Roman one and would have meant nothing pejorative at the time. Amandus provides us with no more of his name or his unit but an *architectus* was a rank normally held only in a legion. If so, he probably served with the VI Legion, then based at York, but seconded to duties on the northern frontier. It has been suggested that he was both one and the same as Valerius

Amandus, a military architect with the I Legion Minervia in Germany in 209, from where he may have been transferred to Britain (or vice versa). We know about Amandus in Britain because he was responsible for carrying out an order to create a dedication to the goddess of the region, Brigantia.[9] Brigantia was depicted in the resulting carved relief in the guise of Minerva and was the personification of the Brigantian tribal region of northern Britain. This means that in reality she might have been a Roman fabrication of a native deity. The dedication was not unique. Among others is one found in total isolation at Greetland near Halifax in Yorkshire. It was a simple, crudely inscribed altar to 'Victoria Brigantia' in the year 208 set up by one Titus Aurelius Aurelianus who proclaimed himself grandly to be 'master of the sacred rites'.[10]

Either way, with her regional identity Brigantia was an important force to appease and to be seen to appease. Other native cults were far more parochial. One of these was the cult of Coventina. She was a water nymph and she 'inhabited' a spring a short distance south-west of the Wall fort at Carrawburgh (Brocolitia), an afterthought installation inserted into the Wall system in late Hadrianic times. The meaning of her name is unknown but perhaps had tenuous links to *covinus*, the word the Romans had acquired from the tribes of Britannia and Gallia Belgica for their notorious war chariots. It is extremely unlikely that the First Cohort of Batavians based here brought Coventina with them since she is unknown anywhere else; instead they probably found the traces of a native shrine and adopted her. At any rate, whatever her powers the soldiers of Brocolitia knew Coventina needed propitiating. Her presence seems to have been regarded as powerful. Thousands of coins, brooches and other offerings were poured into her sacred spring until it was almost choked. They include a relief depicting her lolling on some sort of bed and dedicated by one of the commanding officers, a Titus D[ecimus?] Cosconianus.[11] Other names on altars recovered from the spring give us a taste of the Germanic troops who lived here, such as Vinomathus, Crotus, Vincentius and even Maduhus, who tells us proudly that he was a German, as does Aurelius Crotus. Aurelius Crotus exemplifies that hybrid provincial world. He bore the name of the house of Marcus Aurelius, though in reality this could mean one of many emperors on into the third century, as well as his native moniker.[12]

The most idiosyncratic of all Coventina's adherents was Saturninus Gabinius, son of Felix. Unlike the others who had fashioned, or commissioned, standard small stone altars, Gabinius sat down with some clay and made himself two curious incense burners. He used the same sort of clay the Romans used for tiles. Similar to each other, but not identical and distinctly homemade, they have a kind of almost juvenile charm. The hollow dished pedestals were decorated with inscribed panels. He was very proud of his work and signed them both while the clay was wet, incorporating into the inscription on one that 'Saturninus Gabinius made the votive offering for Coventina Augusta with his own hands'. Both were certainly used, for when first discovered on the occasion the spring was emptied in 1876 they still bore traces of burning. Gabinius was the only one of her followers to have called Coventina 'Augusta'. Neither is dated though the third century has been suggested on the basis of the lettering, but this is hardly conclusive – Gabinius was a man of limited literacy; one of the inscriptions is far more crudely incised than the other. In spite of that his name had some pedigree. Gabinius is the name of a long-established Roman family, which included a proconsular governor of Syria in Caesar's time, though Saturninus can hardly have belonged to them. More likely an ancestor of his was once freed by one of the Gabinii or by someone they had freed. The pieces remain an enigma. Entirely without parallel they commemorate one soldier's personal activities and interests.

To the west along the Wall at Benwell (Condercum) some auxiliary cavalry officers and a centurion of the XX Legion found another god to worship. Antenociticus, like Coventina, is known in only one location. Antenociticus had far fewer attested adherents in his tiny cell-like temple outside the south-east corner of the cavalry fort of Benwell that straddled the Wall. The cult statue bust of the god shows a curious looking young man with horns in his hair. His name defies meaning but its similarity to Antoninus makes it possible he was a hybrid construct made up from a local British deity and allied to some sort of personification of the imperial Antonines of the second century. The altar left by Tineius Longus, prefect of cavalry, provides us with a date. He set up his dedication, abbreviating the god's name to Anociticus, during the governorship of Ulpius Marcellus between 180 and 185.[13] Two other altars were installed before the tiny temple was destroyed, either in a cross-border skirmish or during the time that much of the garrison was away fighting for Clodius Albinus.

The Wall was a phenomenon, then and now. It will have been, by any measure, a sight to see and some wanted a souvenir. Several enamelled bronze vessels have been found which record the names of several of the Wall forts and a schematic representation of the frontier. They are in every sense the Roman frontier equivalent of a model of the Eiffel Tower or the Empire State Building. The most recently found of these, the Staffordshire Moorlands Cup (also known as the Ilam Pan), is by far and away the most interesting. Not only does it record the names of four forts in the western sector but also tells us that the Wall was known as the *Vallum*, the Latin word for a rampart (plate 15). The pan, which is little bigger than a teacup, was either made or owned by a man called Draco or Aelius Draco – we cannot be sure whether Aelius belongs to the Wall's name or Draco.[14] However, since Aelius was Hadrian's *nomen* it is more likely that it was applied to the frontier. If so, it was known as Vallum Aelii ('the Aelian Frontier'). Draco will have been either the manufacturer of the pan, perhaps operating from a small metalworking shop in one of the civilian settlements that clustered round the Wall forts, or a soldier or civilian who visited the Wall and commissioned a personalized souvenir.

The Roman world was gradually shifting its perspective east. That was always where the money had been in the fabulously wealthy provinces of Asia, Syria and Egypt, among others. For some time it had also been where the Romans sought a deeper meaning to their lives. Isis, as we have seen, had reached London by the late first century. Other exotic eastern cults followed. At the military town of Corbridge a man called Pulcher set up an altar to Astarte, the Greek name of a truly ancient Mesopotamian goddess called Ishtar, equated by the Greeks with Aphrodite. Pulcher used Greek for the inscription on the altar. This was unusual for Britain, but not unique. It was accompanied by another, also in Greek, dedicated by a Greek priestess called Diodora.[15] Neither tells us anything specific about their origins but they had undoubtedly come from thousands of miles away, bringing with them an exotic and distant tradition into the incongruous location of the British north. Perhaps Pulcher had some medical skills. Medicine in the Roman world was dominated by Greeks, especially in the army. Antiochos was a doctor at the XX Legion's fortress at Chester, where he set up an altar in Greek in honour of the healing gods Asklepios, Hygeia (health) and Panakeia (all-healing).[16]

One of the most overtly oriental monuments from Britain is the tombstone of Hermes of Commagene, a city in Syria. Hermes died at the age of sixteen and was buried near the fort at Brough-under-Stainmore in Cumbria. No information is given about his parentage but whoever buried him thought well of the boy. The inscription was composed in Hermes' native Greek and told any passer-by to give him greetings for he had swiftly winged his 'way to the land of the Cimmerian people'.[17] The Cimmerians were an Indo-European people who had reached Anatolia by the eighth century BC. Presumably Hermes was a Cimmerian. How he had ended up in northern Britain we cannot now say. He was too young to have been in the army, but might have been brought to Britain as the slave or son of a soldier.

The Roman forts of Britain, especially those of the northern frontier, also became a home for the eastern mystery cult of Mithras, already known to have been worshipped in London (see above). The best-known of Britain's military mithraea today is at the Hadrian's Wall fort of Carrawburgh (Brocolitia). Still visible today in a dank and windswept hollow beside the fort's south-west corner, it once contained several altars. By far and away the most interesting of the three known is the one dedicated by Aulus Cluentius Habitus, prefect of the First Cohort of Batavians. He came from Larinum (modern Larino) in eastern central Italy and tells us it was called Colonia Septimia Aurelia Larinum, which dates his altar to after 193–211.[18] Around 250 years earlier a member of the same family, another Aulus Cluentius Habitus, was famously defended in a complex case by Cicero and it makes for an interesting tale that places the man at Carrawburgh into a broader cultural context. The story started in 74 BC when Habitus accused his stepfather, Oppianicus the elder, of trying to poison him. The idea, apparently, was that had Habitus died his property would have passed to his mother, Sassia, and thus been controlled by Oppianicus. Habitus won that case but at a price. In 66 BC the thwarted Sassia tried to have her revenge on her own son by persuading her stepson, Oppianicus the younger, to accuse Habitus of having poisoned his stepfather. At that point Cicero stepped in to defend Habitus and did so with great success, depicting his client as a man of unequivocal good character and honour and his mother and stepfather as despicable and murderous respectively. In reality Habitus was almost certainly as dishonest and dishonourable as any of the other characters, and had probably bribed his way to success in the first trial.

The story was notorious especially because it was so clear that Cicero had used his skills to misrepresent the truth and was well aware of that. Quintilian, an expert on oratory who lived in the first century AD, said, 'when Cicero boasted that he had thrown dust in the eyes of the jury in the case of Cluentius, he was far from being blinded himself'.[19] It is also worth adding that the Cluentii were considered worthy of a mention by Virgil in Book 5 of the *Aeneid*, where we are told that one of Aeneas' Trojan companions, Cloanthus, was the progenitor of the Cluentii. That suggests that by the late first century BC the Cluentii must have been prominent supporters of Octavian/Augustus.[20] Whether or not any of this was known to the Cluentius Habitus at Carrawburgh in the third century we cannot now tell, but it is likely that he did know and was proud of the fact too. Any of his educated comrades would have been no less aware. Curiously, the outpost fort at Risingham, about 10 miles north-north-east of Carrawburgh on Dere Street, was known as Habitancum, and means something like 'The estate of Habitus'. It was built around the year 140, evidently on land originally owned by a man called Habitus. One explanation is that this Habitus was a Briton with a Latin name but that seems hard to account for in such a remote spot.[21] At any rate, it is a curious coincidence.

Publicius Proculinus was a centurion based at, or passing through, the Wall fort at Housesteads (Vercovicium), the next fort to the west of Carrawburgh, which also had a mithraeum similar to the one at Carrawburgh. In the year 252 Proculinus set up an altar to Mithras at the Housesteads mithraeum and incidentally tells us that it was also in the name of his son Proculus.[22] This is of great interest because it helps paint a picture of soldiers on the northern frontier who had families in

1 The author (right), then aged five, and his brother in 1963 on the edge of the trench which had exposed the Dolphin mosaic at Fishbourne Palace in West Sussex.

2 Bronze bust of Claudius (41–54) or, more probably, the young Nero (54–68) found in the River Alde, Suffolk. The bust probably formed part of a statue displayed in a town, most likely Colchester, and was perhaps removed during the Boudican Revolt of 60–1. This type of individualized portraiture would have been a complete novelty to the natives.

3 The tombstone of Gaius Julius Alpinus Classicianus, procurator of the province of Britannia in the aftermath of the Boudican Revolt. Erected by his wife Julia Pacata, the tomb only survives in fragments today and is shown here as a digital reconstruction.

4 A limestone carving of an eagle devouring a serpent which originally formed part of the tomb of an important person, perhaps an imperial official or wealthy freedman, in a cemetery at the Minories, London. Late first or early second century.

5 Bust of Medusa on a bronze patera from a grave at Faversham in Kent. Classical in concept, the execution is provincial. First century AD.

6 Tile from Kent manufactured by a tiler called Cabriabanus. The name was applied with a roller die while the clay was wet and probably helped identification of his products in kilns or in storage. However, the raised letters also helped the tiles adhere to mortar. Second century?

7 An inscribed plaque recording a dedication to the Imperial Spirits and Mars Camulus by Tiberinius Celerianus who declares himself to be both a citizen of the Gaulish Bellovaci tribe and a Londoner. From a temple precinct at Southwark, London.

8 Bronze statuette of Mars commissioned by the Colasuni brothers, Bruccius and Caratius, and fashioned for them out of bronze by Celatus the coppersmith. Deposited in the Foss Dike (Lincolnshire) explicitly as a votive offering. Height of the figure about 272 mm.

9 Bronze patera made by a bronzesmith called Boduogenus, an unequivocally native name. The level of his skill at manufacturing a thoroughly 'Roman' item is evident from the piece's quality. Found at Prickwillow (Cambridgeshire) and probably deposited as a votive gift, very possibly by Boduogenus himself.

10 Altar erected at Bath (Aquae Sulis) by the 'centurion of the region' Gaius Severius Emeritus to commemorate his repairs of a location that had been desecrated by vandals. Second century.

11 A letter sent by Claudia Severa, wife of Aelius Brocchus, to her friend Sulpicia Lepidina, wife of Flavius Cerealis, commanding officer of the Ninth Cohort of Batavians at Vindolanda. Claudia invites Sulpicia to her birthday party. About AD 97–103.

12 Stone inscription from the River Tyne at Newcastle recording the arrival of reinforcements for all three legions stationed in Britain. The sculptor has miscalculated the lines and has had to make clumsy adjustments to incorporate the necessary text, most noticeably at the end of the fourth line and along the penultimate line. Produced about the year 158 during the governorship of Gnaeus Julius Verus under Antoninus Pius.

13 The two life-size marble busts found at Lullingstone villa. Dating from the mid-second century to early third century, and carved out of marble from the Mediterranean area, they were buried in a subterranean shrine at some point in the third century and venerated for generations. They may represent the ancestors of the villa owner, though it has been suggested that the one on the right may be a portrait of the emperor Pertinax who could have lived at Lullingstone when he was governor of Britain.

14 Detail of the better-preserved Lullingstone bust (above left). The style is mid- to late second century in the time of Antoninus Pius and Marcus Aurelius. It may well be a portrait of an owner of the Lullingstone villa at that time and have been preserved as part of an ancestor cult.

15 Staffordshire Moorlands (Ilam) Cup. An enamelled bronze cup serving as a souvenir of Hadrian's Wall, recording the names of several forts 'strictly according to their order along the Aelian Frontier'. Mid-second century.

16 York Serapeum. Claudius Hieronymianus, commanding officer of the VI Legion at York (Eboracum), commemorates his building of a temple to the Egyptian god Serapis (a Graeco-Roman conflation of Osiris and Apis), reflecting an increasing interest in exotic eastern cults in Britain. Probably *c.* 190–210.

17 The tombstone of Regina, the Catuvellaunian slave girl who was freed and married by her master, Barates the Syrian. She died at the age of thirty. From a cemetery near the fort at South Shields (Arbeia). Early third century.

18 Tombstone of Victor the Moor, freedman and probable catamite of Numerianus, a trooper with the First Cavalry Regiment of Asturians at South Shields (found near the Regina tombstone). Early third century.

19 Sennianus the *mortarium* potter proudly announces that 'Sennianus fired [this] at Durobrivae', identifying this as work manufactured at one of the kiln sites close to the commercial town of Durobrivae (Water Newton) in Cambridgeshire. Late second or early third century.

20 The altar of Marcus Aurelius Lunaris, found at Bordeaux where it was set up in 237 after his voyage from Britain. Lunaris was a priest of the imperial cult at Lincoln and York and thus probably a freedman trader.

21 Silver antoninianus of Gordian III (238–44) from the Dorchester South Street Hoard of 1936. The reverse depicts Laetitia ('Joy'). The coin was one of over 22,000 in the hoard, 8,888 of which were of this emperor alone. Perhaps the property of a merchant in the town.

22 Bronze radiate coin of Carausius (286–93), struck at the 'C' (Colchester?) mint, depicting the rebel emperor's florid features on the obverse and a war galley in his fleet on the reverse. Found at Asthall (Oxfordshire) in 1987, close to the line of the Roman road known as Akeman Street.

23 The so-called 'philosopher' or 'astronomer' on a mosaic floor from the villa at Brading on the Isle of Wight. Mid-fourth century.

24 Panel from a mosaic floor at the villa of Brantingham (Yorkshire). Unidentifiable as any obvious deity or mythological personality, the figure may be a portrait of one of the owner's family. Fourth century.

25 Mosaic at Lullingstone villa, still visible in situ. The design shows Europa being abducted by Jupiter in the guise of a bull. The Latin couplet (see chapter 7) alludes to the opening part of Book I of the *Aeneid* and is thought by some to contain hidden words including the owner's name. Mid-fourth century.

26 Wall painting (detail) from the house church in the villa at Lullingstone (Kent) showing a figure in an attitude of Christian prayer. Although very badly damaged the fresco was restorable and showed a series of figures with their arms outstretched. They may have represented specific individuals from the congregation; this figure was the only one whose face has survived. Late fourth century.

27 Central roundel from the mosaic at Hinton St Mary (Dorset). The Chi-Rho is clearly Christian. The figure may represent Christ or, more controversially, the emperor Magnentius (350–3) (see chapter 7). Either way the composition seems to be clear evidence of the owner of the house having Christian affinities. Mid-fourth century.

28 Part of the mosaic floor from Thruxton (Hampshire) naming Quintus Natalius Natalinus 'and Bodenus', who may have been the villa owner or an esteemed ancestor. Fourth century.

29 Mosaic from Rudston (Yorkshire) depicting Venus being surprised by a merman. The style has been variously interpreted and may represent a mosaicist of native origin attempting to execute a classical concept in vernacular style, or simply incompetence.

30 Gold buckle from the Thetford Treasure, buried in the early fifth century. Height of the plate is 52 mm.

31 A silver votive plaque from the Water Newton (Cambridgeshire) treasure of (largely) Christian plate. The text records the fulfilment of a pagan-style vow with a Christian Chi-Rho by a woman called Iamcilla. The feather was an established component of pagan cult activity but here has been utilized as part of Christian worship, suggesting the existence of a fringe group. Late third century or later.

32 A gilt-silver pepper pot in the form of an empress from the Hoxne Treasure, deposited in the early fifth century, and perhaps once the property of Aurelius Ursicinus and his family. It is 103 mm high.

tow. The family of Proculinus probably lived in the civilian settlement attached to this fort or another, and in due course, if not already, Proculus would have followed his father into the army.

The Housesteads mithraeum attracted support from other passers-by. Some time in the period *c.* 230–50 Litorius Pacatianus was one of many soldiers over the centuries who were detached from their units to serve as members of the governor's staff and bodyguard.[23] Such men were known as *beneficiarii legati*, a wonderfully succinct Latin term which is unbelievably cumbersome in English. It literally meant that they were beneficiaries of the privilege of being exempt from menial duties by virtue of being on the governor's detail. In that capacity Pacatianus erected his own altar to Mithras, describing him, as Proculinus did, as 'the Invincible Sun-God Mithras, Lord of the Ages', which showed how a number of monotheistic concepts were beginning to merge in Roman mystery religious observance. The battle for predominance was already under way and it was little more than half a century before Christianity would start to win out.

In the meantime one of the biggest businesses in Roman Britain was the vast pagan temple-spa complex at Bath, known in antiquity as Aquae Sulis, 'the waters of Sulis [or Sul]'. Bath was already a fully functioning healing and religious centre by the late first century, though the cult buildings would undergo huge modifications in the future. It lay on the Fosse Way and was thus easily accessible from almost all directions. The hot spring had been contained within retaining walls and equipped with sluices and drains. Nearby, the Temple of Sulis-Minerva presided over the comings and goings of pilgrims who hurled offerings and their messages to the god into the bubbling waters. On the other side of the spring a vast baths complex was already operational. Despite having no other major public buildings, the settlement was eventually given defensive walls. The place played host to administrators, staff, priests and pilgrims alike.

Bath was probably established by the Roman army. Its construction of the Fosse Way must have led soldiers to discover the bubbling hot waters in a swamp by the River Avon, and the Britons who venerated the spot. Many of the early visitors were soldiers, or at least those decent enough to commemorate their presence in a way we can access. If the army had been responsible for the initial development of the site it must have been because Bath offered the chance to rest and recuperate or was a place to go in the hope of a final cure from injury and disease. The Roman army liked such places and had developed several other healing spas along the Rhine in the early imperial period from the reign of Tiberius on.[24] Part of the reason was the obvious one that only the army was likely to have the construction and hydraulic skills necessary to create such places, especially in remote frontier provinces. By the second century Bath had evolved into a major religious and healing centre of a type well known across the Roman Empire, like the shrine of Apollo Hylates in Cyprus. Each was unique but the services offered were similar: a cult temple took centre stage amidst a series of facilities such as accommodation and bathing. Here the civilian and military sick, hypochondriacs, priests, soothsayers and charlatans rubbed shoulders with administrators, scribes, souvenir-makers, innkeepers, visitors, thieves and louts.

Aufidius Eutuches was an obsequious freedman, probably of Greek origin, who left two altars to Sulis in the hope that his patron and former master, the VI Legion centurion Aufidius Maximus, would have his welfare and safety protected.[25] If Aufidius Maximus was sick, occasioning the offerings, we do not know whether he got better or not. In some cases we do know. Julius Vitalis was an armourer with the XX Legion, based in Chester, when he arrived at the spa town, probably in the late first or early second century. Born in Gallia Belgica he had joined the legion at the age of twenty. Now aged twenty-nine, he came to Bath, where he died. His armoury colleagues funded the funeral out of the subscriptions paid by his fellow members.[26]

Presumably soldiers continued to arrive in Bath in search of cures, but it is certain that civilians had joined them. Some came for fun, and others came because it was for them literally a matter of life and death. They sought solace in healing from the mineral waters or through religious means. Bath was easily accessible by road from all directions. Many would have come down the Fosse Way from the colony at Gloucester or the civitas capital at Cirencester and from further afield, especially the soldiers arriving from the north.

There was money to be made from pilgrims travelling across Britannia to a major cult centre. Dozens of wayside shrines evolved, sometimes adapting what had evidently once been native cults. Ancaster in Lincolnshire was home to an otherwise unknown local god called Viridios. The shrine itself has not been found but inscriptions prove he was worshipped there at the small town on Ermine Street, the main road north from London to the colony at Lincoln, which lay another day's ride from Ancaster. Trenico was one of the faithful at Ancaster. He paid for an arch which must have served as an entrance to Viridios' precinct.[27] The nature of Viridios can only be guessed at as there is no known representation of him, but a rural hunter god is probably close enough. Not so far away, just to the north-east of Lincoln, stood a shrine to Mars Rigonometis, 'Mars, King of the Sacred Grove', surely an echo of a native cult. Here Quintus Neratius Proximus also paid for an arch. His name and the location suggest he might have been a military veteran now resident at the colony, perhaps being descended from someone related to the governor Lucius Neratius Marcellus, known to have been in charge of the province under Trajan in 103.[28]

Nettleton Scrubb lies on the Fosse Way in Wiltshire. The Fosse Way is a curious road today. Some stretches are now marked out by the dual carriageway of the A46 between Lincoln and Leicester. Other stretches are now no more than cart tracks. At Nettleton Scrubb this once mighty trans-Britannia trunk road is a narrow metalled lane that drops down to cross the small winding valley cut by Broadmead Brook. It lies only a short distance south of the busy M4 motorway but the contrast could not be greater. Here the narrow road becomes even narrower, a sign announcing that it is about to become single track. A passing motorist could cross the tiny valley in seconds and probably not even notice it. To the south-east of the valley the land rises up and to the west the brook trickles and bubbles along through the thick grass and past clusters of trees and bushes. It is, in short, a typical but nondescript piece of pleasant English countryside. There are no grand vistas and, indeed, nothing whatsoever to distinguish it in any significant way from a myriad other valleys, fields and lanes across Britain.

For all that, Nettleton Scrubb remains secluded and intimate. It is tranquil and remote today, bearing not a hint of the inspired architectural experiment to which it once played host. Anyone arriving from the north on the way to Bath would have found this tiny valley to be a hive of activity and cluttered with buildings that lined the road. The high ground to the south-east might still have borne traces of the triple ditches that surrounded a trapezoidal Roman camp, perhaps built by the army or simply as a fortified farmstead enclosure, and in use by the late 40s when the Fosse Way was surveyed and laid out. A number of minor tracks led off the Fosse Way here, just as they would have done in any English medieval village, creating a thoroughly irregular settlement. A little less than a hundred metres to the west an extraordinary building rose on the brook's south bank. It was an octagonal temple built on a podium tucked into the valley's side. Resembling the great church of San Vitale built several centuries later in Ravenna in Italy the Nettleton temple was a radical and unique structure which reached a height of at least 12 metres (around 40 feet) from the base of the podium to the top of any central roof finial. The surrounding buildings must have served as hostelries and service buildings for the cult.

This temple was a precarious architectural conceit designed by someone who had vision but not technical competence. We do not know his name or where his inspiration came from, though a number of military inscriptions record rebuilding and renovations at forts on the northern frontier at this time. However, it is impossible to link the temple to any military archetype. The building was based on a concentric octagonal layout and replaced a simple circular temple which had stood since the 70s until shortly after 250. The revolutionary new design climaxed in a central octagonal lantern which must have exerted substantial downward forces. This would eventually have disastrous consequences, for nothing had been included in the form of buttresses to counter the effect. In the meantime the temple at Nettleton, enhanced by the pastel tones of the weathering stone which gives Cotswold villages today much of their aesthetic charm, must have been a remarkable sight to any Bath pilgrims as they arrived here.

Octagonal structures were known in antiquity but they were not commonplace. There was the so-called Tower of the Winds in Athens (also known as the Horologeion of Andronicus), built in the late first century BC, but this was no more than a simple tower, with no internal radiating chambers or central lantern. Even Nero's octagonal fountain hall in his Golden House in Rome, built in the 60s, was essentially simpler and not freestanding as Nettleton's temple was. The fact that Nettleton was freestanding was crucial. Instead of being an internal feature, supported and contained by surrounding structures, Nettleton's temple was gloriously on show and clearly intended to impress, but it had nothing except blind ambition and audacity to keep it standing – in the end, neither of these would be enough. For the moment, though, the temple enjoyed a high summer of around half a century, presiding over a settlement that was otherwise made up exclusively of very ordinary looking houses and service buildings.

Unusual though it may have been, Nettleton was not entirely alone. Other octagonal Romano-British temples were built, for example at Pagans Hill, Chew Stoke, in Somerset. However, there was a crucial difference. These other temples were simply octagonal versions of the Romano-Celtic concentric square plan: the central cella was represented by solid walls in a square supporting the superstructure with a surrounding ambulatory and no radial chambers. At Nettleton there were no solid inner cella walls. The octagonal cella lantern was supported only by the innermost parts of the radial walls, as at San Vitale. Instead of being a separate self-contained chamber, the cella at Nettleton was also initially open to all eight radial chambers. San Vitale still stands because it has external buttresses which counteract the forces created by the lantern. Another difference is that it was possible at San Vitale to move around the building from each radial chamber to the next because of the use of weight-relieving arches in the internal radial walls. At Nettleton these internal radial walls were solid.

Nettleton eventually collapsed because no buttresses were installed when it was built. Remedial measures merely patched up the damage and failed to arrest the structural disintegration. It remains a fascinating experiment and clearly was the work of someone with imagination and flair whose work may well ultimately have inspired early church architecture, however indirectly. It is interesting to note that at Lufton in the fourth century an octagonal *frigidarium* was built at a villa baths, on a very similar design but with buttresses. By the fifth century the concept had been used in the Lateran Baptistery at Rome, with external structures acting as buttresses. San Vitale at Ravenna followed in the sixth century, employing buttresses and external structures to counteract forces. Nettleton, however, remains a pioneering attempt at the basic design, but fatally flawed.

The Nettleton shrine was dedicated to Apollo conflated with a native god called Cunomaglos, who had probably been worshipped there before the Romans arrived. Cunomaglos is a native name with many echoes in pre-Roman British culture. 'Cuno-' means 'hound', and appears in tribal royalty with the name Cunobelinus, the Catuvellaunian leader who died shortly before the invasion of 43. 'Cunomaglos' means something like 'hound prince'. The name survives thanks to a woman called Corotica who passed through this place at some point in its history. She was the daughter of a man called Iutus and at Nettleton she asked Apollo Cunomaglos for some unknown favour which seems to have been granted. She repaid the god with an altar.[29] Corotica's name is unequivocally native and she must have been of some independent means if she was able to pay for the altar. It survives because in the temple's later days, by which time the structure had partially collapsed thanks to its flawed design, the altar was used as a perfunctory fireside seat by squatters.

Although there was some accommodation at Nettleton it was not a place suitable for a long stay. Corotica was probably on the way to somewhere else, and Bath is a distinct possibility. If so, she may well have been in search of a cure, for Bath above all was a healing shrine. However competent some aspects of Greek medicine in antiquity were, the outcome of disease often remained the focus of superstitious hopes. The ancient world was littered with healing shrines of all types, with natural hot springs being a particular favourite. To these places came pilgrims with all sorts of ailments and grievances. Typical were Vettius Romulus and his wife Victoria Sabina who brought their daughter Successa Petronia to Bath. Her curious name, which means 'one who succeeded another', must have been chosen because the couple had already lost a child. We do not know when Vettius Romulus and his wife arrived in Bath, or why, but it is entirely plausible that they brought Successa Petronia here because she was ill and they hoped that she would find a cure. Their efforts were in vain. Before they left they buried their 'dearest daughter', who had died aged three years, four months and nine days.[30] We do not know where this family had come from. At least the inscription is fairly clear; sometimes they are tantalizingly cryptic. Another family tragedy at Bath involved an infant girl called Merc(. . .) who expired aged one year, six months and twelve days.[31] She is described as having been an *alumna* ('foster daughter') and possibly a 'freedwoman of Magnus'. This unusual text suggests that the little girl had been born to a slave woman in Magnus' possession, both of whom had been freed by him, only for the child to die. Perhaps the text was a convenient way of disguising the fact that she was his real daughter. However, the text can be read another way entirely. Although *alumna* appears in full, the translation of 'freedwoman of Magnus' relies on expanding MAGNIL as *Magni Liberta*, though in fact it may be a single word and thus represent the name Magnilla. In this case the child might have been 'Merc(. . .), foster-daughter of Magnilla'.

Some pilgrims had come from overseas. Peregrinus of Trier left his dedication to Mars Loucetius and Nemetona, evidently patronizing one of the other cults available in the town offering visitors further opportunities to part with their cash. Mars Loucetius and Nemetona were 'Celtic' deities usually worshipped together. Priscus, son of Toutius, was a stonemason from the Carnutes tribe in the Chartres area of Gaul; he chose to make his offering to Sulis.[32] Sulinus was more likely a local man since his name alone suggests an origin in the town where Sulis was worshipped. He is extremely unusual, though not unique, among the Romano-British population for turning up on more than one inscription in separate places, though his profession, like that of Priscus, made him more likely than most to turn up at all. At Bath Sulinus erected an offering to some mother goddesses called the 'Suleviae' in the form of a statue mounted on an inscribed statue base, and tells us that he was a sculptor and the son of someone called Brucetus or Brucetius. At Cirencester he erected an altar to the same gods and confirms his identity by including the reference to his father.[33] No doubt the quarries of Cotswold stone in the area had attracted him there, though it is possible he worked at both places and anywhere in between where his services were required.

Men like Peregrinus, Sulinus and Priscus were finalizing part of the deal they had struck with the gods of their choice. They were fulfilling the vow they had made when they transmitted their initial request to the deity. Those initial requests are scarcely ever found because they were cryptic, secret communications with the gods and were never meant to be seen. At Bath many were scrawled on sheets of lead by scribes on behalf of the visiting pilgrim, rolled up and hurled into the bubbling waters of the sacred spring. These so-called 'curse tablets' have for many years been among the most celebrated remnants of Roman Britain, though in reality the vast majority are incomplete, incoherent or no better than tiny fragments. Only a few have coherent and complete messages. Among them is the story of Docimedis, a man who had suffered the theft of a pair of gloves. It is faintly remarkable that anyone who had experienced such a trivial loss would have bothered to make an issue of it, but puerility on this scale was a routine characteristic of Roman religious establishments. Docimedis thought it would be appropriate for the miscreant 'to lose his minds (*sic*) and eyes'.[34] Docilianus had been deprived of his hooded cloak by another thief and wanted the culprit never to sleep again or have children until the cloak was returned.[35]

It is disappointing that we do not know where these people came from but their names had been manufactured from the Roman name Docilis. This tells us nothing about their origins other than to suggest they were probably British but belonged to families that had absorbed Latin-based names into their dynastic traditions. One family seems to have sworn an oath at the shrine. Uricalus arrived at Bath to swear this oath before Sulis with his wife Docilosa and their children Docilis and Docilina, as well as Uricalus' brother Decentinus and Decentinus' wife Alogiosa.[36] Decentinus is unequivocally Latin in its origins, though a very unusual variant on Decens, but Uricalus is a native name. If the two really were blood brothers we have a family that quite contentedly combined both traditions; if so, perhaps one of their parents had been a Briton and the other an immigrant Roman or Romanized provincial. A pewter plate also found in the sacred spring lists a series of names, including the very Roman Severianus 'son of Brigomalla', a variant on many native names that started with *Brigo-* though this one unusually is female. It was as if an English woman called Ethelburga in the twelfth century had given her son a Norman name like William or Richard but even that assumes here we could be sure Brigomalla was a Briton. On the same plate appears the native name of Catonius, son of Potentinus, a name that had its origins in the Latin *potens* for 'power'.[37] Such examples show us that it really is quite impossible to draw firm conclusions about the ethnic origin of any Romano-Briton from an individual name. We need either an inscription that specifies ethnic origin, or physical remains which can be chemically analysed. Just to complicate the issue further, Alogiosa's name is likely to originate somewhere in Greek.

All these visitors to Bath had cause to engage the services of the various priests and officials who ran the spa and shrine. Lucius Marcius Memor was a soothsayer (*haruspex*) of some note at the spa. He set up a statue to the goddess Sulis in the temple precinct and identified himself as such on its plinth.[38] He is unique in Roman Britain's history as the only example of a *haruspex* known in the province. Since no others are known, even at Bath, it is possible he was only passing through; it has been suggested he was on the governor's staff. If so, he would only have been in Britain for a few years at most.

Bath of course was not the only place at which a deity could be appealed to by this form of communication It simply happens to be the best known. About 22 miles away, and almost precisely due north, in Gloucestershire was the shrine of Mercury and other gods at Uley. Dozens of lead curse tablets have been found here as well, many utilizing the same formulaic structure and style as the Bath examples. Unlike Bath, this was a rural temple surrounded by a cluster of service buildings. Here a woman called Saturnina sought the return of linen cloth with the help of Mercury and Silvanus. Biccus was less specific about what he had lost but very much less unequivocal about the desired punishments for the thief. These punishments should include preventing the culprit urinating, defecating, speaking, sleeping, staying awake, and then he was not to have good health either, a final demand which seems unnecessarily superfluous. Cenacus was able to identify Vitalinus and his son Natalinus as the thieves of his draught animal and simply requested that their health be threatened if they did not return it.[39] As with the Bath examples, many of the Uley curses are garbled and incomplete, though they still include the tantalizing traces of individuals and their strange and memorable names such as Vicariana, Varicillus, Mellossus and Senebellena.[40]

Wherever visitors to places like Bath or Uley came from, they generally communicated with the goddess through the medium of Latin and this is what is almost always found. Native languages and dialects had no formal written form, though it was perfectly possible for native names and words to be transliterated with Latin characters and absorbed into the language, *moritex* (shipper) being one of the best examples.[41] In theory this ought to have been feasible for the whole of any native language. In Roman Britain the practice is all but unknown, although, oddly, such transliteration did occur after the Roman period; moreover, native texts were transcribed with Latin letters in Gaul during the Roman period, albeit rarely. However, one Bath curse tablet just might be a native text written with Latin letters.[42] As such it has defied translation but it remains a reminder that many of the Romano-British were accustomed to the idea that the public side of their lives was conducted in verbal and written Latin and their private affairs in a spoken British dialect. This may have been as a result of some legal prohibition, or of custom and practice derived from some sort of taboo. Either way, this suggests once more a form of discrimination against native culture in Britain. The scarcity of examples might also be taken to imply that perhaps most native Britons were illiterate and were no better able to express themselves in written Latin than their own language.

Established cults like those of Sulis-Minerva and Mercury were increasingly competing with the influx of exotic cults from the East. By the late second century the cult of a Graeco-Roman hybrid Egyptian god called Serapis, conflated from Osiris and Apis, had arrived in the great legionary fortress and colony of York. Claudius Hieronymianus, commander of the VI Legion, built a new temple to Serapis. The temple itself has never been found but the dedication slab has survived. His name is as unusual for Britain as the god of his new temple (plate 16). Of Greek origin, its most familiar manifestation to the Romans was in the ruling dynasty of Hiero in Syracuse. Our Hieronymianus, who may have come from Sicily, had quite possibly spent some of his time to date in the East acquiring an exotic taste in cult. If so, Hieronymianus was well and truly in touch with the Roman zeitgeist in the 190s. The new emperor Septimius Severus (193–211) was not only a North African but also beguiled by the exotic superstitions and mysteries of the East. Indeed, the temple may even have been built to please him. In any event, by the end of the second century Hieronymianus had moved on and become governor of Cappadocia. Meanwhile, Britain would shortly play host to the new emperor and provide him with a place to die.

Times were also changing. Roman Britain from the outset had been, not surprisingly, unequivocally pagan, whether that meant worshipping Coventina, Jupiter, Mithras or Isis. Christianity was known in Rome by the 60s at the latest and its gradual spread can be tracked through a number of ways, including for example the celebrated letters of the younger Pliny to the emperor Trajan during his time as governor of the province of Bithynia and Pontus. One of the Bath curse tablets was written by Annianus, son of Matutina, because he had suffered the theft of six silver coins from his purse. The text, which is extraordinarily difficult to read because it has many omitted letters and was written backwards starting from the bottom, begins *seu gentilis seu Christianus*, 'whether of the national [faith] or Christian . . .' It is only a passing reference to Christians but they are already marked out as a recognizably different caste from mainstream Roman society. Unfortunately, it is completely impossible to date the curse tablet. Not even the names of the suspects help us. Annianus listed eighteen potential wrongdoers, ten of them with Latin or Greek-based names and eight with native names. There is no indication which, if any, were Christian.[43] In the end, of course, Christianity would be the ultimate curse of Sulis-Minerva and all other pagan cults in Britannia. Appropriately enough the cult temple of Sulis-Minerva now lies beneath a precinct overlooked by Bath's abbey church of St Peter and St Paul.

Roman Bath was a massive commercial enterprise, but there was money to be made out of religion on a far smaller scale. The Snettisham (Norfolk) hoard is one of the most interesting collections of material ever found in Britain. We know nothing about the man, and it probably was a man, who buried it but we know something of his life, his skills and his interests. The Snettisham hoard is a jeweller's stock-in-trade, though why it was buried will forever remain a mystery. It was found in 1985 during building work on a new housing estate. Despite being exposed with a mechanical digger it was only slightly damaged and instead was carefully removed and examined by one of the builders, a man called George Onslow. As he examined the contents Mr Onslow had the great privilege of reaching out and touching a moment in Roman Britain's history. He found coins, jewellery, gemstones and other items packed into a globular grey ware jar about 17.5 centimetres high. The location had some rather inconclusive evidence of light Roman industrial activity, with more general traces of Roman occupation in the area, and was about 800 metres from a villa.[44]

The coins provide the date. There were 83 silver coins and 27 bronze. The latest silver coin was a worn one of around the year 155, which makes it likely the hoard was buried in the 160s or 170s. The majority of the silver coins had been carefully chosen from those struck in the period 85–96 when the fineness was 93.5 per cent silver to copper. This is very close to sterling silver (92.5 per cent), where the ratio of silver to copper offers the optimum combination of purity and hardness. The silver coins had almost certainly been chosen to melt down to make jewellery, which is what most of the rest of the hoard consisted of, including rings, snake-rings, bracelets, necklaces and gemstones. The rest was made up of other rings, scrap and ingots, as well as the bronze coins which were probably simply loose change, though they could also have been used for casting cheaper jewellery. There was no indication that the jeweller worked in bronze, though obviously he could have done. Most of the manufactured metal was silver, but a small amount was gold, as was some of the scrap.

The hoard preserves a livelihood. The Snettisham jeweller may have been based there or was an itinerant, like the Old Buckenham (Norfolk) brooch maker who buried his stock-in-trade and manufacturing equipment there and never recovered it. The Snettisham jeweller may have been both, working up stock to tote around at villas and towns or to sell on to travelling tinkers. It is no less possible that he sold his work at a shrine site, since so much of it bears images of deities. The 117 gemstones had been bought in. They seem to have been made by at least three different people, perhaps working nearby or in the vicinity; certainly the style and technique suggest their wares were sold around Britain but not beyond. It is conceivable these workers were slaves, or at any rate that slaves played a part in the process. At Malton there was a goldsmith's shop, now known only from a crudely carved dedication to the Genius of the Place and bearing an invocation to the 'young slave' to use the 'goldsmith's shop' to his 'good fortune'.[45]

Whoever these artisans were, the subject matter of the work they made shows a monopoly of Roman deities and personifications, with twenty-seven of the Snettisham gemstones depicting Bonus Eventus and twenty Ceres alone. This in no way precludes the possibility that persons of local British origin were responsible. Since time immemorial commercial enterprises have proved themselves able to service the available markets rather than impose their own tastes on unwilling customers. It is a matter of interest that discoveries of Iron Age jewellery, including gold torcs nearby, might point to the existence of a very long-established manufactory that adapted across generations to new tastes and demands. The jewellery in the Snettisham jeweller's hoard was good quality but not exceptional, and its taste and style fairly routine for the Roman world. However, the pieces would still have been suitable for persons of high status and it is interesting to wonder if the customers were also descendants of an Iron Age aristocracy that now sought to display its wealth through Roman-styled goods rather than the torcs of two centuries before. In other words we may have here an individual who preserved his own family's tradition of jewellery manufacture for the benefit of the descendants of their tribe's aristocratic forbears.

The jeweller himself clearly intended to return to his work. The unused gemstones and the ingots prove that much. We can never know why he did not and it is perhaps even more mysterious that the hoard remained in the ground in antiquity, in spite of being deposited in what seems to have been a busy and industrious location. His work was simply part of the broader industrial and commercial base of a province that was now integrated into the Roman economy and which was also completely expressed in a Roman idiom. Roman religion and religious iconography above all epitomize Britain's cultural transition. By the fourth century religious tensions had taken on an unprecedented form and would provide us with some of our most evocative and memorable links with the Romano-British. Before then, however, a century of turmoil lay ahead.

CHAPTER SIX

DEATH, DISRUPTION AND DECLINE IN THE THIRD CENTURY

In 197 once he had defeated Clodius Albinus (see chapter 5) Septimius Severus took total control of the Empire from that moment. He was utterly ruthless and determined to establish his own dynasty. In 208 he arrived in Britain with a vast army and made his own fatal error. He embarked on a campaign deep into Scotland, determined to toughen up his sons, Caracalla and Geta, and involve them in a prestigious victory on Britain's northern frontier. The effort of leading the campaign and controlling his eldest son, Caracalla, would kill him in 211 at York. Thereafter, Caracalla's abandonment of any land Septimius Severus had seized rendered the whole effort entirely futile, but it marked the end of half a century more of sporadic warfare in the north, which only then seems to have quieted down.

The coming of the Severan war of northern conquest in 208 was the occasion of a vast amount of military activity in Britain, probably in fact the greatest single influx of men and materials since the Claudian invasion over 160 years previously. The preparations had already started. By 205–7 the governor Lucius Alfenus Senecio was overseeing restoration and repair along the frontier forts, assisted (unusually) by the procurator Marcus Oclatinius Adventus. Oclatinius Adventus had had an extremely successful career. Not only does he turn up on several inscriptions in Britain but he also merited a mention in the histories of Cassius

Dio for his ambitious rise to fame. Oclatinius Adventus had come from nowhere to be a mercenary spy (during which time he acted, among other things, as an executioner) before reaching equestrian status and procuratorships, which was when he came to Britain. Under Caracalla he was promoted further and became a senator. Cassius Dio was mystified because Adventus was allegedly both uneducated and too inexperienced for high office. His name appears alongside that of Senecio on an elaborate inscription from the outpost fort at Risingham.[1] For a man like Adventus a few years in Britain were simply part of his curriculum vitae. As so often, Britain was no more than a posting and not a way of life; however, the route was opened up for more job opportunities with Severus' decision to divide the province in two.

There was scarcely any pretext for the war in Britain beyond waking up an indolent frontier garrison. Severus wanted his sons, Caracalla and Geta, to experience a proper war and to divert them from the fleshpots of Rome. A war in Britain provided a relatively safe opportunity. A disaster would not result in barbarians flooding across into Europe, though it is a mark of his confidence that Severus was prepared to relocate the imperial household, including his wife Julia Domna, across the Channel to Britain for several years.

The war would last several years, and cost a vast amount. Thousands of Roman soldiers paid the ultimate price too, many set upon in the forbidding swamps and forests of Caledonia, bewildered and disoriented by the environment and systematically wrong-footed by an enemy that knew every last pool, clump of heather and grove. Among those soldiers was a centurion called Gaius Cesennius Senecio. Cesennius Senecio was a centurion of the Praetorian Guard, Rome's emperor-makers and topplers, and probably had a very good idea of how the Guard had behaved in 193. He set out to Britain with his paymaster emperor, presumably exhilarated by the prospect of an adventure which would enhance his status and provide him with a tale to tell and money to spend. In 205 he had been a centurion with Rome's *vigiles*, the fire service, and must therefore have been promoted, perhaps expressly so that he could go to Britain. In the event Cesennius Senecio expired somewhere in Britain and his body had to be taken back to Rome by a man called Zoticus so that his obliging freedman Caius Cesernius

Zonysius could see to the burial; this must mean that he had already been cremated and that his ashes were what Zoticus brought to Rome.[2]

The imperial entourage that arrived with Severus was huge. Apart from his sons and members of the court it also included his wife, the empress Julia Domna. The Caledonians agreed to a peace treaty, which clearly included a face-to-face meeting between the Roman imperial family and a leading Caledonian called Argentocoxus and his wife. Argentocoxus' wife is unnamed but she was gently mocked by Julia Domna for the manner in which British women were shared among their menfolk, something that Caesar had described more than 250 years earlier.[3] The wife of Argentocoxus tartly retorted that women like her were free to 'consort openly with the best men' in contrast to Roman women who were debauched by the vilest Roman men in secret.[4] It was a mark of the far greater degree of equality enjoyed by British women compared to their Roman counterparts and an interesting echo of how more than 150 years previously Caratacus and his family had paid the same level of homage to Agrippina as they had to her husband, the emperor Claudius.[5] Julia Domna's answer, if there was one, is unrecorded but she might have taken some small consolation from the fact that Argentocoxus' name had clearly been manufactured in part from the Latin word for silver, *argentum*. Nonetheless, the anecdote remains a unique glimpse of a conversation between a Roman empress and a British chieftain's wife. It also enshrines a fragment of scathing Wildean wit in the most surprising context.

Caracalla's pathological brutality had already emerged during his father's reign, and at one point he had even lunged towards his father with a sword. The aftermath of Severus' death saw the immediate execution of various members of the imperial entourage.[6] The clear implication from the historical sources is that the killings took place before Caracalla left Britain for good. His victims on this occasion included the praetorian prefect Papinian and his tutor Euodus. One possibility is that a mass grave of around forty decapitated males of this date in York discovered in 2004–5 might include some or all of his victims.[7] Since none of the skeletons can be tied to any specific individual through tombstone evidence it is impossible to say whether they are any of his victims, though none of them is thought to have been older than in their mid-forties. They may simply be criminals or even gladiators and need not even necessarily have been buried at exactly the same time. However, they were very well built and taller than average for the period.

In a sense it does not matter. It is certain that Caracalla killed members of his household and that there were other victims in Britain. Another was Gaius Julius Marcus, made governor of the newly constituted Britannia Inferior by 213. Being given a job by Caracalla was hardly something to rejoice over. Julius Marcus initiated a programme of rebuilding and restoration at auxiliary forts across the north and ensured that the inscriptions which recorded this work swore allegiance to Caracalla. However, the erasure of his name from many of these inscriptions suggests he had fallen rapidly out of favour and was probably arrested and executed, a fate which certainly befell the governor of Gallia Narbonensis.[8]

Some members of the British garrison paid with their lives for the emperors of this period in different ways. Tadius Exuperatus 'died on the German expedition' at the age of thirty-seven according to the monument at Caerleon to both him and his mother, Tadia Vallaunius, set up by his sister Tadia Exuperata.[9] Vallaunius is a native female name; along with the fact that the soldier had a family at Caerleon, it makes it likely he was a son of a legionary who had taken a local woman as his wife, joining the II Augusta himself when he was old enough. The tombstone and the *Expeditione Germanica* cannot be dated with any certainty but in 213 Caracalla led a campaign against the Alamanni, a tribe of the Upper Rhine, and this may be where Tadius met his end.

Quite a few of the other governors of Britannia Inferior are known to us by name thanks to the army's predilection for producing commemorative inscriptions in this period. One is more prominent than the others. Tiberius Claudius Paulinus was a successful career senator whose first position of importance was as commander of the II Legion Augusta at Caerleon in Britannia Superior, a post he probably held during the reign of Septimius Severus or shortly afterwards. From there he was promoted to be proconsular governor of Gallia Narbonensis, and then governor of Gallia Lugdunensis. His name suggests that he might have belonged to one of the Gallic families enfranchised under Claudius and subsequently promoted to senatorial status as part of that emperor's policy. Paulinus was evidently remembered with respect in Britain because the town council at Caerwent, the civitas tribal capital known as Venta Silurum, only a few miles from Caerleon, erected a statue there to commemorate his career to date.

The setting up of statues of local worthies was a very well-established Roman urban tradition, though it is scarcely known in Britain. It was the way in which communities expressed their gratitude for the vast sums of money such men had paid out as part of their obligations as magistrates and councillors, providing public buildings, facilities and services. Pliny the Elder called it a 'civilized sense of rivalry' which meant that a man's achievements were not only recounted on his tomb but also in a public place, and said that 'statues adorn the forums in all municipal towns'.[10] The forum at Pompeii was littered with the bases of statues of city magistrates who had been awarded this privilege, usually by a council decree. Very few statues themselves remained; any of those still standing after the earthquake of 62 were removed by scavengers following the eruption of Vesuvius in 79 which finally destroyed Pompeii. However, the statue bases do survive, as does that of Tiberius Claudius Paulinus at Caerwent, and they bear witness to these men's careers and contributions to their town. The obvious question must be then whether his was a rarity or whether Romano-British towns were just as likely to feature these commemorations. Unfortunately, we cannot answer that, but if the council at Caerwent was inclined to make such a gesture it is unlikely that others did not or that Caerwent never commemorated anyone else this way. Such municipal fame was very transitory. The odds in Britain were stacked against such monuments surviving through the late or post-Roman period. Before the Roman era was over, the statue of Paulinus had been removed and, if it was made of bronze, melted down, probably by men who had either never heard of Paulinus or who had more pressing priorities. The redundant base was dragged off and turned upside down to form part of a late Roman stone platform of unknown purpose, where it was found in 1903.

The statue of Paulinus must have been set up around the time of Caracalla (211–17).[11] We can be fairly confident about that because by 220 Paulinus was back in Britain as governor of Britannia Inferior, a post that brought with it the command of the VI Legion at York, during the reign of Elagabalus (218–22). He was recorded on an inscription of that date found at High Rochester (Bremenium), an outpost fort of Hadrian's Wall, which commemorates the construction of an 'artillery platform' (*ballistarium*) there.[12] Exceptionally, we know a little more about his time in Britain. While he was at York one of his favoured advisers and friends was Titus Sennius Sollemnis of the Viducasses tribe in Gaul to whom Paulinus owed a favour: Sollemnis had used his influence as a member of the provincial Council of the Gauls to obstruct a motion which could have led to the destruction of Paulinus' career. Paulinus, while still in post in Britain, was unable to repay the favour immediately by giving Sollemnis a position so in the first instance he sent his saviour various gifts, which included among other things a bejewelled golden brooch (*fibulam auream cum gemmis*), a British cloak (*tossiam Britannicam*), and the equivalent of 25,000 sesterces in gold. He wrote to Sollemnis from a place called Tampium, which must be in Britain, and presumably northern Britain at that, but no such location has yet been identified. What we do not know is whether Paulinus had done something genuinely wrong or was the victim of a malicious personal campaign.

Sollemnis continued to benefit; he was subsequently made Paulinus' adviser (*assessor*) in Britain. All this information is recorded on an honorific inscription on a statue base from Vieux in Gaul which itemizes the career and achievements of Sollemnis and also includes the text of two letters, one by Paulinus and one by another governor of Gallia Lugdunensis, Aedius Julianus. What is perhaps most remarkable to us is that it was apparently quite in order to record this sort of mutual back-scratching on a public monument.[13] But the whole story is another reminder to us that for persons of this class Britain was an important, but only transient experience. Britain was also an imperial resource, a place to be exploited as it had always been. Around this time one villa at Combe Down in Somerset seems to have been administered by an imperial freedman, working as 'assistant to the procurators', called Naevius.[14] The inscription is unique but may stand for many other rural estates that were effectively being run by what we might call farm managers or bailiffs for the benefit of the state and state officials.

Paulinus was one of the most important people in Britain during his times in both provinces. Beneath him was a teetering edifice of administrators down to very local levels, very few of whom are known to us. The Roman fleet in Britain, the *classis Britannica*, was still busily supplying the Roman army with iron from the vast sprawling ironworks in the Weald of Kent. The fleet bathhouse which lay at the heart of the Beauport Park sector of the works (near Battle) was still in operation and around this time was enlarged and improved. A fragmentary inscription records building work there by a man called Bassus or Bassianus who was probably a military architect. His name is an interesting echo of Caracalla's birth name which was Bassianus. Caracalla was renamed Marcus Aurelius Antoninus after his father seized power. If the Beauport Park Bassianus was named by his parents in honour of Caracalla he did not live up to their aspirations. The work he oversaw at the bathhouse was shoddy compared to the original Hadrianic structure.[15] It was just as well that before too long the enormous slagheap that had been injudiciously allowed to accumulate nearby finally collapsed and buried the baths. Perhaps one of the men who used the baths was Olus Cornelius Candidus, an equerry on the governor's staff probably in the early third century, to judge from the style of the altar he set up to the mother goddesses of Italy at Dover.[16] Dover (Dubris) was one of the fleet's coastal forts. Cornelius Candidus had built a shrine to his favoured goddesses; he probably came from Italy and may have arrived at Dover with a new governor.

This was an age when conspicuous obsequiousness was an even more essential part of survival than hitherto. This is probably why an extensive series of inscriptions over the next twenty to thirty years was erected in Britain's forts. The units, like the First Cohort of Lingones at Lanchester, in County Durham, adopted the emperor's name. The Lingones, a tribe from eastern Gaul, became 'the First Cohort of Gordian's own Lingones' during the reign of Gordian III (238–44). We do not know his name but Marcus Aurelius Quirinus, the unit's commanding officer, clearly had the services of an unusually stylish and flamboyant mason on his force. This man was responsible for at least two inscriptions, clearly carved by someone with a taste for playing around with lettering.[17] His predilection was for the selective minimization of vowels, and occasionally consonants, as a space-saving style feature. The texts commemorate the building of a baths, and the restoration of the headquarters building and armouries. An irregular detachment of Suebians from Germany, based at Lanchester too and also calling themselves 'Gordian's own', set up an altar to their goddess Garmangabis. The lettering style on the altar looks very much like that of the other two inscriptions mentioned above and must have been carved by the same mason. It is a shame that none of the other inscriptions from the fort, some of which are clearly private individual dedications, provides us with his name. It was, we might note in passing, now two hundred years since the invasion of Britain.

There is a curious instance of honour being paid to the emperor from around this period. Lossio Veda, son of Vepogenus, was a Caledonian, which means that he came from what we now call Scotland. During the reign of Severus Alexander (222–35) Lossio Veda was, incongruously, in Colchester where he made a dedication to the god Mars Medocius and also the Victory of Severus Alexander.[18] He tells us nothing about his reasons for being there but he could have been a merchant, a soldier, a traveller, an envoy seeking Roman help of some form, or even a hostage of high status allowed some everyday liberty. However, the remarkable fact is that this man who was by definition someone from beyond the Roman frontier was apparently not only travelling freely within the Empire but also paying appropriate respects to the emperor, and at his own expense. He is a reminder that Britain included other peoples who were outside the Empire but whose lives nonetheless were affected in every way by their proximity to the Roman world. When an individual like Lossio Veda adopted aspects of the Roman system he allowed himself to become visible in the record. One wonders how he appeared to the citizens of Colchester: did he dress as a Roman or did he proudly wear his tribal apparel? Much later, in the late fourth century, the poet Claudian described Britain as being 'dressed in the skin of some Caledonian beast, and with tattooed cheeks', an image which suggested that the popular Roman perception of Britain and the Britons remained modelled on people like Lossio from beyond the frontier rather than within the province.[19] While Lossio is very unusual, Roman Britain must have played host to numerous individuals who flitted in and out of the Roman province throughout its history. They also help explain the scattered finds of Roman goods in northern Scotland and Ireland, carried there by trade or by returning travellers.

Earlier we met Sulpicia Lepidina and her friend Claudia Severa and their efforts to sustain polite society on the northern frontier in the late first century. By the standards of the day, as officers' wives, they had a moderate chance of doing so but they still faced great difficulties if things went wrong. The deaths of their children or their husbands were both unavoidably serious possibilities, the latter being a potential disaster so far from their unknown homes. We have no idea what happened to them but in other cases we do. A woman with a similar name, Aelia Severa, and described as being an *honesta femina*, 'honourable lady', died at York aged twenty-seven years, nine months and four days. She was already a widow for she was described as being 'formerly the wife of Caecilius Rufus' – the text on her coffin uses the word *quondam* for 'formerly' and in this context this usually denoted a connection to someone deceased.[20] Fortunately she had the protection of her husband's freedman Caecilius Musicus, who made sure his dead master's widow was properly buried. His name meant 'musician' or 'poet' and may be a literal record of his profession; alternatively it was simply an allusion to a prolific and highly esteemed Gallo-Roman comic poet and playwright of the second century BC called Caecilius Statius. Either way, the name serves as a reminder that, however vivid the written record, apart from the last century or so we cannot 'hear' the past even if we can read the surviving poetry. The Romano-British, like every other human society, will have enjoyed music which is entirely lost.

Sadly, Aelia Severa was not allowed to rest in peace. At some point Aelia Severa's coffin was exhumed and her remains were turfed out and replaced with those of an anonymous man. This same grave of the funerary-recycling man also reused as a lid a family tombstone which had been set up by a veteran of the VI Legion at York, Gaius Aeresius Saenus, to his family and, in anticipation of his own demise, himself. This grieving man had had to say farewell to his wife Flavia Augustina, who expired aged thirty-nine years, seven months and eleven days, his son Saenius Augustinus, who had survived just one year and three days, and a daughter, whose name is lost, who lived for one year, nine months and five days.[21] Flavia Augustina, like so many mothers of that time and since, had had to endure the tragedy of losing two infant children. The tombstone, however, was not a bespoke piece. The family is depicted with the parents standing behind their children, but the latter are figures more appropriate to a son and daughter of around eight and six years respectively. It was clearly purchased 'off the shelf' and an appropriate inscription inserted in the blank space. Robbing tombs for their stone was customary in the Roman world. Visitors to the fourth-century House of the Porch at Ostia in Italy in Roman times, and today, were greeted by a drain cover in the corridor around the middle of the house that was adapted from a second- or third-century inscription from a tomb, with drain perforations insouciantly cut straight through the names of the deceased and his wife. During the lifespan of a family lineage, ancestors and their graves were accorded enormous respect by their descendants, freedmen and associates. Once a line died out it was soon forgotten and their monuments were liable to be treated as quarries. In Rome the remains of the grand roadside tomb of the great Republican Scipio family was built over with a house in the third century AD. In the same way the tomb of the procurator Classicianus was dismantled and the stone used in London's late Roman defences. At the legionary fortress of Chester the soldiers thought nothing of tearing up an earlier cemetery of their predecessors and using the tombstones, often cutting them down to size, to help rebuild the walls. This had the happy consequence of preserving them and many were found in 1891.

Outside the supply fort, with its port at South Shields on the south bank of the Tyne just near where it enters the North Sea, Barates from Palmyra buried his wife and former slave Regina. Apart from Boudica, Regina is the most famous of all Romano-British women for the touching commemoration left her by Barates and the elegant eastern-style classical tombstone he commissioned for her in the manner of the early third century (plate 17).[22] She was thirty and had been born into the Catuvellaunian tribe, whose region where Hertfordshire and Essex are now had once been the most powerful of all the British tribal zones. Regina is exceptional in the record for being apparently unequivocally British. Almost inevitably she comes down to us through the medium of someone else who had absorbed the Roman traditions of Latin literacy and the need to express himself that way. Her face has been destroyed, rendering her a visual anonymity, which has done nothing to dent the symbolism of her life. She is in every sense our model of Britannia, a woman violated, enslaved and even named by Rome, yet who found presumably a kind of happiness in the time left to her. Her survival in the record exemplifies the essential paradox of her existence: a Briton known only to us through a Roman idiom.

Regina was the wife of a Romanized Syrian, without whose care and effort we would or could know nothing of her, since like almost all the Britons she did not seek to perpetuate her memory herself in any other way. The fort's Roman name was Arbeia, a name now thought by some to have been derived from *Arabi*, the Latin for Arabs. In that sense it probably means something like 'Arabtown' much as today we use the word 'Chinatown' to denote a part of a modern city inhabited predominantly by a Chinese immigrant community. If that is correct, it is interesting that in the fourth century the garrison of the fort was a unit of bargemen from the Tigris where modern Iraq is now.[23] Barates is likely one and the same with a Barates, 'the flag-bearer' whose tombstone survives at Corbridge.[24] Barates himself was as much a product of the Roman world as his wife. He recorded his wife's death in Latin but also included a partial transcription of the text in Palmyrene, a version of Aramaic, and clearly his own tongue. He is a reminder that Roman Britain, with its exotic mix of peoples, was also a place where people spoke anything from the variant forms of indigenous dialects to eastern languages. Latin was the lingua franca in the Western Empire and Greek in the East that held the Roman world together. Probably a soldier or at least for some of his life a trader, we can imagine Barates coming across Regina in some desultory slave market in a ramshackle town in the military north and buying her, though she may of course have been acquired further south while he was en route to the north. Barates may have bought her simply to perform practical duties or he may have liked the look of her and thought her a potential wife and mother for the children he hoped to have. That Regina was sold into slavery at all is a hollow echo of the fictitious speech of Calgacus composed by Tacitus a century or more earlier. Calgacus was attributed with cursing the Romans for their enslavement of the Britons; long after Calgacus and his Caledonian tribes were defeated by Agricola in 83–4 Britons were still susceptible to a lifetime of servitude. There is no indication that Regina ever had the children of Barates but at the age of thirty it is certainly possible she had.

Whatever his plans, in the event Barates and Regina would not grow old together. Regina now presides in an appropriately regal manner over the collection in the museum at South Shields. Regardless of what else Barates did for his beloved wife, his greatest gesture was to guarantee her immortality. Her monument makes her special to us but at the time their relationship must have been quite normal. Male soldiers, traders and travellers have always consorted with women they found in the places where they were stationed, indulging in relationships that varied from the casual and fleeting to the permanent.

Regina was not the only slave woman in Roman Britain to have been freed into marriage. Around the same time that she passed away a priest called Calpurnius Receptus died at Bath. He must have worked at the cult centre of Sulis-Minerva for his tombstone says he was a priest of Sulis. He was seventy-five years old, a considerable and unusual age but not unique. At some point in his long life he had freed one of his slave women called Trifosa. She took the name Calpurnia from her former master and married him. As Calpurnia Trifosa at some point in the early third century she buried her priest husband at Bath.[25] The practice was not unusual in the Roman world and it is indicative of how different slavery could be compared to the racial slavery of the southern states in America before the 1860s.

In the Roman world homosexuality was widely accepted, even when it involved relations between adults and young people or children, and was considered almost a kind of leisure pastime for mature men. The historian Cassius Dio said of the emperor Trajan (98–117) that he 'was devoted to boys' but 'harmed no one' in the course of his relationships with them, escaping any censure as a result.[26] In Roman Britain, while there is no example that is explicitly homosexual, another tombstone from South Shields is a likely candidate. It is a remarkably elaborate piece of sculpture, possibly carved by the same mason who made Regina's. It shows the figure of Victor, a Moor, who had died aged twenty, lounging on a dining couch and framed by a pair of pilasters supporting a pediment with a lion's head (plate 18). Like Regina, Victor had once been enslaved and was now buried by the man who freed him, in this case Numerianus, a trooper of the First Cavalry Wing of Asturians who were garrisoned at the fort. At the top left and right of the tombstone is a pair of *imagines clipeatae*, perhaps showing Victor and Numerianus.[27] Was Victor Numerianus' catamite? It is altogether too elaborate and affectionate a monument for a mere freedman.

The enslavement of provincials was endemic in the Roman world. Britain was not specially selected for this. These slaves were connected to the army and were firmly associated with forts in the military zone. But the army's reach stretched far further and was a ubiquitous aspect of such a remote and heavily garrisoned province. The army also had vast demands for food and supplies, evidenced by no better source than the Vindolanda letters from the end of the first century.

The villa at Yewden, near Hambleden in Buckinghamshire, has earned for itself a certain amount of notoriety. The villa itself faces an enclosed courtyard which contains several farm buildings. In a yard to the north of the villa buildings a total of ninety-seven infant burials were excavated a century ago. Their remains indicate that the majority at least died at around the time of a normal birth, rather than prematurely, which suggests then that their deaths were deliberate. This has led to several suggestions, including one that the villa was used not only as a farm estate but also as a military brothel with the babies being disposed of as unwanted offspring. Another is that the villa was used as an important military supply estate where it was essential to keep slave workers productive, and the children were exposed at birth accordingly. Certainly, the number of writing styli found on site might attest to a great deal of administration and record-keeping going on, which would certainly be commensurate with an installation working for the state. In one or two instances cut marks on the bones suggest that some were killed violently or may be evidence of medical intervention in a difficult birth. DNA analysis showed that both male and female offspring were involved, while finds from the site have been taken to indicate that the main period of death was the late second century between about 150 and 200, though in reality these finds were not specifically associated with the individual burials.[28] A further suggestion is that the place was in some way dedicated to a mother goddess cult and was a place where women came to give birth in the confident knowledge that professional help would be at hand.

Artefacts suggest that a large number of adult females lived here, which one might have expected with all the babies, though it is difficult to imagine a brothel doing such a roaring trade in what was quite a remote location. However, the villa was in use for a long time and in reality these babies might represent just one or two stillbirths per annum, something that could be expected in the natural course of events on an estate where many workers were involved or if many women were coming on a regular basis to give birth. Moreover, the area where the babies were found is outside the immediate confines of the main building complex and is the sort of area not usually explored during villa excavations. In other words, Yewden may not have been as unusual as it now seems. The villa site at Frocester has produced at least thirty-seven burials of perinatal infants from the several centuries that the site was in occupation. Moreover, what we do not and cannot know is how many children lived, making evaluating the significance of the number of deaths very hard. If they were slaves it is worth remembering that the literal meaning of the Latin word *proletarius* is of a person at the bottom of the heap and so poor that their only contribution to society was the ability to reproduce and provide more labour. Nonetheless, whatever the truth, the dead babies are a reminder that infant mortality was and always had been a chronic aspect of most human societies until the modern age.

The war of Severus was already long enough ago to be no more than the half-remembered stories of old men. The great Wall of Hadrian was over a century old, and the invasion of Claudius eighty more years before that. Quirinus and his troops at Lanchester were just one unit in one fort of dozens of units scattered across the north. They will never have heard of Flavius Cerealis and his wife Sulpicia Lepidina at Vindolanda, who were as long ago to them as the soldiers of the Zulu War of the 1870s are to us, yet their lives will have been little different. They built and repaired their forts, went out on patrol, occasionally fought but probably spent most of their time squabbling bitterly with rival units, swaggering on parade, hunting, cooking, foraging, praying, drinking, carousing and moaning.

An altar from Bollihope Common, near Stanhope in County Durham, which is not so far south of Vindolanda, is dedicated to Silvanus and records a similar hunting expedition to the one the Vindolanda officers had engaged in a century or more before. It paints a vivid picture of life on the frontier for officers with time to spare. Gaius Tetius Veturius Micianus was the commanding officer of a cavalry wing of Gaulish Sebosians. He triumphantly bagged a boar that apparently had fought off any attempts by his predecessors to capture it. Since his unit at that date may actually have been based as far away as Lancaster, the text suggests that the officers in these northern forts were quite able to spend significant amounts of time away on hunting expeditions competing with one another.[29]

The commanding officer at Lanchester, Marcus Aurelius Quirinus, like the officers who bagged the boar on Bollihope Common, also had time to spare. At Eastgate, also in County Durham, he set up an altar to the god Silvanus on the banks of a beck that feeds into the River Wear.[30] The wives and children of many soldiers lived in the scattered settlements beyond this and many other forts, providing some comforts and increasingly a ready supply of new recruits. They were still paid with the emperor's coin though many will have noticed a steady process of debasement underway. By Gordian III's time the coins still looked silver though there was a good deal less actual silver in each piece. Within another twenty years the silver would have disappeared for good. That mattered more than it might seem today in our age of token coinage. For the Roman army the purity of coin they were paid could cause them to make or break a regime.

In these isolated communities all sorts of tensions must have arisen with consequences that seem on occasion to have escaped discovery. Murder was, of course, well known in the Roman world. It could range from the merciless killing of a slave to slaves killing their masters, political murders, and crimes of passion. At Vindolanda, some time around the middle of the third century, a small girl aged about eight to eleven years old was buried in a pit in the corner of a barracks, apparently with her hands tied. Chemical analysis of her teeth after her discovery in 2010 suggested that she had been born on the continent and lived there till she was around seven.[31] With only the skeletal remains surviving it is impossible now to know how she died. The implications of a girl this age being buried in a barracks which would have been occupied by men are extremely unpleasant, especially in our own time when more and more focus has been placed on the systemic abuse of children in some circumstances. Had the episode been a normal death of a child, the burial would have taken place outside the fort and its attendant settlement; burial within the living area was illegal so whoever placed her there must be under suspicion. Moreover, the little girl was buried just 35 centimetres below the floor surface, a grave so shallow that she must have been deposited there in haste. Other murder victims met their end at Housesteads fort some time during the following hundred years (see below).

London's streets and those of other towns in Britain must have been as prone to dark deeds in the Roman period as they have been ever since. In the early third century a coin forger was at work. There was nothing especially unusual about this. Coin forging was endemic in the ancient world. The dividends from being able to pass off base metal coins as silver or gold were considerable. This London forger had a small collection of genuine second-century bronze and brass coins, one genuine brand new silver coin of Caracalla (dated 213–17) and some clay moulds for making copies of silver coins of Septimius Severus, Caracalla and Geta. He must have planned to melt down the bronze and brass coins and use the metal to cast his counterfeit 'silver' coins. His nefarious scheme to rip off Roman Londoners was therefore under way around the year 220. But he was caught, or feared he was about to be caught. His forging equipment was all thrown into rubbish dumped on the floor of a tower in London's new city walls, conveniently telling us that they must have been built by that date. Strangely, fragments of a human skull were found with the forger's materials in a macabre but unresolved twist.

Money, whether authentic or fake, was an essential part of the Roman economy. London would have been the perfect place to circulate counterfeit coinage because it was still a major mercantile centre. All the major towns of Roman Britain thrived on commerce. Indeed, they could not have existed without it. No one exemplifies this better than the merchants of the third century who plied the North Sea trade routes between Britain and Europe. Lucius Viducius Placidus and Marcus Aurelius Lunaris were freedman who had done well. They were not unusual. The inscriptions from Pompeii, Herculaneum and Ostia are filled with references to ostentatious ex-slaves who had made small fortunes after their liberation. Since the Roman senatorial aristocracy did not sully its hands with commerce, at least directly, the way was open for former members of the servile class who had no such reservations. Pompeii and Herculaneum had been destroyed in 79 but it is clear the world so vividly recorded there had continued to exist across the Empire.

Lucius Viducius Placidus was a Gaul from the Rouen area in the territory of the Veliocasses tribe. He made his money out of trading with Britain in the early third century and may well have been a freedman. Nevertheless, he will have become a Roman citizen in 212 (whatever his status), thanks to Caracalla's edict of universal citizenship that year. Placidus means as it sounds: placid or gentle, perhaps a comment on his personality as a newborn or wishful thinking on the part of his parents. It is a remarkable fact that two dedications by this man have survived. The first lacks the *tria nomina* of a citizen so probably dates to before 212. It was found at Colijnsplaat in Holland where the Scheldt meets the North Sea and commemorated a local goddess called Nehalennia. Lucius Viducius Placidus also paid in the year 221 for an arch and gate to a temple precinct in York dedicated to the Genius of the Place and other, uncertain, deities.[32] It was almost certainly the case that this man plied the North Sea between York and the Low Countries importing and exporting a variety of goods. Perhaps these included pottery; Marcus Secundinius Silvanus was another merchant on the Britain run who left an altar at Nehalennia's shrine. He calls himself a *negotiator cretarius*, 'pottery trader'.[33]

Their clients might have included men like the potter Sennianus, a man whose name is native in origin. Sennianus worked in the sprawling potteries that clustered round the small town at Durobrivae (Water Newton) on Ermine Street. Apart from defences, the town had none of the features of the formal colonies or civitas capitals; it has all the hallmarks of a place that grew up spontaneously around a junction on a major road and a river crossing. It was, after all, precisely how London began. The Roman world seems to have spawned towns like Durobrivae effortlessly. The location was ideal. Relatively central and with excellent communications as well as all the resources needed to make pottery, it clearly attracted those with the skills needed to make the most of it. It was in every sense the Stoke-on-Trent of its day. Kiln sites clustered in and around the town and the air must have been thick with smoke from the firings. Vast quantities of pottery were made here, especially in the late second century and on into the third as the samian potteries of Gaul went into decline. The products were shipped around the province and abroad.

But the Durobrivae potters produced more than imitative fine wares. They also churned out *mortaria*, those highly specialized Roman grinding bowls that defined the era and which had been the main product of a variety of dedicated production centres in Britain almost from the moment the Roman invasion had begun. Sennianus was a *mortaria* potter but, unlike all the others working at Durobrivae, he decided to paint his name on one of his bowls (plate 19). The words read *Sennianus Durobrivis vri*(. . .). The last word is annoyingly incomplete, allowing for inconclusive academic debate which includes rejecting '*vrit*' even though that is the most likely reconstruction. The reason for rejecting '*vrit*' (which means 'heated' or 'dried by heating'), apparently, is that its use to mean firing pottery is otherwise unknown. Since the Roman world is full of examples of such 'rules' not being obeyed, it is rather bizarre to reject the most obvious explanation of the word for such arcane reasons. If it does read '*vrit*' then the meaning is 'Sennianus fired [this *mortarium*] at Durobrivae', which has the advantage of being obviously plausible. Since we are not party to obscure colloquial use of Latin words, this is as good as any other suggestion and certainly better than no suggestion, which appears to be the main scholarly offering.[34] Sennianus was the only one known to record himself like this but another man from the area stamped his *mortaria* with *Cunoarus fecit vico Duro*(*brivae*), 'Cunoarus made [this] at the town of Durobrivae'. Cunoarus is also an unequivocally native name, echoing Cunobelinus, the Catuvellaunian king who died about AD 41–2, which makes it possible that the potters here were at least partly men of local origins.

By 237 Marcus Aurelius Lunaris was a *sevir Augustalis*, a priest of the imperial cult, serving at both York and Lincoln. He was probably at least in his thirties or forties and had evidently done well enough to hold this position in two of the province's greatest colonies. Such men were not career priests. This priesthood was an honorific mark of status often held by freedmen because their status denied them access to elected civic magistracies; a position in this priestly college gave freedmen a prestigious position in Roman urban and commercial culture. Lunaris would have officiated in ceremonies according to a calendar of rites, along with other men like himself. Such freedmen were almost always traders or businessmen. Like Placidus, his name probably commemorates enfranchisement in Caracalla's edict of 212, though he may already have been freed. Alternatively, he could have been freed and enfranchised during the reigns of Caracalla's successors Elagabalus (218–22) and Severus Alexander (222–35), both of whose names began 'Marcus Aurelius'. Lunaris means, quite simply, 'of the moon'. Pregnancies were measured by the Romans as the passage of nine moons;[35] perhaps Lunaris or a forbear was born on the night of a prominent full moon.

The year 237 was the third in the reign of Maximinus I (235–8), one of the military thugs who took control of the Empire in the third century and lasted only a few years before being killed. Lunaris would have had little interest in such distant goings-on. In 237 he arranged a journey to Bordeaux in Gaul. Before he left he collected a block of Yorkshire millstone grit and had it packed onto the ship, which must have sailed out of the Humber estuary, rounded East Anglia and headed down through the Channel to western France. Perhaps he and Placidus were able to call on the services of a man like Marcus Minucius Audens. Minucius Audens was a legionary helmsman, in Latin a *gubernator*, from which our word 'governor' comes.[36] He had made an offering to a variety of mother goddesses at York during his service with the VI Legion there, perhaps helping with the massive amount of men and materials arriving there during the Severan campaigns of twenty-five years previously. Marcus Aurelius Lunaris successfully reached Bordeaux, a journey he may well have made several times before, or at least presumably intended to make again. To give thanks for his safe deliverance from the high seas he had the block of millstone grit carved into an altar with an inscription which recorded his name, his position and a consular date for 237, and dedicated it to the 'tutelary goddess Boudiga' (plate 20).[37] The name is probably a slip for Bourdiga, the divine identity of Bordeaux where the altar was found. For all that, 'Boudiga' is a curious echo of Boudica, the only such possible connection, but it is unlikely that any reference to her was intended.

Such people were the international businessmen of their day, of the type who now gather in Britain's airports early in the morning to catch flights to the commercial centres of north-west Europe, returning the same day or later in the week. There must have been thousands of similar men who risked everything on dangerous voyages over difficult and unpredictable seas. Many will have been ruined by a single disastrous voyage, while others made fortunes. The Pudding Pan Rock in the Thames Estuary was the occasion of at least one, and probably several, such catastrophes. It is so-called because of the fishermen in more modern times who dredged up pottery, much of it barnacle-encrusted Gaulish samian ware and evidently once the cargo of a ship or ships that came to grief in the second or early third centuries.

These traders were increasingly susceptible to attacks by seaborne pirates who plagued the North Sea and the English Channel. Exactly who these marauders were we do not know for certain but they probably sailed out from the coasts of northern Germany and Denmark, beyond the borders of the Roman Empire. They were attracted by the rich pickings of the trade routes between Britain and Gaul. By the early third century steps were being taken to secure the coastline with forts and fortified compounds. One of the earliest was at Reculver, on the north coast of Kent, where a governor of Britannia Superior, probably called Quintus Aradius Rufinus, erected a shrine in the headquarters building at the fort sometime in the 230s or 240s.[38] The fragmentary inscription that records his name was found in the building's strongroom. The fort overlooked ships as they headed up the Thames to London. Over the next sixty years or so more forts and fortified sites would be added; the remains of several are some of the most prominent Roman remains in Britain today, but apart from at Reculver, no names of any of the men involved in building them are known.

The kind of fortunes made by the lucky traders who escaped pirates and shipwrecks can only be guessed at but perhaps the Shapwick Hoard found in 1998 and the Dorchester South Street Hoard found in 1936 provide a clue. Most coin hoards turn up in locations that provide not the slightest hint of where the owner lived and worked. This is hardly surprising – hiding one's wealth under the proverbial mattress is a risky business. However, the Shapwick Hoard was found in what turned out to be a room in a hitherto unknown second-century Roman villa in Somerset. It consisted of 9,238 silver coins dating from Mark Antony (31 BC) to AD 224 in the reign of Severus Alexander.[39] They were perhaps earned and accumulated from the produce of a rural estate, though the wide date spread of the coins indicates that this took place over a long period of time, perhaps two or more generations, before the hoard's final loss in the mid to late 220s. The coins had been stored in rolls of cloth or leather and probably packed into a sack before being buried.[40] For some unknown reason, at least the west range of the house seems to have been demolished (not long after the hoard was concealed in that part of the building), evidently by persons unaware of the hoard's existence, and it remained undiscovered until modern times when ploughing brought some of it to the surface and a metal detector was used on the field.

The Dorchester South Street Hoard turned up in the backyard of a Roman townhouse of Durnovaria, a major town in the tribal canton of the Dumnonii in south-western England. It is not unreasonable to suggest that this was the home of a merchant or businessman of some sort who chose his back garden as the safest place to secure his wealth. There was at least no risk of forgetting where he had buried it. Over 22,000 silver coins were involved and had been placed in a bronze jug, bronze basin and a small wooden barrel. They dated from the reign of Caracalla to the year 257 and included 8,888 silver coins of Gordian III (238–44) and 4,939 of Philip I (244–9) alone (plate 21).[41] This suggests that the bulk of the wealth had been accumulated in the 240s and early 250s. The reason for non-recovery in both cases is obviously unknown but modern examples of hoards where the hoarder is known do include cases of individuals who died before ever revealing the location of their wealth, which only turned up later through chance discoveries. The

Dorchester coins involved were of debased silver, characteristic of the mid-third century, but enough bullion content remained to make this a significant and valuable deposit, certainly by comparison with most of the 'silver' coinage issued thereafter. The Shapwick coins were mostly of much higher purity and thus their bullion value was around as great as the Dorchester coins, despite their being fewer in number. These hoards were not recovered by their owners. The vast majority will have been recovered and thus are undetectable – any man of substance will have been prone to episodic hoarding as and when necessary. Marcus Aurelius Lunaris and others of his kind will have been accustomed to the routine practice of hoarding.

By the time the Dorchester hoarder had buried his coins Britain had been a Roman province for more than two hundred years. Indeed, since Septimius Severus' time it had been two provinces. The forts and fortresses had been around for long enough to need renovations and rebuilding and the same applied to the towns. The Vindolanda tablets lay buried in the subterranean anaerobic swamps that lurked below the later fort and settlement and their oblivious inhabitants, recording the lives on the northern frontier more than 150 years previously. By this time we start really to leave the world of inscriptions. Why, we do not know. The habit seemed to dwindle in Britain and eventually virtually die out, though this is by no means a phenomenon limited to Britain. However, it had always been something of a preserve of the immigrant soldiers, traders and administrators. This necessarily has the consequence that we know a good deal less about individuals as the third century faded into the fourth, but for all that some of the most flamboyant and idiosyncratic characters belong to this era.

The murder of Commodus on the last day of 192 had heralded in an era of imperial turmoil despite Septimius Severus' efforts to establish his own dynasty. By the middle of the third century it had become routine for emperors to have risen up through the ranks and then seize power at the head of part of the army, fight it out for supreme power, only to topple after a very few years, or in some cases weeks or months. This chronic instability must have afflicted Britain in some ways but the archaeological evidence gives us little idea of how. There is no evidence of particular change or decay and, if anything, the northern frontier seems to have enjoyed a period of relative peace and quiet in spite of the chronic political instability that plagued the Empire in the third century.

The greatest political disruption came in the form of the Gallic Empire. In 259 Marcus Cassianus Latinius Postumus seized power in the north-western provinces. Like so many usurpers of the era, Postumus (a name, incidentally, usually applied to a man who was born after his father's death) had risen from total obscurity through the ranks of the army and had been made commander of the Rhine army by the emperor Valerian (253–60). Valerian had ruled jointly with his son Gallienus but had had to leave Rome in 256 to deal with a threat from Persia. Many other frontier threats undermined the regime. Meanwhile, Postumus established what he had the audacity to announce was a legitimate Roman Empire. In 260 Valerian was humiliatingly captured by the Persians, adding insult to injury because there was already a breakaway regime in the East led by Odaenathus of Palmyra in Syria. Gallienus was now in no position to challenge Postumus.

Postumus marked himself out as an official Roman emperor in every respect. He held consulships and his coins promoted stock Roman virtues, personifications and aspirations. He and then his successors bumbled through the next thirteen years, experiencing murder and usurpation just like the 'real' Roman Empire. For the average Roman Briton, life would have seemed very little different apart from the coins that trickled through his or her fingers and the names on milestones that popped up along Britannia's highways naming Postumus and his successors Victorinus, Tetricus I, and his son Tetricus II (as well as several other fleeting figures). Although Britain was absorbed back into the Roman Empire after the Gallic Empire's fall in 273, the breakaway regime retained a visible presence in its abundant and increasingly decrepit coinage, which to this day dominates site finds of the period.

In the time of the Gallic Empire those on the military north began to see the long period of stability start to deteriorate. At the fort of Lancaster in around 262–6 the resident unit of Sebosian cavalry was commanded by Flavius Ammausius during the governorship of Octavius Sabinus. Octavius Sabinus will have been the governor of Britannia Inferior and thus also the legionary legate commanding the VI Legion at York. Ammausius had organized the rebuilding of the baths and its basilican exercise hall. This was an opportunity to record the current loyalty to Postumus of the unit, which was now called the Ala Sebossiana Postumiana, or the 'Sebosian Cavalry Wing, Postumus' own'. The inscription is partly remarkable for recording one of the last gasps of apparent normality and convention. Ammausius is stated to be the prefect of cavalry and Octavius Sabinus to be of senatorial rank. Moreover, the inscription even cites a consular date – it was dedicated on 22 August in the year of the second consulship of both Censor and Lepidus, though it is undoubtedly referring to members of Postumus' senate, which was not in Rome but at Cologne.[42]

This was indicative of the sustained need to show instant loyalty to the current regime. At the Hadrian's Wall fort of Birdoswald, Marcius Gallicus, then commanding the First Aelian Cohort of Dacians, set up an altar to Jupiter and added his unit's new *Postumiana* epithet, as did Probius Augendus, who either preceded or followed Marcius Gallicus. Before long one of their successors, Pomponius Desideratus, found himself with the unit now restyled the First Aelian Cohort of Tetrician Dacians.[43] Things moved fast in the Gallic Empire. In 268 Postumus was murdered, only to be followed by a rapid succession of replacements. By 270 Tetricus I had taken over and managed the startling achievement of ruling for three years before abdicating at the behest of the official emperor Aurelian in 273. No doubt this game was played almost everywhere on the northern frontier. Meanwhile the ordinary civilians of the south were familiarized with the new regime through the simple expedient of updating milestones, which now brandished the names of various rulers of the Gallic Empire in locations as far apart as Breage in Cornwall (Postumus) and Bitterne in Hampshire (Tetricus).[44] The milestones are among the only inscriptions known from the later part of Roman Britain's history.

Just how concrete this loyalty was we cannot say but it is more than likely the army units did not all automatically follow whoever the latest emperor was, with some inevitably backing the wrong side, though with Roman imperial politics moving at a breakneck pace this might not always have caused serious problems. However, at Ambleside in Cumbria a most remarkable tombstone turned up in 1962 in a garden near the fort of Galava. It is very crudely carved but quite legible. The text records the death at the age of fifty-five of a retired centurion called Flavius Fuscinus, and at the age of thirty-five Flavius Romanus, a record clerk (*actuarius*) who had been 'killed in the fort by enemies'.[45] The men might have been father and son or simply compatriots joined in the unfortunate circumstances of their deaths. The text is very tantalizing because it does not specify who the enemies were – were they rebellious Britons who burst into the fort and killed the men, or were they members of a faction either within the fort's resident unit or from another fort? The tombstone might belong to almost any point in the third or fourth century when siding with the right usurper might mean the difference between life or death. Their names belonged to innocuous Roman tradition and, as so often, tell us nothing about their origins. A Fuscinus was a friend of the poet Juvenal and the name itself derived from the Roman name Fuscus, with the first-century BC poet Horace counting a Fuscus among his friends. 'Romanus' means simply 'the Roman'.

Flavius Romanus met a violent end at the hands of an unknown enemy. Violence was endemic in the Roman world, either in military or civilian contexts. An impression of just how violent life could be emerges from excavations in a fourth-century cemetery outside the Bath (south-west) gate of the major Roman town at Cirencester, indeed the very gate that pilgrims to the spa would have travelled through to Bath on a journey which would have included passing the shrine of Apollo Cunomaglos at Nettleton. By this time inhumation was the normal practice of burial; this of course means that there is a better chance of identifying either the cause of death or injuries inflicted during life. The number of male skeletons featuring evidence of violence caused the archaeologist recording the finds to say that 'fighting . . . was a commonplace event with these people'. One man had been struck with such force on the right-hand side of his head that a triangular piece of skull had broken away and sunk towards the brain, which presumably arrested further movement. Suspended here the fragment healed but remained in a depressed position, perhaps causing some brain damage. This would explain additional evidence from the skull for a trepanning operation.[46] His remains bear witness to a dramatic experience which may well have hastened his end, and which seems to have been just one of many traumatic injuries experienced by him and others.

The civilian context of the cemetery makes it unlikely these were inflicted during warfare, which means we might have to assume that town life for some adult males had the potential to be a thoroughly unpleasant and violent experience. This in fact should really not be any surprise in the context of any Roman town. In 59 a vicious riot broke out at the amphitheatre in Pompeii during gladiatorial displays when the locals decided to attack rival supporters from nearby Nuceria, resulting in numerous fatalities and serious casualties.[47] Cirencester's own amphitheatre lay a few yards from the Bath Gate cemetery. Many forts and other towns in Britain had amphitheatres, among them Silchester and London. Sextius (or Sextilius) Marcianus, the Chester centurion and (perhaps) part-time gladiator whom we met earlier, is one of the few individuals we know to have fought in such places in Britain. At York a man called Victor was buried with a small bone label laid on his chest. It said 'Lord Victor, may you have a lucky win!', an exhortation applied either to gladiators or charioteers.[48] Cirencester's Skeleton no. 305 could have been a gladiator, a gladiatorial supporter or simply the victim of a drunken tavern brawl or a street mugging of the type described by Juvenal as endemic in Rome in the early second century.[49] It is worth adding here that whether or not one considers the evidence of tombstones or the physical remains in graves, female burials are always rarer. The tombstones can be explained by a male-dominated society where male status was a social determinant, but this does not explain why there are so few female burials in cemeteries. They exist, but never in the same numbers as male burials.

The small girl who seems to have been murdered at the fort of Vindolanda around the middle of the third century was not the only such victim. Another murder, this time of two adults, took place at the fort of Housesteads on Hadrian's Wall sometime between the late third century and mid-fourth century. One of the buildings excavated in the fort vicus in the 1930s yielded an unpleasant secret. There were two skeletons, one evidently a well-built middle-aged man and the other probably a woman.[50] They had been buried on the floor of a room at the back of the building used as a tavern and then sealed beneath a layer of clay. Burial within a building in an occupation area was both taboo and illegal in the Roman world so the mere presence of adult human remains in this context is suspicious enough. But the male skeleton preserved part of a knife blade between his ribs, and it is reasonable to conclude that was how he had died. As with the little girl at Vindolanda, the likelihood is that the killer lived on the premises. Burying his victims here saved him the trouble of having to dispose of the bodies elsewhere and the risk of being apprehended while doing so. As for a motive, perhaps robbery or jealousy lay behind the killing. Britain's modern and eccentric love of murder mysteries has led to this unfortunate occasion now being the subject of a schoolchildren's investigative exercise at the fort today.

The Roman world was no stranger to state-sanctioned violence either. Another personality of this era may have been Albanus the martyr. He is known to us only through the Christian tradition of his martyrdom at the hands of the imperial authorities.[51] The episode is undated but best fits the time of the Tetrarchy, the period of rule by a college of emperors initiated by Diocletian (see the Carausian episode at the end of this chapter). Between 303 and 311 a sustained programme of Christian persecution was operated, initiated by Diocletian, which intensified.[52] This included a requirement that priests be forced to make a pagan sacrifice in order to be released, which undoubtedly fits the Albanus story. The story is a strange one since it involves a resident of Verulamium (St Albans) taking in a priest and protecting him, only to be so beguiled by the man's faith that he not only adopted it himself but decided to take the rap when imperial officials arrived, with no indication that the priest was prepared to stand up for his own faith. Albanus refused the chance to make a pagan sacrifice and was executed on a hill outside the city. The site of his martyrdom subsequently attracted a drift of settlement, with the result that the medieval abbey of St Alban was built there and became the centre of the later town.

The other possibility is that the abbey of St Alban stands on top of a pagan shrine that was appropriated by the Christian Church, which then fabricated a tale of martyrdom in order to create a convincing pedigree for the spot; the name 'Albanus' means white, which suggests an appropriate degree of purity for a martyr. It is unlikely, though, that this could possibly have worked had it been a complete work of fiction; in reality a germ of truth probably lies buried in the story somewhere. What is certain is that there was an active Christian community in Britain by the early 300s. Christianity was a potent exotic cult and it arrived by the same routes that brought Mithras, Isis and Serapis. If Albanus himself did not exist in the form recorded, he almost certainly represents a version of a real event or the conflation of several episodes.

This was also the era when some of Britain's villas began to show signs of significant development. Some of the villa owners had always been able to indulge in some improvements, such as adding corridors and wings or installing an indifferent mosaic or two in the prime reception rooms. The investments reflected a slowly improving financial state for a very small element in the province's rural social structure. But in the late third century some families appear to have embarked on an era of rapidly accumulating wealth, resulting in palatial villa establishments that presided over the most fertile regions in Britain's landscape. These were predominantly in the Cotswolds and south-west, but with many other concentrations across a vast central swathe that stretched from Exeter to Lincolnshire and across to the south and east, and even had outliers into south Wales and Yorkshire.

There is an exceptionally rare instance of a precisely dated named individual at a villa. He was found at the villa of Tarrant Hinton in Dorset. Cupitus, the son of Verus, died on 26 August in the year 258. The inscription which records him was a building stone rather than a tombstone so it must have come from a tomb built near the villa house in a family cemetery, though it ended up in the filling of a well.[53] Cupitus was in his thirty-ninth year, and thus had been born in late 219 or the first half of 220. This was old enough for his demise to cause significant practical problems for his family, though in his case there is no indication that he was either married or a father. Cupitus is extremely unusual in being someone from a villa whom we can name and also know a little about. Although the name is Latin in form, it probably contains a native element in the Cup-; if so it might be a small piece of very tenuous evidence for a villa estate being owned by a family of native origin. Having said that, the name Verus is very distinctly Roman and in any case we cannot be certain that he did own the villa.

Death, of course, could come in many different forms and at different ages. Around this time a tragedy befell the occupants of the villa house at Lullingstone in Kent. It had been in existence since the late first century and may well have stood on the site of an Iron Age farmstead. Behind the house, a little higher up the slope of the valley side that overlooks the River Darenth, a structure was built that in plan resembles the so-called Romano-Celtic temple with a concentric square cella and ambulatory. It had an entrance which faced south and was so close to the house that it was quite obviously an integral feature of the immediate environs. Unlike a conventional temple, though, this example had been built to stand on top of a square tomb chamber that was over 3.3 metres deep. The project was quite a complicated one and had involved levelling the hillside to create a terraced plot for the mausoleum, presumably in some haste.

Within the tomb were two graves and it was quite clear from the structural remains that the temple-mausoleum had been custom-built to accommodate these two burials and these two alone. The bodies were placed into two lead coffins along with various grave goods and then protected by a wooden sarcophagus placed over the assemblage. This was high enough to leave an ill-conceived void 1.22 metres tall between the tops of the coffins and the sarcophagus cover. Over that a packing of gravel and chalk was used to fill up the chamber to ground level. This would have inevitable consequences once the wooden sarcophagus rotted. The construction of the temple-mausoleum then followed after the burials had been sealed, a phase that seems to have taken some time to complete. Eventually, the sarcophagus decomposed to the point where it could no longer support the fill above and it collapsed, allowing the fill to subside and squash the coffins beneath.

Unfortunately, one of the Lullingstone burials was disturbed in antiquity. The other survived to be excavated but had been badly damaged once the sarcophagus roof collapsed. It contained the skeleton of a male in his early twenties. The disturbed fragments of the other body seemed to be those of a woman of similar age. The grave goods included a pair of flagons and two pairs of glass bottles, as well as a gaming board and pieces, and a bone disc representing Medusa to ward off evil.

The burials were, and remain, very unusual and it is particularly unfortunate that no inscription survived to provide the slightest hint of what had happened here. It is likely that the couple had died at around the same time. They were presumably either married or were brother and sister – the remains have never been subjected to DNA analysis and are probably too contaminated for that ever to happen now. Their deaths may simply have been a tragic coincidence or had been caused by the same agent, perhaps disease. There would have been nothing particularly unusual about that but their case was clearly considered so special a loss that exceptional arrangements were made to commemorate them. The temple-mausoleum was evidently constructed where it was so that the memory of the young people could be venerated by the rest of the family for the foreseeable future, and so that their tomb would remain a conspicuous feature of the villa's setting. However, the later history of the house would see an unexpected development for the pagan temple-mausoleum.

In London at around this time another anonymous young person was buried with some ceremony in an area now known as Spitalfields. A young woman in her twenties was buried, like the Lullingstone couple, in a lead coffin decorated with a scallop shell design, though in this case inserted into a more resilient stone sarcophagus. Evidently from a family of some status, she was buried with a number of grave goods, including clothing which was decorated with gold thread, glass and jet phials, cosmetic equipment and ointments. The burial probably originally lay beneath another mausoleum but the urban context of the discovery not surprisingly meant that any trace of this had long since been cleared away, along with any record of her identity, age, origins or connections.

The Lullingstone couple must have been members of the owner's family; they would never have been accorded such a privileged monument had they been lesser mortals. Unfortunately, there is usually little opportunity to extract any meaningful evidence of individual lives when it comes to the vast mass of the Romano-British rural population. Whoever the villa-owning families were, it is self-evident that they can only ever have constituted a tiny fraction of the population. There were around a thousand villas in third- and fourth-century Britain, most of which were little more than well-heeled farmsteads. If we generously allocate to each an average of thirty people to account for an extended family, slaves and estate workers, that accounts for 30,000 people. If we assume that there were around three million people in fourth-century Roman Britain, a figure that might have varied by as much as one or two million either way, then those villas account for no more than roughly 1 per cent of the population, most of whom will have worked on the land. These included slaves, free-born estate workers and farmers operating smallholdings or larger, but still modest, farms.

Very few rural sites have produced much in the way of burials, largely because excavations focus on the main structures, which, not surprisingly, are unlikely to yield human burials apart from the remains of miscarried infants, as at Lullingstone in Kent where several were found. Moreover, the preference for cremation in the first and second centuries can leave us none the wiser about some grave occupants. The 'small town' (what we could call a village now) at Neatham in Hampshire grew up around a road junction and river crossing on the main road between the civitas capitals at Silchester (Calleva Atrebatum) and Chichester (Noviomagus Reginorum). It was a nondescript and fairly typical roadside settlement which benefited from the constant traffic passing by. Gaulish pottery and amphorae were among the imported goods which arrived here. Some found their way into a small number of burials found on the site. One of these was placed in a pit less than half a square metre in size. The cremated remains of an unknown individual were placed in a wooden casket and were accompanied by several pottery vessels, a pair of shoes, a bracelet of twisted bronze wire and a brooch from the mid-first century. The bracelet suggests the deceased was a woman but it is impossible to know.[54] It was a poor grave but it belonged to a community in which even modest individuals could be honoured with goods for the afterlife. One striking artefact from Neatham is a fragment of a wooden 'keyhole' toilet seat.[55] The latrine block at Housesteads fort on Hadrian's Wall, with its arrangements for communal relief and a constant flow of water to flush excrement out of the fort, is well known. It resembles examples found at, for example, the Roman port town of Ostia where seating made of stone actually survives. However, it is no great surprise to find a similar facility in a Roman fort. The Neatham wooden toilet seat fragment is a remarkable chance survival in a very much more mundane location. It suggests that even the most ordinary Roman Briton might at least have been able to enjoy some sedentary comforts while relieving himself or herself, though in this case the toilet is likely only to have involved a cesspit rather than a system of sewers.

By the third and fourth centuries inhumation had become much more common and this helps us understand the rural population better. At the villa at Bletsoe in Bedfordshire, fifty-four fourth-century graves were uncovered in the 1930s and 1960s thanks to the fact that the villa building is buried under a modern house. That allowed archaeological attention to be diverted to the villa's cemetery, apparently occupied by those who worked on the villa estate (rather than the higher status owners of the estate), most of whom died in their thirties or forties. All these adults suffered from arthritis and many had traces of fractures which might be expected in a working rural agricultural environment. They seem to have eaten well, their teeth suggesting a diet which included the regular consumption of meat. One man showed evidence of a severe infection in his tibiae followed by new bone growth; he is thought to have contracted leprosy, which was just starting to show its early signs.[56] Since the disease spreads only where people are concentrated in large numbers, one possibility is that he had come to Bletsoe as a slave to work on the estate, having originally lived in a city.

Frocester villa in Gloucestershire has already been mentioned in connection with the remarkable phenomenon of infant burials at Yewden. The long-term and extensive excavations at Frocester tracked the development and decline of a modest rural villa site which ran from the Iron Age through to the early fifth century. Sixty burials were found in and around the villa site, most of which were of Roman date. Thirty-seven of the burials were infants. The remaining twenty-three were children or adults. The thirty-seven babies are easily accounted for by considering the likelihood of infant mortality and the length of time involved, but the number of adults and older children is too few, indicating that the remains of the majority of people who lived there have never been found. Conversely, the villa at Gadebridge Park in

Hertfordshire, a far bigger and more elaborate establishment, has produced no burials at all because they must have taken place too far away from the villa house to have been found.

Like Bletsoe, some of the Frocester inhumation graves give us a modest idea of some of the lives led in and around this small rural settlement because it was possible to identify a degree of pathology in some of them. Two of the bodies, both middle-aged females, had signs of Paget's Disease, a condition that results in misshapen and enlarged bones. A teenage boy's skull suggested that he may have had a mental abnormality. Other skeletons found at Frocester have traces of accidents, infection and even a ruptured aneurysm.[57] In reality most of these conditions could have affected anyone of any background at the time. This may not tell us much but it does remind us that no two of these individuals had had the same life – their experiences, like those in the Bath Gate cemetery at Cirencester, were unique and individual.

In a more curious variant, one of the Frocester burials included a young man who seemed not only to have been subjected to post-mortem decapitation but also to have had his body left exposed for some time before burial. The decapitated burial is by no means unusual in Roman pagan inhumation contexts, though no conclusive explanation has been offered for the phenomenon. Another example was found in a grave just 35 metres away from the villa buildings at Bradford on Avon in a very late-Roman context.[58] One possibility is that post-mortem decapitation was intended to prevent the deceased exhuming himself or herself and returning to plague the living rather in the manner of zombies beloved of latter-day makers of a particular genre of films and television series, or, in a more metaphysical sense, prevent the spirit of the deceased from haunting the living. Whatever the motivation, the macabre process involved in decapitating a corpse and burying the separated head and body is difficult to contemplate now and must reflect to some degree the sort of threats the Romano-British believed stalked their world.

In 286, around thirteen years after Tetricus I and his son Tetricus II abdicated and handed over the Gallic Empire to the emperor Aurelian, Britain became the subject of the most remarkable event in its whole history as a Roman province. Into the story at this stage bursts the ebullient, almost comically pugnacious-looking figure of Carausius. A preposterous character by any measure, this brazen pretender to the Roman throne declared himself emperor in the Empire's remotest province. His vast bull-necked portrait looks like a caricature, a sort of cartoon pirate that only makes his conceits the more extraordinary, for here we have a man who declared himself to be a messianic figure. This was the man who said he would oversee the restoration of the Roman world in Britain, a new Augustus to pull the Empire out of the hideous mire into which it had sunk over the fifty or more years leading up to 286. It was by then the 1,034th year of Rome and the 313th since Octavian was declared to be Augustus, but to listen to Carausius one would have thought the clock had been restarted.

Carausius rose to fame, as so many thugs of his era did, in the Roman army. By the mid-280s the Roman world was ruled by Diocletian, a man bent on reforming rule of the Empire. In 286 he divided the Empire in two so he could rule the East while his colleague Maximianus would rule the West. It was simply intended to be more efficient in an age of increasing instability and frontier threats. Meanwhile, Carausius had served in Gaul, leading troops against bands of landless peasants called the Bagaudae. For his success he was rewarded with command of the Roman fleet in the North Sea and English Channel, charged with clearing the waters of Germanic pirates who sailed down raiding coastal settlements in Britain and Gaul.

Carausius came from Menapia, equivalent roughly to modern Belgium. He must have grown up familiar with the coastline and he also grew up at a time of endemic instability. His formative years must have witnessed the reign of Postumus, whom he undoubtedly regarded with considerable admiration. Carausius recognized that by 286 not only was his personal prestige high thanks to the success he had had with the pirates, but he also had the opportunity to seize power in Britain and part of northern Gaul. So he did. It is also possible that he was involved in some sort of prestigious victory in Britain while still in the pay of Diocletian, who in 285 adopted the title Britannicus Maximus.

Within a very short space of time Carausius was manufacturing his own coinage, at first overstruck on existing pieces sourced from coins in circulation, but soon on new flans made for the purpose (plate 22).

Crucially, he laid his hands on enough bullion to start striking quality silver and gold coins with a series of reverses that celebrated proper Roman virtues, and one that depicted him as a messianic figure being greeted by Britannia. Carausius, or at any rate someone on his staff, was well read. The coins include many literary allusions but none more so than in the cryptic exergue legend that appears on many of the silver coins: RSR. This was short for *Redeunt Saturnia Regna*, 'The Golden Age is back', from Virgil's Fourth Eclogue. If that was not enough, he issued medallions, one of which repeats the RSR and the other which has INPCDA, the next line of the Fourth Eclogue. It expands to *Iam Nova Progenies Caelo Demittitur Alto*, 'Now a new generation is let down from heaven above'. Such extravagant claims make the silver type he issued with a legend *Expectate Veni*, 'oh, come the awaited one', adapted from Virgil's *Aeneid*, all the easier to understand.[59]

The silver was probably issued to Carausius' willing troops and the quotes from Virgil were probably part of their loyalist chants at parades. Carausian coins were struck at London, Rouen and one other, as yet unknown, mint in Britain. To the average Roman Briton the Carausian era must initially have amounted to little more than yet another thug on the coins. But Carausian power spread across Britain. One milestone survives from near Carlisle, recording his name and showing either that Carausius held sway even that far north or that the local troops thought they had better pay him lip service.[60] In the end, though, his reign was no more than one more brief episode in a turbulent history. He courted favour with Diocletian and Maximianus and brazenly struck coins in their names, including one type that shows him with the other two as a triumvirate college of emperors. They ignored him and planned their revenge. But time ran out for Carausius in 293. He was murdered in a palace coup and replaced by his finance minister Allectus in 293. In the same year Diocletian and Maximianus appointed junior assistant emperors called Caesars, who in time were supposed to replace them when they abdicated. The new system was called the Tetrarchy ('Four Rulers'). In 296 Maximianus' Caesar, Constantius Chlorus, arrived in Britain with an imperial army and defeated and killed Allectus. A few years later the milestone of Carausius was extracted from the ground and a new inscription carved on the bottom end to provide the name and titles for Constantius Chlorus in 306–7. The milestone was then replaced in the ground with Carausius' name on the bottom end. It was a fitting indignity for his audacity but also ensured the preservation of his name and the conceit with which he had styled himself Marcus Aurelius Mausaeus Carausius Pius Felix Invictus Augustus.[61]

Beyond the extraordinary events at the court of Carausius we have really very little idea how much he impacted on the ordinary Romano-British. The astonishing hoard found at Frome in Somerset in 2010 turned out to consist of an epic 52,503 coins of the late third century. Of these, a record-breaking 766 were struck by Carausius, making it the largest group of his coins ever found. The hoard was so huge, and the pot which contained them so large, that it was evident the hoard could never have been removed wholesale in antiquity, or even deposited complete without the pot shattering. Clearly the coins had been accumulated in an already buried vessel over some time. It is never possible to identify motive and purpose from a hoard and Frome is no exception. Speculation that this was a votive deposit is no more or less valid than suggesting it was simply a miser's savings bank. Occasional examples of more modern hoards where the hoarder and his or her history is known only serve to prove how completely irrational and unpredictable hoarding activity can be.[62] But the Carausian coins are of special interest. The latest dated coin in the hoard belongs to 305, showing that it cannot have been abandoned until after that date. However, the Carausian coins include five silver denarii in extremely good condition and with little trace of wear. These are so rare in this condition it is more than likely they were buried together by the same person. Since the Carausian silver coins are all but unused, their owner probably acquired them directly from the Carausian state. If so, the most likely individual would have been a soldier, probably an officer, who had received a donative to purchase his loyalty. Unfortunately, it is impossible to know if the Frome hoard belonged to one person, a family, a religious cult, a guild or some other organization.

The whole episode must have involved large numbers of soldiers being withdrawn from the north to fight for Carausius and later for Allectus in his last battle. That probably led to some deterioration along the frontier. The Tetrarchy had to arrange for repair work through the governor of northern Britain, a man called Aurelius Arpagius. Flavius Martinus has the honour of being the last known centurion in the now-ancient garrison of Roman Britain. He was based at Birdoswald on Hadrian's Wall. Here he oversaw extensive rebuilding work in the name of Aurelius Arpagius at some point between 296 and 305, arranging for the headquarters building, the baths and the commandant's house to be rebuilt.[63] It was more than 250 years since the Claudian army had arrived, after which soldiers were to dominate the record of the province's population, but now they more or less disappear from the record as the habit of monumental inscriptions faded.

CHAPTER SEVEN

ROMAN BRITAIN'S HIGH SUMMER, AD 307–410

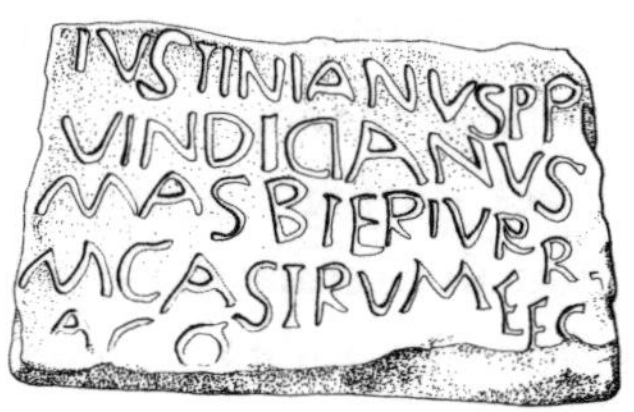

The fourth century was the time when Roman Britain, at least for some, came of age. But in the eyes of other members of the Roman Empire Britons were still at the bottom of the ladder. Silvius Bonus, a Romano-British poet, is only known to us from the bile heaped on him by the Gallo-Roman poet Ausonius. In the year 382 Ausonius published his epigrams, which included his cruel mockery of Silvius Bonus. The joke, as far as Ausonius was concerned, was that his Romano-British counterpart had the absurdly ironic name of Silvius 'the Good'. How, Ausonius asked, in an echo of the disparaging term *Brittunculi* on the Vindolanda writing tablet from three centuries before, could a Briton possibly also be good? Silvius had had the effrontery to criticize Ausonius' poetry and was dismissed with lines such as *nemo bonus Brito est*, 'no good man is a Briton'.[1] The diatribe goes beyond the purely personal; it is quite obvious that Ausonius was tapping into a seam of engrained anti-British prejudice, which might suggest that he would have regarded the Latinate content of the mosaics of Romano-British villas with the same distaste as the way Petronius mocked the ostentatious and pretentious wall paintings in the houses of overgrown and suddenly moneyed freedmen in his *Satyricon* three centuries earlier. Perhaps Silvius had the last laugh – after all, without Ausonius' sneers we might never have heard of Silvius Bonus, for good or ill.

In 306 Roman Britain played one of its occasional centre-stage roles in the history of the Roman world. Constantine I was declared emperor by the army at York, overturning Diocletian's collegiate system of emperors. His father, Constantius I, had just died there while on campaign. The soldiers were sticking rigidly to the Roman military tradition of dynastic loyalty which went back to the day the Praetorian Guard made Claudius, the only eligible member of the Julio-Claudian family, emperor in 41.

Constantine I spent little time in Britain but his reign would have an astonishing impact on the province and provide a strange echo a century later in Britannia's last act during the reign of its last rebel ruler, Constantine III. By the fourth century the Roman army in Britain was under the control of several new military commands. The duke of the Britons (*dux Britanniarum*) had supreme charge of the main garrison of legions and auxiliary units, while a count (*comes*) oversaw the fortified compounds and garrisons of the Saxon Shore, a series of installations around the south and east coast designed to deal with the consequences of coastal raiding by Germanic pirates. Another count commanded cavalry units whose remit was to move swiftly to any point of trouble. Britain itself, divided into two provinces by Septimius Severus to inhibit the chances of any further adventurous governors, had been divided into four provinces by Diocletian after the debacle of the Carausius–Allectus episode: Britannia Prima (Wales and the south-west), Britannia Secunda (the north), Flavia Caesariensis (East Midlands, Lincolnshire and Norfolk), and Maxima Caesariensis (the south-east).

The individual members of the military units of this era are almost all but unknown to us. The army ceases to be a useful source of information about individual lives, with a very small number of exceptions. A garbled, and crudely carved, inscription from the late Roman signal station at Ravenscar on the Yorkshire coast near Scarborough is practically the only piece of evidence we have. It carries no dating information, no emperor's name and no record of affiliation even to an army unit. Justinianus, the *praepositus*, and Vindicianus, *masbier* (an unknown word which must be a misunderstood transcription perhaps by a semi-literate mason for *magister*, 'master'), are stated to have built a tower and fort from the ground up. With no parallels it is impossible to be certain of its date other than that it appears to belong to a time when the Roman administrative system was still in operation, but this could take it to as late as the early 400s.

The inscription is poorly laid out, with clumsily carved letters, and is in marked contrast to the elegant inscriptions of the first and second centuries or the stylish work of the Lanchester mason working in Gordian III's time. There is a tone of autonomy to the slab in its total lack of deference even to a provincial governor. The traditional formulaic protocols have almost completely disappeared, though even bothering to create an inscription at all was fairly remarkable. The name Justinianus is a Latin adjective and means 'of Justinus' or 'belonging to Justinus', which can include 'son of Justinus'. Vindicianus must be similarly derived from Vindicius. Both names are Latinate, unlike that on the building stone discovered in the western sector of Hadrian's Wall at Drumburgh. Here a man called Vindomorucus recorded a length of wall, either of the frontier or a fort that he had built or overseen.[2] Several building stones from other stretches of the Wall are thought to belong to a late date, bearing the names of tribal cantons from the south such as the Catuvellauni. Apparently, working parties had been sent north to help repair the Wall in the face of raids by transborder tribes; perhaps Vindomorucus belonged to one of them. His name is overtly native, with *vindo*- meaning anything from 'white' or 'bright' to 'fortunate', and is well known from place names in Britain. It provides the ultimate origin of our 'winter', with the clear allusion to the brightness of snow in winter sunshine. The latter part of the name suggests something to do with the sea, with *mor*- sharing the same remoter origin as the Latin word *mare* ('sea').

These men worked for an army that the invading force of 43 would not have recognized. It was also an army that was increasingly inclined to participate in risings. Between 350 and 353 Britain formed part of yet another breakaway empire, this time run by Magnentius, of whom more later. Thirty years later on, another generation of Romano-British troops decided to nominate one of their own as emperor. Magnus Maximus, a Spaniard by birth, promptly decided to set off in 383 for the continent to pursue his claim, and took much of the British garrison with him. Maximus was not equal either to his ambitions or his circumstances and he was defeated at the Battle of Poetovio on 28 July 388. Oddly, he seems to have been regarded with some fondness in western Britain, where he was remembered as Macsen Wledig, a progenitor of some of the Welsh ruling dynasties in the Middle Ages.[3] If any of that is true then he represents one of the very few routes by which anyone living today in Britain could try to trace their origins back to the Roman period. Maximus was followed by more adventurers in the early 400s. The last was called Constantine III, yet another member of the British garrison whose name seems to have been his greatest asset. He appears to have been elevated quite literally because of his famous namesake, declared emperor in York a century earlier. He did what all other usurpers did and used the army to support his claim. By 411 he was dead too, killed on a continental battlefield. By then Britain was no longer a Roman province, having been cast adrift in 410 by the legitimate western emperor Honorius.

One of the great paradoxes of Romano-British history is that while an increasingly denuded and beleaguered provincial army struggled against barbarian incursions, the Romano-British elite seem to have enjoyed a high summer. An exceptionally privileged few became the possessors of very considerable wealth, much of which was ploughed into the construction or embellishment of extravagant rural houses. These buildings had their conceptual origins in the villas of Italy in the first and second centuries AD and there was a very self-conscious attempt in Britain to emulate the architectural and decorative ostentation of such houses. They seem to have gone hand in hand with a very deliberate reactionary movement to celebrate the art, iconography and rituals of traditional pagan cults. It is in some of these houses and cult centres that we find evidence for Roman Britain's real lives in the fourth century, and in the form of some of the most celebrated treasure hoards ever discovered in the Roman Empire.

In archaeological terms the fourth century has traditionally been the preserve of the great villas of Roman Britain's last decades, regardless of the fact that the vast majority of the population had nothing to do with villas. The towns have much to tell us archaeologically but they were no longer places in which grand public building projects were under way, and nor were they home to immigrants, or retired soldiers who obligingly recorded themselves and their loved ones on inscriptions. A significant number of Britain's rural houses were subjected to a slow process of architectural and decorative embellishment from the late third century on. By the 350s some of the houses, like Woodchester, had acquired the proportions of grand country houses; even lesser houses were prone to have at least one or two prestigiously appointed reception rooms. In some of these places we can, with difficulty, track a little of the nature of the people who lived there.

However, this was also a time of enormous political instability and religious change. Britain played host to a number of rebel emperors, especially in the latter years of the fourth century and into the fifth. The legitimization of Christianity by Constantine I in the Edict of Toleration at Milan in 313 transformed the political climate and the expression of status, though in some respects it only confirmed what had already become an unavoidable truth: the Empire was steadily converting to Christianity. In 311 the persecution of Christians begun in 303 by Diocletian was stopped by his successor Galerius, occasioned when he succumbed to a serious illness. By 314 three bishops from Britain were able to attend the Council of Arles. These were Eborius, bishop of York, Restitutus, bishop of London, and Adelphius of 'Colonia Londenensium', which is probably a copyist's mistake for Lindum (Lincoln). The delegates also included a *presbyter* (priest) called Sacerdus and a deacon called Arminius. Eborius' name must be derived from the Roman name for York, Eboracum, suggesting he was local, unless the name was fabricated for him. Of the others, nothing can be said except to observe that the name Adelphius was of Greek origin. It is very unlikely that these five men were the only senior officials of the whole Christian Church in Britain; there must have been many more, of which these were the ones nominated to attend the Council at Arles.

There is a curious story to bring in at this point: the strange case of Bishop Exuperius and the Risley Park lanx. The lanx, a large rectangular silver dish, was discovered in the eighteenth century at Risley Park in Derbyshire but, despite the growing enthusiasm for the classical world at the time, it was rapidly hacked up into pieces so that the metal could be shared out before any of the local antiquarian cognoscenti had heard about it. An engraving was made, based on the surviving pieces, and a record made of the inscription on it. A replica, apparently made up from the fragments, resurfaced in recent times but was soon exposed as a forgery, though it probably includes some decorative features copied from the original engraving. The lanx also bore an inscription saying it was a gift of Bishop Exuperius to the church at Bogium or Bagiensum. It is conceivable that there was a Romano-British place called something like this, and that there was a British bishop called Exuperius, but it and he are otherwise unknown. Perhaps rather more convincing is that it was a garbled and mistranscribed version of the Roman name of Bayeux, *civitas* Baiocassensis. If so, then instead of referring to a bishop from Britain, the lanx inscription would be for Exuperius, bishop of Bayeux, who died around the year 405. The lanx is therefore more likely to have come to Britain in medieval times.

This was a curious age, which is just as well for without the evidence of religious activities we would otherwise have a tiny fraction of the names of ordinary people compared to earlier in Roman Britain's history. However, the record for late Roman Britain is very different from that of earlier in the period. Gone are the prolific offerings by soldiers along the northern frontier and at other forts, at least so far as we can guess from the style and content of what has been found. The towns are similarly silent for the moment. The epigraphic habit had largely died out in either context.

One rare exception is the remarkable inscribed column base from Cirencester. Cirencester, by the fourth century, was one of the largest towns in Roman Britain and was the capital of Britannia Prima. Britannia Prima was one of the four provinces into which Britain had been divided by Diocletian as part of his programme of administrative reorganization. Given the pleasing qualities of Cotswold stone, the town buildings must by then have weathered into colours and textures for which the area is well known today. The inscription is one of the last from Roman Britain. It refers to someone called Lucius Septimius (. . .) (the latter part of his name is lost), governor (*praeses*) of the province of Britannia Prima, who has restored the statue and column base 'erected under the ancient religion'. The monument was probably a 'Jupiter column', an unequivocally traditional homage to the state cult of Rome's guardian god.

Lucius Septimius is the last governor of any part of Britain to be recorded this way and was clearly in post no earlier than the 290s. He has expressly restored a pagan monument and since he refers to the 'ancient religion', the implication is that this took place in Christian times; indeed, the very act of inscribing the column base at all was implicitly pagan in its tone, which makes the most plausible date sometime in the reign of Julian the Apostate (360–3), when temples and other pagan monuments were officially restored in an effort to turn back the clock and undo the Christianization of the Roman Empire. Lucius Septimius also tells us that he was a citizen of Reims in Gaul, or so at any rate the inscription has been restored to read.[4] Little had changed in Britain. It was still the case that Gallo-Roman administrators were being sent to Britain, yet not a single demonstrable ethnic Romano-Briton of equivalent status has been identified, even in the fourth century.

Julian's reign represented a brief convulsive reversal in what was by then an unstoppable process. Christianity, however, was far from stable in its own right. Its legitimization and adoption as the state cult simply exposed further its own divisions, with fragmentation on liturgical lines following as interest groups squabbled for political power. In the fourth century it mattered not only that one posed as a Christian, but also which type of Christian. In 350 the legitimate emperor in the West was Constans, and in the East his brother Constantius II, sons of Constantine I. Constantius' pedigree as a Christian emperor was secure enough, but he was an Arian. Orthodox Christians regarded God the Father and Jesus as God the Son as wholly equal in every respect. For the Arians, Jesus had been created by God the Father and was therefore by definition a subordinate or lesser being. Orthodox and Arian Christians refuted each other's scriptural evidence and their division became the most important basis of fracturing among Christians at the time and for some time thereafter. Quite apart from the scriptural 'evidence', it was probably the case that the idea of an inequality between father and son deities was more plausible to some members of a population still in some respects wedded to pagan traditions of a pantheon of gods linked by family connections.

In the year 350, Magnentius, a successful army general, was proclaimed emperor in the West in a direct challenge to Constans, who was soon murdered, and seized power over Britain and Gaul and other western provinces. Magnentius posed as an Orthodox Christian. He did this in part because it gave him a manifesto that distinguished him from Constantius II. Magnentius issued coins that showed him bareheaded on one side and on the other depicted a large Chi-Rho, the symbol of Christ based on the first two letters of Christ's name in Greek, the X (Chi) and P (Rho). By 351 he had made the disastrous mistake of trying to expand his rule to the East and was soon defeated and had to withdraw. In August 353 he committed suicide in Gaul.

In the aftermath Constantius II sent an imperial secretary (*notarius*) called Paulus, a Spaniard, to Britain to weed out Magnentian supporters. The purge was Stalinist in its ruthlessness and mendacious denunciations. Paulus was said to have gone totally beyond his remit and indulged in an orgy of false accusations which he used to destroy large numbers of 'freeborn men and even degrading some with manacles'.[5] The implication is that men of high status were being wiped out, though for what purpose is simply not clear. So appallingly unfair was the process that the vicar of Britain, Martinus, attempted personally to kill Paulus but without success and had to commit suicide. Paulus then returned to Constantius' court, taking with him a number of men who were subjected to torture, exile or execution.

The story of Paulus is an extraordinary one and, assuming it is true, some of its consequences might have a chance of being detectable in the archaeological record. The villa at Gadebridge Park in Hertfordshire is known to have been comprehensively demolished at around this time. Stock enclosures were built over the site of the house, so apparently farming continued there, reflected in continued coin loss on the site but at a far lower rate than earlier in the fourth century.[6] The process was so systematic that it is hard not to believe it was the result of some punitive edict. We know nothing about the owner but in this instance it is reasonable to suggest that he was one the victims of Paulus, his estate at Gadebridge Park being confiscated and operated thereafter for the benefit of the public purse or granted to a supporter of Constantius' regime. The measures were, in the words of the historian Ammianus Marcellinus, an 'eternal mark of infamy' (*nota sempiterna*) on the reign of Constantius.

By the late fourth century Britain was nominally as Christianized as anywhere else in the Roman Empire. But the island played host to a remarkable cycle of pagan revivalist cults, characterized by a self-conscious classical posturing in name, words and habits. One of the most curious was at Lydney Park in Gloucestershire. Here by the late fourth century a shrine was built on the site of an old Iron Age hill-fort, a place that presumably retained some lingering presence in local lore. The centrepiece was the temple building, an unusual hybrid building that combined the basilican form with that of the concentric square layout of the Romano-Celtic temple. It stood in the middle of the old hill-fort's irregular plot, surrounded by a precinct wall which also contained a baths and hostelry as well as a row of individual chalets immediately beside the temple. The place was dedicated to the worship of the healing god Mars-Nodens, a conflated Romano-Celtic cult almost unknown elsewhere.[7] The temple had a mosaic floor, now sadly lost, with a remarkable inscription in the design. It was located in front of a shrine in the north-west part of the temple's cella, itself extremely unusual; mosaics are otherwise unknown in Romano-British temples apart from plain tessellated floors. The inscription, happily, was recorded prior to its loss. It read, 'To the God Mars Nodens, Titus Flavius Senilis, superintendent of the cult, had (this mosaic) laid from the offerings with assistance from Victorinus the interpreter'.[8]

Of course, the inscription is more cryptic than that translation suggests. Titus Flavius Senilis' title is abbreviated to PR REL, which was once thought to be short for *praepositus reliquationis*, 'superintendent of the fleet supply-depot', a suggestion which is so disconnected from the context of the mosaic that it is, in hindsight, faintly amazing that it was ever taken seriously. But it reflected an age when military interpretations were preferred. *Praepositus religionis*, 'superintendent of the cult', is also far from certain but does at least fit the context. Even the god's name is abbreviated to DNM, expandable to *Deo Marti Nodenti* ('to the God Mars Nodens') on the basis of other inscriptions recording him elsewhere on the site. Titus Flavius Senilis appears mostly in full so there is no real doubt about his name, or that of his assistant Victorinus. Victorinus, though, has an equally mysterious occupation. *Interpretiante* is taken here to mean an 'interpreter of dreams', though the dream part of the title is entirely speculative. Nevertheless, it also fits the context, especially when considering the architecture of the temple and its accompanying chalets. Niches in the temple may have been where the faithful spent the night in the presence of the god, probably after consumption of substances like alcohol to induce more vivid and revealing oneiric experiences. Pausanias, who wrote a description of Greece in the second century, makes an explicit reference to similar facilities at the healing shrine of Asklepios at Epidaurus, saying 'beyond the temple is the place where the suppliants sleep'.[9]

We can do no better than assume that this was what was going on at Lydney. If so, we have a very unusual instance in Roman Britain of the names of people actually operating a cult. Flavius Senilis was a citizen but at that date this was of no significance at all since it was long after Caracalla's edict of universal citizenship. Victorinus might recall the short reign of Marcus Piavvonius Victorinus of the Gallic Empire who ruled from 268 to 270. The two men's names are not distinctive and tell us little, but they make an interesting classicized contrast with the obscure native cult of Nodens, regardless of the fact that he was conflated with Mars. Silvianus was one of the visitors to Lydney. His main concern was the fact that he had lost a ring and evidently suspected the culprit to be a man called Senicianus. He wished for Senicianus not to be allowed health until the ring was returned and had this fact recorded on a lead curse tablet.[10] Silvianus' problem was typical of similar curse tablets from Bath though, unlike those flung into the sacred spring there, Silvianus' curse seems to have remained on show, probably pinned to the temple wall. Someone seems to have added to its text at a later date the word *rediviva*, '(the curse) comes into force again', presumably because the miscreant Senicianus had failed to give up the ring.

Silvianus is probably typical of the men and women with whom Flavius Senilis and Victorinus had to deal, but it is a remarkable fact that such a traditional form of pagan cult activity had been revived in Britain in so remote a place. Flavius Blandinus was another pilgrim who visited the shrine at Lydney and willingly fulfilled his vow to the gods. He added the word *armatura* to the standard formula which was punched into a small bronze plate that was nailed to the wall of one of the temple buildings. It either means he was a military drill instructor or he had fulfilled his vow 'with (a gift of) armour'.[11] This raises the interesting question of exactly who these people were. These names are for the most part unequivocally Roman, but at such a late date they are all likely to have been provincial in origin, their remoter forbears being entirely buried beneath their Latinate identities. If so, perhaps they were indulging in a curious form of second-hand nostalgia for classical culture, almost certainly thanks to the uncertainty of the times in which they lived.

It is easy to refer glibly to 'villa owners' when in reality we have no idea in any one instance who owned a villa and its land and whether or not that person even lived there. Some of the great fourth-century Romano-British villa estates will, of course, have passed through several different hands over the course of many decades for a variety of reasons, including purchase, or confiscation, so even if we knew the name of an owner it would only represent a small part of that villa's life. The place name Villa Faustini ('Villa of Faustinus'), listed in the fifth route of the Antonine Itinerary, compiled in the early third century, presents just this sort of problem.[12] The position of the Villa Faustini in that route's sequence places it somewhere in eastern Suffolk or Norfolk but it cannot be linked to any known villa structure. Presumably someone called Faustinus owned it when it was built, but there is no reason to assume that it remained in his family. The ruins of the Villa Quintilii stand today by the Appian Way outside Rome. Two exceptionally wealthy brothers, Sextus Quintilius Maximus and Sextus Quintilius Condianus, owned it in the mid-second century but they were destroyed and executed by the jealous emperor Commodus (180–92), who took the site over and enjoyed its luxurious facilities. It continued to be known as the Villa of the Quintilii and still is today.

At some locations we can discover something about the owners. The owners of the known villas of Britain must have included the descendants of the indigenous tribal elite, retired soldiers and administrators, absentee continental landlords, or even the army or the state. These people are largely nameless and faceless to us. At the Poundbury cemetery outside the town at Dorchester (Durnovaria) a fourth-century mausoleum yielded some painted wall-plaster which appears to have depicted a number of men of various ages engaged in a procession or assembly; none of them had the attributes of gods or mythological figures but they carried staffs. They were clearly depicted as individuals, with varying treatment of hair and some with beards and some without. One plausible suggestion is that therefore the mausoleum belonged to a local elite family and that the figures are perhaps a parade of ancestors who had served in civic office. However, although only fragments survived there was sufficient room for around one hundred, exactly enough to account for the decurions who served on the town council so it may represent the men in office at one time when the occupant, perhaps one of their number, died.[13] However, there is no indication of any name or origin of these men.

Whoever the elite of late Roman Britain were, it must have been all too easy to look back at the age of Augustus and see it as a time of comparative peace, stability and reconciliation. In that context, traditional pagan culture with its pantheon of gods and an unlimited cast of mythological heroes, images and associations must have seemed an attractive route through which that era could once again be accessed. Even Christians often retained a love of classical imagery in art and literature. A love of Latinate pretensions is wonderfully illustrated in two quite different mosaic floors from the villas at Low Ham in Dorset and Brading on the Isle of Wight. Low Ham's floor is almost a cartoon strip, depicting in a series of panels episodes from Book 4 of Virgil's *Aeneid*. Brading's is a cycle of esoteric mythological scenes, including the bizarre panel depicting a strange cockerel-headed figure. Low Ham was a courtyard villa but only the western range has ever been explored. This was kitted out with a bath suite in the fourth century, the *frigidarium* of which was enlarged around the year 340. The purpose, or consequence, was to enable it to accommodate both a mosaic floor depicting the scenes from the *Aeneid* and a plunge bath from which, presumably, bathers could view the floor. The design is a clumsy one and consists of three rectangular zones. The lateral rectangles contain action friezes, one depicting Aeneas' fleet arriving at Carthage, the other Aeneas, Dido and Cupid (disguised as Aeneas' son Ascanius) setting out on the fateful hunt. The central zone is divided into three smaller panels. One of these was designed to be seen by those entering the bath and shows Aeneas, Ascanius, Venus and Dido. The other two panels faced those in the bath and showed, in the centre of the mosaic, Venus with a pair of cupids, and in the panel nearest to the bathers, Aeneas and Dido gripped in an embrace. The story of Book 4 is concerned with how Aeneas becomes embroiled with Dido as part of the mischief-making deal cut by Juno and Venus. The two mortals are the victims of the callous goddesses and both risk capitulating to the forces of emotion, a thoroughly un-Roman quality. During the hunt a storm blows up and they take shelter in a cave where they consummate their passionate relationship. This is as far as the mosaic gets.

In the *Aeneid* Dido gives way recklessly to infatuation, and Aeneas is reminded by Jupiter, via Mercury, of his destiny. He abandons Dido, who implodes in a fit of frenzied rage and commits suicide in a graphic and ostentatious manner. Aeneas, obliviously, sets off from Carthage only to meet the deceased Dido once more on his visit to the Underworld in Book 6. The Low Ham mosaic thus depicts only the first 172 lines of Book 4. It was, and remains, the most memorable of all the books of the *Aeneid* and inspired Henry Purcell's *Dido and Aeneas* some seventeen centuries after it was written. The *Aeneid*'s tortuous plot and reliance on a divinely inspired foregone conclusion have always made it a challenging piece of work. Book 4, however, stands apart and this must reflect its choice as subject matter for a mosaic floor by the Low Ham villa's owner, though in this respect it remains unique apart from a possible rendition of Aeneas in a mosaic panel at Frampton. The Low Ham panels look very much as if they have been assembled from copies of a series of paintings and this would reflect their clumsy arrangement on the floor, for which they were probably never originally composed; it has been suggested that the owner of the villa was in possession of an illuminated manuscript of the text and commissioned mosaic renditions of selected scenes.[14] There are a number of stylistic features, such as the design of the horses, which link it to mosaics in North Africa.[15]

What is particularly striking about the Low Ham floor is not only that Venus is depicted naked but so also is Dido, whereas Aeneas is conspicuously not, even at the notorious climax of the sequence. Dido and Venus are both thus presented as temptresses. More than a century later the Gallo-Roman bishop Sidonius Apollinaris wrote a letter to a friend to describe his own country villa. At one point he describes the baths and proudly points out that 'no indecent story is exposed [*turpis prostat historia*] by the nude beauty of pictured bodies'.[16] This is evidently a sideswipe at villa owners who had had their baths unnecessarily decorated with naked figures participating in shameful stories, presumably reflecting the more repressive Christian sensibilities that proliferated throughout the Empire. We do not know what Sidonius would have thought of the Low Ham floor but he would probably have disapproved. Virgil's original intentions were more elevated. Dido's abandonment of self-control was what Virgil called 'the first [day] of death'. His Dido had succumbed in a thoroughly 'un-Roman' way to temptation and her loss of restraint was a tragic attempt to entice Aeneas into decadence and dereliction of duty; it was a reminder to any self-respecting Roman to put duty before indulgence. In that sense the Low Ham floor portrayed a worthy message. Of course, it is also possible the Low Ham owner enjoyed the excuse to include some titillating features.

The Brading villa mosaics on the Isle of Wight are altogether more obscure and represent a remarkable cycle of arcane mythological scenes, heavy with obscure symbolism. They include Orpheus and Medusa, who are familiar enough from many other mosaics, but also the enigmatic so-called 'philosopher' with a sundial and a further panel with a bizarre cock-headed figure accompanied by griffins. The latter is part of a badly damaged floor, the centrepiece of which was a bust of Bacchus. No conclusive explanation has ever been offered for the cock-headed figure. Apart from the cock-head the figure is anthropomorphic and stands to one side of a small temple-like building reached by stairs or a ladder. On the right-hand side stand two griffins, one facing the cock-headed figure, the other facing away towards the side of the panel. One possibility is that the figure represents an initiate to the cult of a gnostic deity called Abrasax (sometimes spelled Abraxas), also known as Iao. Other suggestions include the idea that the figure has been misrepresented by an uncomprehending mosaicist trying to use a pattern book depicting animals or beings he did not recognize.[17] However, the Brading villa lies only a few yards from a coastline famous since the nineteenth century as a source of both dinosaur bones and footprints. Since the villa owner and his family can scarcely have failed to be aware of these phenomena they would probably at the very least have been impressed by 'evidence' that verified the former presence of fantastic beasts, perhaps contributing to some of the topics chosen for the mosaics.

The 'philosopher' or 'astronomer' figure at Brading is perhaps a portrait of the owner himself (plate 23). It is quite conceivable that other figures on some mosaics are depictions either of the family members at the time the floors were commissioned or of their ancestors. A large floor from the mid-fourth century in the villa at Brantingham in Yorkshire included eight panels in the form of arched frames containing depictions of the upper body and face of eight individuals (plate 24). Although they could symbolize the nine Muses together with another figure placed in the floor's centre, they might have been modelled on real people, though without any inscription to verify the fact we cannot be certain.

The owner of the house at Lullingstone at this time remains unknown with any certainty despite the abstruse efforts by some scholars to extract his name from the Latin couplet on the mid-fourth-century mosaic floor (plate 25).[18] The structural arrangements are difficult to unravel. By this date the old house had been reduced in size but the main reception rooms had been extended with an apse that protruded from the western side of the house towards the steep hillside that overlooked the building. A suite of rooms associated with Christian worship seems to have been created in the later fourth century, perhaps around 360, being apparently self-contained and accessible only from outside. They occupied part of an upper storey over a long-sealed cellar where a shrine to some water nymphs and the two ancestor marble busts discussed earlier had been left untouched for generations. Offerings still seem to have been made to them, suggesting that older pagan powers could not be comfortably ignored. The rooms have been identified only from the wall-paintings depicting a Chi-Rho symbol, which represents the first two Greek letters of the name of Christ, and several figures in an attitude of prayer (plate 26). They clearly represent Christian worshippers and are perhaps portraits of the actual people concerned. The owner must have been a Christian and had made over part of his home to make a 'house church' where an itinerant priest could officiate in the presence of local Christians who would have gathered there for the purpose.

The temple-mausoleum built close by the house at Lullingstone at the beginning of the fourth century had been allowed to fall into disuse, presumably because of its pagan associations, or perhaps because the house was now owned by a different family. Curiously, around this time someone invaded the remains of the temple-mausoleum, dug down and violated one of the burials by stealing the lead coffin and throwing the bones back into the grave. This is difficult to account for if the residents belonged to the same dynasty as the deceased, since regardless of conversion to Christianity there would have been no good reason to abuse the burial of a pagan forbear. Indeed, there would have been a powerful taboo; perhaps the discovery of a grave was unexpected. Moreover, the grave-robbing can hardly have occurred without the owners knowing about it unless they only visited Lullingstone occasionally. The purpose seems to have been to extract the valuable lead used for the coffin but that only makes it more mysterious the other burial was left untouched. However, the memory of the building remained long after, for its remains were used as the footings for part of a Saxon church which was built on the site in later centuries and still existed in a ruinous state in the 1700s. Presumably some local lore preserved knowledge of the fact that Christian worship had gone on here in Roman times, but by then nothing of the house remained to be seen, whereas parts of the temple-mausoleum on its terrace must have still been visible and were mistaken for the site of the house church.

The Hinton St Mary villa in Dorset has a mosaic with both a Chi-Rho behind the figure usually interpreted as being Christ and a panel depicting Bellerophon riding on Pegasus to kill the Chimaera, well known as an allegorical depiction of good triumphing over evil (plate 27). Part of Lullingstone's mosaic floor also depicts this scene and was only a few yards from the rooms with the Christian paintings, though it preceded those by some decades. However, Bellerophon's exploits would have been familiar to an educated Roman or Greek in the most innocuous of pagan contexts, too, since the story features in Book 6 of the *Iliad*. It also made for an attractive scene in its own right, with the subject matter of a human riding a fantastic animal through the air balancing, at Lullingstone, the apsidal panel in the next room which depicts Europa being carried off through water by Jupiter in the guise of a bull. It is the

Latin couplet that accompanies the Europa scene at Lullingstone which has been the occasion of most speculation.

> INVIDA SI TAVRI VIDISSET IVNO NATATVS
> IVSTIVS AEOLIAS ISSET ADVSQVE DOMOS[19]

This is not a quote from Virgil's *Aeneid* but famously alludes to one of the earliest scenes in Book 1 of that poem. Juno, queen of the gods, loather of Trojans and supporter of the Carthaginians, is disgusted at the thought that a Trojan prince is on his way to establish a future race of Romans who will destroy the Carthaginians. So she appeals to Aeolus, god of the winds, to blow Aeneas off course and drown him. The Lullingstone couplet means, 'If jealous Juno had seen the swimming of the bull, she would have gone as far as the halls of Aeolus with more justice', or, in other words, Aeolus' winds would have been better utilized by Juno in putting her unfaithful husband Jupiter off course than by trying to thwart Aeneas.

The Lullingstone Latin does not come from any known poem but it was clearly composed by someone who knew his or her Latin verse well and is considered by some to imitate the style of Ovid. The reasons for this judgment are described as 'cumulative rather than conclusive', relying on the position of the word *adusque* ('as far as') and the general idea that if a mythical figure had acted in a certain way then something else would have followed.[20] The sense then is a kind of stylistic homage which was either deliberate or simply the result of unconscious emulation as a consequence of education. It may have been composed by the owner of the house or, perhaps, by a poet whose works have been completely lost. If the latter, the poet may have been someone for whom the owner acted as patron. However, the message was possibly less esoteric; its purpose may have been to suggest humorously that wives who paid more attention to what was going on around them would have a better chance of catching their husbands misbehaving. Either way, it was a witty allusion to a scene no educated Roman could have failed to understand, though once the novelty had worn off it is difficult to imagine visitors paying much attention to it. Sidonius had phrases from verse painted on the walls of his villa baths to entertain people and nothing more.[21]

This is at odds with the amount of significance some scholars see in the words, with some being convinced that hidden messages and words, including the owner's name, were cryptically concealed within it. The name extracted by starting with the last letter of the first word and counting each eighth letter following produces Avitus.[22] Applying the same principle to starting, this time, with the first letter of the second line allegedly produces IESVS, thus apparently demonstrating the Christian affiliations of Avitus, though inconveniently for the theorists the latter S is in fact not there since the line is not long enough to supply a fifth letter. There is little merit in the process since there is absolutely no certainty about the sequential 'method' used to find the name, which may simply be coincidence and which is not matched anywhere else. All sorts of processes can be applied to 'discover' hidden words this way and many more can be extracted from Lullingstone's mosaic.[23] In reality there may have been some sort of concealed private joke or allusion but it is unlikely that we would have easy access to it since we have no detailed knowledge of the people who lived there. The mosaic at Frampton is even more obscure in its metrical Latin couplets with references to Neptune and Cupid, associated with another Bellerophon scene and a Chi-Rho, where no amount of playing with the letters has generated any hidden words at all.[24]

At Thruxton in Hampshire a name is not in doubt. Here the mosaic floor, now badly damaged but preserved in the British Museum, had for its central motif a picture of Bacchus sitting on a leopard, a popular device and known from a number of mosaics. However, the floor also included a panel at the top with the inscription:

QUINTVS NATALIVS NATALINVS ET BODENI

There is no doubt about the first three words (plate 28). We have here a Roman citizen called Quintus Natalius Natalinus.[25] It cannot possibly be the name of the mosaicist as the panel stretches almost the whole 3.54 metres of the width of the floor; mosaicists who signed their work were rarely allowed anything beyond a discreet monogram such as the 'TER' for Terentius or Tertius at Bignor.[26]

So Natalinus may have been the owner in either the late third or fourth century when the floor was laid. A second inscription once mirrored this one at the other end of the mosaic but unfortunately, by the time the floor was lifted in 1899, this had been destroyed and there is no hope of its ever being reliably restored, though a couple of letters survive. The building was not in the least typical of any normal Roman rural house and this complicates an understanding of the significance of the mosaic. The house consisted of an aisled hall which in fact was almost square. Attached to one end of the hall was a suite of three rooms which together were slightly longer than the width of the hall, creating a building which resembles a reversed 'L'. The mosaic floor occupied the most westerly of the three rooms and formed the foot of the reversed L. The most convincing interpretation of the inscription is that this was a man called Quintus Natalius Natalinus who was also known as Bodenus. If so, this suggests a man of native origin who was still known by what we would now call a 'Celtic' name but whose official name was now a thoroughly Roman one. Why he should have felt the need to record the fact thus is a mystery since there is no equivalent instance with a more complete text to explain the purpose. Nevertheless, in the Roman world, such inscriptions could have a more prosaic function. At Pompeii, Aulus Umbricius Scaurus, purveyor of *garum* (fish sauce), had his name and wares depicted on the mosaic floor of his atrium to impress his guests in a vulgar display of commercial success.

However, a first-century grave was found close by and a more interesting possibility is that the mosaic was laid in commemoration of an ancestor, with the room being used as a shrine to their memory.[27] In that instance perhaps Quintus Natalius Natalinus was an esteemed first-century ancestor who adopted a Roman name when made a citizen, or he may have been a descendant who owned the late Roman structure and honoured his ancestor Bodenus. Either way the double name is a reminder that many other individuals bearing Romanized names were probably indigenous Britons in their origins.

Part of the purpose of any of these floors was competitive ostentation. They were there to be seen and to be admired. This reaches a climax in the case of the Orphic floor at Woodchester, where the central part of the north range of the building was modified to incorporate a very large room to accommodate the floor. At 225 square metres it is the largest villa room known in Britain. Column bases attest to an elaborate roofing arrangement and probably an upper-floor gallery from where to view the mosaic, which would have been overwhelming and incoherent at ground-level. There was nothing especially unusual about having a design that depicted Orpheus charming the animals with his music; the theme was a popular one at the time. What was unusual was the sheer scale. The man who commissioned this alteration to his house was creating a showcase villa designed to advertise his status in the main public reception room; this was derived from both the fashionable literary and mythological content of the floor as well as the audacity and financial ability to commission a mosaic on that scale. We know nothing about the owner, but the location of the house makes it likely he was a dominant figure in civic politics in both the colony at Gloucester and the civitas capital at Cirencester, each of which is only 10 miles away. This then would be the grand public room in which he and his descendants after him greeted clients or petitioners in surroundings that would have emphasized and amplified the family's wealth and exalted position in the province's hierarchy.

It is one thing to try and disentangle something of the personalities behind the choice of expensive and prestigious mosaic floors and quite another to disentangle something of the people who actually made and laid the floors. Mosaicists scarcely ever signed their work. In the social structure of the Roman world they were persons of little consequence, with many being slaves or freedmen. Even architects of major public buildings are almost always unknown to us. The Aldgate-Pulborough Potter sticks out in the history of ceramics for his ineptitude. Alongside him we should place the mosaicist commissioned to lay a floor in a villa at Croughton in Northamptonshire. What seems to have happened here is that the mosaicist's team set to work some time in the fourth century to lay a complicated geometrical floor consisting of the usual bands of guilloches defining panels and zones. The central feature was marked out as an octagon containing two superimposed squares offset by 45 degrees to create an eight-pointed star and an inner octagon. Within that inner octagon was supposed to go a circular medallion depicting Bellerophon killing the Chimaera. Being the focal point of the floor, the Bellerophon scene was almost certainly prefabricated at the mosaicist's workshop and transported to the site, whereupon, no doubt to frustrated and worried incredulity on the part of the mosaicists, it turned out to be too big for the octagonal area left for it. The mosaicists adopted a pragmatic solution which totally ignored the integrity of the design and simply removed the border around the medallion from approximately one o'clock to five o'clock and wedged in the Bellerophon panel. Even the Chimaera has distinctly truncated forelimbs.[28]

The result was a mosaic that at a casual glance looks acceptably executed but which on closer inspection turns out to have been appallingly badly laid. It is difficult to know whether to be more astonished by the mosaicists' incompetence or the customer's willingness to be fobbed off with such a poor piece of workmanship. Even the bands of guilloches exhibit clumsy joints where two bands meet. The owner of the Croughton villa clearly wanted to own something that qualified him as a member of the educated villa-owning set but lacked the contacts, the know-how, or perhaps the funds, to commission a mosaic from a reliable craftsman and his team. However, one should not assume that mosaics were otherwise universally well laid. Minor errors are common enough, but Croughton remains exceptionally poor.

The mosaicist hired to install a floor at Rudston in Yorkshire was not inept in quite the same way. His design was essentially simpler and consisted of a floor featuring animals from the arena in individual panels around the edge. In the middle a circular panel depicted Venus dropping her mirror after having been startled by a merman. There is no doubt about the identity of the main character or her classical attributes but the execution is remarkable to a modern eye. Is it some sort of idiosyncratic native stylistic variant, or simply very poor workmanship? Venus is a pigeon-chested scarecrow of a goddess with bloated thighs and unbalanced limbs, while the wretched merman resembles a distended newt and is contorted through 90 degrees to fit into the available space (plate 29). There is nothing else like it in Britain or anywhere else. It can be argued that Venus' features might be intended to emphasize aspects of fertility but this is rather a generous interpretation. One thing is for certain – had Paris encountered this Aphrodite when judging which goddess was the most beautiful, then the Trojan War might never have been fought.

These houses and their decoration, whether competently or incompetently executed, reflect in very different ways veneration for the antique of a type that was common in the fourth-century Empire. It was a time of great uncertainty with enormous cultural changes as Christianity took full control of imperial government and brought with it a raft of new tensions. Some found solace in those older traditions. A similar cherishing of the antique appears in other late Roman contexts in Britain. The Thetford Treasure belongs to the last years of the fourth century at a time when Britain's role as a formal Roman province was soon to come to an end (plate 30). It is, by any standards, a remarkable collection which broadly speaking consists of various pieces of jewellery and a group of objects, some of which are inscribed silver spoons, explicitly associated with the cult of an ancient Latin woodland god called Faunus, best known to the Romans from Virgil's *Aeneid* and the works of Horace, both written more than four centuries earlier.

The Thetford Treasure's survival is itself an extraordinary story. Found by a metal-detectorist called Arthur Brooks and his wife Greta in 1979 on a building site on Gallows Hill, Thetford, in Norfolk, some of the treasure was contained in a small shale box and the rest clustered around it. It was a place that had already proved productive to metal detector users but the discovery was a shock to the finder. What happened next is not relevant to this book but it took till the summer of 1980 for the treasure to be declared and for it, or at least almost all of it, to arrive at the British Museum. Tragically, in the intervening period the site was built on and the original context lost, probably along with some small missing additional components; however, it is undoubtedly true that had the treasure not been already found then it would have been lost forever, since previous archaeological work had missed it. The inclusion of a small number of coins of the rebel emperor Magnus Maximus (383–8) is almost certain but has never been proven and now never will be, though they fit the estimated date of the rest of the hoard. The coins were dispersed before the hoard was reported.

In a sense, even the finding of the Thetford Treasure is part of Roman Britain's real lives. The original owners would never know the circumstances in which their property would be found but now they and the finders are inextricably linked. No doubt the original owners stole onto that hill one dark night and furtively buried the treasure, carefully covering their tracks. Sixteen centuries later another furtive nocturnal visit to that hill resulted in its abrupt removal, an act which probably also saved it from destruction by the site developers. It is the inscriptions on the spoons that are of the greatest importance here. They show an extraordinary conflation of the ancient Latin god Faunus and a series of native epithets which are equally likely to be of British or Gaulish origin. One of the most vivid is *Dei Fauni Medigenii*, which appears on three of the spoons. It means '(spoon) of the god Faunus, the mead-begotten'. To a modern eye this suggests that Faunus was mythically conceived in the unedifying circumstances of parental intoxication but this is wholly inappropriate. In antiquity drunkenness was regarded as a state of enlightenment in which higher awareness might be achieved. There is every possibility that the visitors to Nodens' shrine at Lydney sought their nocturnal revelations in the same way. Another inscription reads *Dei Fauni Nari*, '(spoon) of the god Faunus, the mighty'. Some of the spoons feature personal names and these must be the members of the cult: Ingenuus, Primigenia, Silviola, Auspicius, Agrestius, and Persevera, together with the invocation *vivas* for 'may you live [long]'. One is anonymous and simply reads 'Good man, may you live long'.[29]

Faunus was in myth an ancient king of Latium in Italy. He was the son of Picus and Venilia, and grandson of Saturn, though he was also said to be the son of Mars. He was believed to have had a special liking for agriculture, which meant that he became venerated as an Italian country god with oracular powers who protected agriculture, especially pastoral, and property in a broader sense. Horace offered Faunus the sacrifice of a young goat and wine in return for a propitious production of young animals as part of a festive rural celebration held in December in the meadows.[30] The image is typical of the tradition of an idealized rural mythical past which the Romans indulged in throughout their history. In the *Aeneid*, the king Latinus visits the oracle of his father, Faunus, where the priestess 'lies under the silent night on the outspread fleeces of slaughtered sheep and woos slumber' in order to speak to the gods.[31] Virgil adds also a cryptic reference to 'a deadly vapour' emanating from the forest. This may be a quite literal, but uncomprehending, reference to a natural gas like ethylene which causes hallucinations. This is now believed by some to have lain behind the oracular pronouncements in the temple of Apollo at Delphi, which lies over a natural fissure from which subterranean gases escape.[32]

Of course it is now impossible to know really what was going on in Norfolk in the 390s, not least because little is known about the Faunus cult at any time, even though there was a temple to him in Rome. In spite of the Faunus label, perhaps the Thetford worshippers were following a far more ancient native rural cult that had adopted classical pagan labels and identities, much as ancient mother goddess cults became identified first with Isis, who was herself then absorbed into the veneration of the Virgin Mary; the names change but the underlying beliefs remain much the same. The Thetford Treasure is the only evidence for a Faunus cult in late antiquity apart from an anti-pagan work written by Arnobius of Sicca in the fourth century which mentions the god. Ingenuus and his associates may have been members of an arcane and esoteric late Roman cult in Norfolk in the early fifth century who buried their precious cult equipment out of fear of the Christian authorities. They may customarily have used it in an actual temple, now completely lost, or in a natural setting which would now be undetectable. On the other hand, the objects may have been second-hand (perhaps even having been stolen) by the time they were buried and were owned by the jeweller whose rings, finished and incomplete, and bracelets made up much of the rest of the hoard. In this case the Faunus worshippers would probably have lived elsewhere in Britain or even in Gaul. Perhaps the jewellery belonged to the cult and was used by members as part of their equipage, or maybe the jeweller was a cult member and took charge of the hoard on behalf of the others.

Whatever the truth, paganism by this time was under assault. Constantine's Edict of Toleration in 313 was just that – an edict of toleration: it did not impose Christianity at the expense of other cults. But in the century that followed, paganism was subjected to increasing legal penalties. Unfortunately, many citizens of the Roman Empire were painfully aware that Christianity had not only failed to prevent the barbarian raids across the frontiers but also was subject to its own internecine strife in the form of heresies. It was this that turned many back to paganism, even if they maintained a public Christian face, which threatened the cohesiveness of the state. Pagan cults were also, by their very nature, the repositories of considerable wealth in the form of temple plate and offerings. In 391 the emperor Theodosius issued an edict which ordered the closure of temples and banned sacrifice, followed by a ban on other pagan rituals in 392.[33] It is easy to see how anyone in possession of these overtly pagan ritual objects might see fit to hide them before they were confiscated. What is certain is that Ingenuus and the others had turned away from the official Christianity of their era, perhaps even actively refuting it as apostates. But they were already so far detached from ancient paganism that they found their revivalist cult in the literature that educated Latinate people knew intimately. In that sense the Faunus cult is a reflection of the broader elite Romano-British society with their indulgence in pretentious mosaic floors and other depictions of classical art.

The pagan traditions of the Faunus cult had found a new esoteric popularity in part because of disaffection with Christianity. Nevertheless, pagan habits died hard, and this included a taste for elegant classical silverware often decorated with mythological scenes. The Mildenhall Treasure has for its main piece the vast silver Great Dish which is over 60 centimetres wide and weighs over 8 kilograms. The dish's central feature is the face of Oceanus, recalling the gorgon's head from the pediment of the temple of Sulis-Minerva at Bath, surrounded by Nereids, marine beasts and a Bacchic frenzy involving Bacchus and various associates. Yet the treasure also included three spoons engraved with the Chi-Rho monogram, and two others with inscriptions, one reading 'may you live long Papittedo', the other 'may you live long Pascentia'.[34] Such invocations were not explicitly Christian, with several being included in the Thetford Treasure, but they are often found in contexts with Christian associations, as in this case. Evidently a man and a woman, it is tempting to wonder if these are the names of a very wealthy married couple of the Romano-British elite whose treasure once decorated their villa. Of course it is impossible to know that, and even if they ever lived in Britain the silver may have passed through several owners before it was buried and may also have been made up of the property of several different households or individuals. If this seems gratuitous speculation one need only remember that today it is possible to find old silver spoons which carry the obsolete monogram or initials of an original owner, perhaps from the 1700s or 1800s, yet remain serviceable, valuable, and desirable items in the twenty-first century.

Pascentia is distinctly Latinate, with origins in the word *pascare*, 'to feed' or 'to pasture'. Papittedo is more obscure but probably has links to *pappare*, 'to eat'. Pascentia and Papittedo may have been members of a Christian congregation somewhere and in fact there is no need to reject the idea that they lived in Britain. Since we know that at the Council of Arles in 314 there were already bishops from Britain who were able to attend, there must by then have been a significant number of active Christian congregations in Britain. Moreover, educated Christians, such as the fifth-century Gallo-Roman bishop Sidonius, whose letters survive, seem often to have had little issue with the aesthetic appeal of pagan imagery, either in pictorial or literary form, which they both enjoyed and circulated.

Two of the Mildenhall silver plates are engraved with the name Eutherios.[35] Eutherios is Greek and was the name of the chief chamberlain of the emperor Julian, known to have been in Gaul in the mid-fourth century. It is a technical possibility that Julian's Eutherios was once the owner of part or all of the treasure, since someone of his status would have had access to this level of wealth. However, this is an enormous amount to read into a name, not least because there is no easy explanation for his property being in Britain, though of course it need not have been in his ownership by the time it was buried.

Until the Edict of Milan in 313, and indeed even thereafter, Christianity's variant forms were increasingly subject to proscription by the Church. The treasure from Water Newton (also known as Chesterton) in Cambridgeshire is a remarkable example of early Christian plate. The area centres on the Roman town of Durobrivae, today just off the A1 road near Peterborough. Ploughing in 1975 turned up the hoard, which consisted of twenty-seven silver objects and one of gold. Many of them bear unequivocal references to Christianity but some of the pieces are distinctly pagan in style (plate 31). They seem to form a collection of plate used by some Christian sect that had retained some adherence to pagan tradition. The members of the group included Innocentia and Viventia, who contributed a silver cup inscribed with their names and the Chi-Rho symbol.[36] Perhaps sisters, or mother and daughter, they are reminiscent of the important role played by women in the early Church and described in, for example, the letters of the early church father St Jerome. Another man, called Publianus, announced on another silver cup, 'prostrating myself, Lord, I honour your sacred sanctuary'.[37] This is a clear reference to a church of some sort, though in practice at the time this was more likely to have been part of a private residence.

Part of the treasure included a number of votive feathers embossed with the Chi-Rho symbol. Votive feathers were pagan and belong to a long-established tradition of similar items found at pagan temples, often declaring the name of the dedicant and the god or goddess to whom he or she was making the offering. Such feathers were probably nailed to the walls of temples. Innocentia and Viventia seem to have belonged to a sect that used pagan forms of worship in Christian rites. This would have provoked outright revulsion among hardline Christians and in that sort of context it becomes easier to imagine why the plate was gathered up and buried, perhaps before it was seized by church authorities and the church where it was displayed taken over.

Much church influence came from the Eastern Empire. At Carlisle, some time perhaps in the fourth century, Flavius Antigonus Papias, a citizen with a combined Latin and Greek name, was buried, with a tombstone set up by a woman called Septimia, presumably his wife, that commemorated his impressive life of 'sixty years, more or less'.[38] The insouciant imprecision of this score reflects a more Christianized attitude to earthly existence, seen merely as a sordid and uncomfortable prelude, the 'vale of tears', to the glories of the afterlife. Was he a Christian? The answer is: quite possibly. The tombstone is a very unusual survival from so late a date, estimated from its very different style from that of earlier funerary inscriptions. Indeed, if it were not for the fact that it is recorded as being found in a Roman cemetery in 1892 at Carlisle, it might well have been thought to be a modern import from the Eastern Empire. It begins with the traditional pagan abbreviation DM for 'to the spirits of the departed', but it also says that Papias 'restored to the Fates the soul' he had been lent for his threescore years, a phrase that is also more Christian in tone. In Latin this is a metrical phrase and reads *fatis animam recovavit*. It may have been taken from some sort of poetic prayer. Moreover, his name recalls that of Papias, bishop of Hierapolis in Asia Minor, an early Christian apostolic father who lived around the beginning of the second century and produced an important collection of works on the sayings of Christ.

The Roman Britain that all these people lived in, whether resident in a northern frontier military town, like Antigonus Papias, a rural farm-worker or an owner of a grandiose villa estate, had by the end of the fourth century little time to run. The process was gradual and in some places the transition was possibly hard to detect at the time, but eventually the dwindling of towns as markets and sources of goods was matched by a political deterioration which resulted in Britain being formally given up by the Empire.

CHAPTER EIGHT

LOOKING BACK ON THE WORLD OF GIANTS, AD 410 AND AFTER

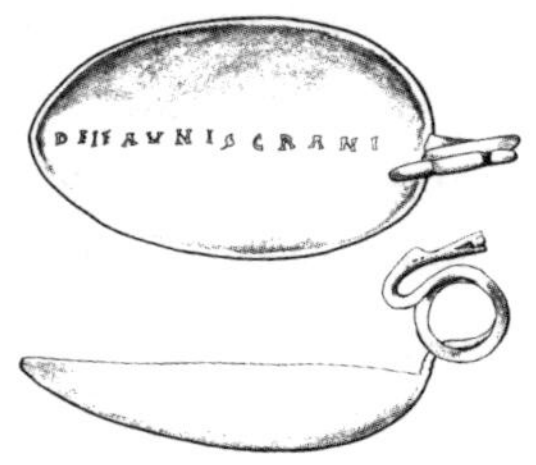

One of the few individual Britons from the fifth century about whom we know anything at all is Pelagius, though it is possible he actually came from Ireland. Pelagius was born some time in the later fourth century and might have entered a monastery. However, Pelagius began to devise his own special brand of Christianity, drawing on both pagan and Christian traditions. By the end of the fourth century at the latest he had travelled to Rome and begun to challenge orthodox teaching. Pelagius rejected the view that God had predetermined who would be eligible to enter Heaven (the 'elect') and who would not, publishing his beliefs in a treatise called *De Natura*. This was an idea promoted by Augustine, bishop of Hippo in North Africa (from 396), but Pelagius regarded this as a logical absurdity. Pelagius believed that anyone could influence his or her destiny through deeds and actions, something obviously derived from the pagan idea of making a contract with a deity. In other words, Pelagius believed that free will allowed a human being to decide to do good works and thus earn a posthumous future in paradise. Augustine believed that one had to be selected by the grace of God and that was the determining factor; a person not so selected could do nothing to alter that, regardless of good works.

Augustine was, quite literally, revolted by Pelagius and hurled a fusillade of written verbal abuse at him. By 409 Pelagius was actively circulating his ideas, which, not surprisingly, were quite attractive to those Christians who felt that from the Augustinian perspective they had no hope of going to heaven. By 417 Pelagius had been excommunicated and the following year he was declared a heretic, the usual punishments imposed by the totalitarian Church on anyone who dared to challenge its rules. This did nothing to dampen the appeal of Pelagius to people whose only alternative was accepting they were not members of the 'elect' and thus would be denied access to heaven. By 429 the heresy had taken deep root in Britain and this must in part have been linked to a conceptual relationship with paganism that had enjoyed something of a renaissance there in the late fourth century. Pelagius himself disappears from the story, but his legacy was a problem for the Church that lasted for generations. The bile heaped on him by Augustine was almost certainly a manifestation, at least in part, of what we would call the prevailing racist dismissal of the Britons as an inferior breed. This seems to have been particularly true of Romanized provincials, who used the abuse as a means to enhance their own Romanized credentials.

The early fifth century must have been a very strange time for those whom Pelagius left behind in Roman Britain. Some of the institutional and physical paraphernalia of the province was still in existence but it is abundantly clear from the archaeological evidence that much was not, or if it was it was derelict. The townsfolk of Wroxeter used timber public buildings installed in the ruins of what had once been the imposing masonry remains of the town baths. Public buildings in other towns, even if they were still visible, were falling into decay. Some villas were still being used but their once lavish mosaic floors were worn and damaged, sometimes serving as threshing surfaces. Many others were already in ruins, their owners already long gone and long forgotten.

The soldiers on Hadrian's Wall, at least those who were left, occupied semi-derelict forts patched up with any available stone. One of these was the fort at Birdoswald. Known as Banna in antiquity, this may be the 'Bannavem' where St Patrick was born in or around the year 389. He was the son of a church deacon called Calpurnius, a reminder that in these less certain times church organizations and administrative positions may have been the main form of social order in the Romano-British settlements. Some time around the year 405 Patrick was seized by pirates and enslaved, being taken to Ireland; after several years he escaped and went to pursue a monastic career in Gaul before evangelizing Ireland. Patrick's impact on British and Irish history would come after the Roman period but his experiences provide us with a glimpse of the insecurity of the period. Birdoswald was a shadow of its former self and archaeology has shown that in the fifth century it seems to have become the stronghold of a chieftain-type ruler, perhaps leading the descendants of the old garrison in a world where self-sufficiency in every respect had become the only means of survival.

St Patrick's story comes down to us through early Church writings.[1] Many of the conventional sources of information about individuals, which have played a crucial part in this book, were simply no longer in use, severing much of our communication with the period. It is left to stories like this or chance discoveries of exceptional artefacts to fill a little of the gap. The wealth that had subsisted in the form of extravagant rural properties, like the Woodchester villa, had evaporated as power and status in a conventional Roman idiom dwindled. Wealth now relied on the possession and retention of portable valuables, material that could be hidden in the hope of better times to come. Some of the other last names from Roman Britain survive in a remarkable hoard of such bullion. The Hoxne Treasure was found in a field in Suffolk in 1992. It included gold jewellery, silver vessels, spoons, utensils and other items, as well as 15,234 gold and silver coins (plate 32). The latest of the coins were struck between 407 and 408; they provide a *terminus post quem* for the burial of the treasure, which must have been buried around 409–10 or very soon afterwards. However, it is as well to be careful with any finds of this date involving coins. Imperial coinage was no longer shipped after 410 to Britain, which had had no mint of its own since about 325. If the hoard was, say, buried in 430 there would have been little or no chance of coins dated 410–30 being available to add to the hoard. Moreover, most of the silver *siliquae* coins in the hoard had been clipped, a phenomenon associated with a period of diminishing or absent coin supply. That alone suggests that a number of years passed after their striking dates before they were buried.

It is impossible (and unreasonable) to refute the likelihood that the Hoxne Treasure's burial and non-recovery in antiquity are in some way connected with the turmoil surrounding the cessation of the administration of Roman Britain by the Empire. This was exacerbated by the withdrawal of much of the garrison to support the bid by Constantine III to become the legitimate emperor in the West. Having said that, it is equally impossible to know what the precise circumstances of its burial were. There is no obvious Roman structure or settlement of the high status that would be commensurate with the exceptional nature and wealth of the treasure, though it is worth noting that a now-lost hoard of Roman gold coins of this date was found in 1732 less than four miles away at Eye in Suffolk. It is quite conceivable that the Eye hoard was buried by the same people engaged in dispersing their wealth in a number of locations to reduce the chances of losing it all.

Although the Hoxne Treasure is of major importance from every possible perspective, what matters here is that it included inscribed items. We cannot now know if they were all once owned by the same family, whether that included successive generations or contemporaneous members of that family, or were the property of several different households. In either case it is still not possible to say whether or not the family or families, or their personal agents, were responsible for the cache. It may have been buried by thieves, or by imperial officials who had requisitioned the goods in order to pay bribes to barbarian warriors. We know that the latter took place because of the hoards of Roman treasure found beyond imperial frontiers, such as that recovered from Traprain Law in Scotland, which were crudely cut up into conveniently sized chunks by the recipients, to whom the bullion was only valuable as bullion, not as manufactured objects.

The Hoxne Treasure, happily, had never got that far, even if that was the intention. Although the original wooden container had long since rotted away, the treasure was found more or less in its original location and as intact as could be hoped. The owners included *Domina* Juliane, 'the Lady Juliane', whose name appears on a gold bracelet, and Aurelius Ursicinus, whose name was inscribed on a set of ten silver spoons. His name had connotations of being 'old' by the time the treasure was buried. Lucius Septimius, the governor named on the Cirencester column base, had a name that harked back 150 years or more to the time of Septimius Severus. Aurelius Ursicinus' name also belonged to that era, echoing that adopted by anyone enfranchised between the time of Marcus Aurelius (161–80) and the edict of universal citizenship issued by Caracalla (whose formal name was Marcus Aurelius Antoninus) in 212. Both men perhaps then came from families that regarded themselves as having well-established pedigrees, though there is no obvious conclusion that can be drawn about their position in Romano-British society from this.

Another set of ten spoons in the Hoxne Treasure was originally owned by Peregrinus, a name that meant literally 'stranger' or 'foreigner' and which was also quite common. Four more spoons belonged to Silvicola, 'woodland dweller', which shares its prefix with a number of other names found in Britain. However, the most remarkable parallel is the very similar name Silviola which appears on some of the stylistically related spoons from the Thetford Treasure, though the metal analysis shows that the spoons were from quite separate productions and cannot therefore be demonstrably related. Some of the other spoons bear anonymous invocations such as 'long life to you, good man'; together with some additional names, like Datianus which appears on one spoon, there is an unavoidable feeling that the collection of items has been rather haphazardly accumulated purely for the sake of its value. It is more reminiscent of the stock of a dealer in valuable bullion items, a pile of silver items scattered across a market stall and accumulated from dozens of sources. Spoons, utensils and vessels might be inscribed for an original owner but thereafter their lives normally consist of being handed down and sold through various hands. It should be remembered that the majority of the treasure was not inscribed. It included, apart from the coins, variously a gold body chain that was at least thirty or more years old when buried, a silver handle in the form of a tigress and several elaborate pepper pots. Even if it did all belong to one household when buried, it is quite conceivable that it had been acquired as a gift of bullion, a theory given some credibility by the fact that parts of the treasure weigh very close to rounded figures. The gold coins, for example, weigh almost exactly eight Roman pounds, and the silver coins almost exactly 56 Roman pounds, itself obviously a multiple of eight. There was no overt religious association apart from a Chi-Rho on one of the bracelets; no meaningful conclusion can be drawn from its presence since by that date in the Christianized Empire it was an entirely routine decorative element.

Another interesting theory is based on the curious selection of items in the treasure, which excludes many of the most popular or common jewellery items such as brooches, earrings or pieces inlaid with gemstones, but includes such unusual and luxurious items as the pepper pots. Pepper was an expensive commodity and not likely to be one easily obtainable at a time of endemic insecurity; nor would it have been of major importance. This gives the hoard the look of a collection of low-priority items – valuable, but not necessarily favoured material. It is certainly extremely unlikely that whoever had owned some of the pieces which were found had not also owned classes of jewellery that were not included. In short, the Hoxne hoard is perhaps material which could be chanced with burial or which had been given up to a government agent requisitioning bullion by weight, while the owners retained their preferred possessions.

It has been pointed out that the treasure, once it was packed into its box, must have weighed around 40 kilograms when buried, which alone implies that more than one person was involved in its concealment, unless the hoard was built up in the course of several visits.[2] The results of the excavation suggested that the items had been carefully packed into the box, which makes it likely therefore that it was prepared in its entirety somewhere else and then brought to the site. It is absolutely impossible now to know how far it was brought, whether the decision to bury it was an expedient temporary solution intended to conceal it for a few days, or whether it was intended to bury it for the long term until whatever circumstances had provoked the preparation of the hoard had changed.

In the end the 'real life', or 'lives', that the Hoxne Treasure enshrines remain a consummate mystery. We might assume that Aurelius Ursicinus and the other names from the hoard are those of members of the Romano-British elite and that they were real people whose experience of life in Britain was at around the highest standard available at the time. But whether all or any of them were involved in the treasure's burial, or even still alive when this occurred, it is quite impossible to say. There may have been no specific plan to recover it; if there was an all-prevailing sense of the ill shape of things to come in the early 400s then the purpose may have been more to prevent a third party in the form of thieves or the government (usually under such circumstances regarded as one and the same thing) from seizing it. All we do know for certain is that whoever placed the treasure in the ground never returned to collect it and as a result it survived to become yet another of the remarkable series of late Roman hoards discovered in Britain in modern times, which is itself a peculiar feature of this remote province and shared with nowhere else in the Empire.[3] It is worth noting the phenomenon of treasure concealment which the Anglo-Saxon Chronicle recorded thus: '418. In this year the Romans collected all the treasures which were in Britain and hid some in the earth so that no one afterwards could find them.' This is a fascinating comment, if inconclusive: it suggests an enduring tradition that the upheaval of the period had led to a significant amount of deliberate concealment of bullion goods. Evidently it was widely believed this had occurred and must have been based on sustained anecdotal evidence and, no doubt, chance discoveries of some of the less well-hidden hoards during the Saxon period.

At some point in the fourth or fifth century AD an elderly man was buried in what would one day be known as the village of Ancaster in Lincolnshire, very close to where the medieval church was later built. He was buried in a grave that was oriented east–west and he was laid with his head to the west. This was a Christian configuration and would have allowed him to rise up and greet the Second Coming. The grave was located to the west of the late Roman fortifications that created a defensible enclave in what had once been a straggling settlement along Ermine Street, the great Roman highway that headed out north from London towards Lincoln. That road was probably laid out by soldiers of the IX Legion in the first century. By the time the grave was dug the area was susceptible to coastal raiders, the very people who would subsequently settle in Britain and establish a permanent Germanic presence.

Ancaster's principal industry had been, apart from farming, its limestone which was quarried and freighted round Britannia and is indeed still today an important industry. It was also the home of the shrine of Viridios, an otherwise unknown god who seems to have been some sort of local rural warrior deity. His shrine has yet to be located but an inscription found near the village church refers to the donation of an arch by a man called Trenico, as mentioned earlier. Another partial inscription, naming the god, was found in the anonymous elderly man's grave. It was used as one of the slabs that created his sarcophagus and was carefully laid with the name of Viridios beside the man's head.

The old man and his grave in many ways stand for so many of the millions of Romano-British whose name and identity are lost to us, but who are found in a context that defines the era they lived in. His grave preserved the name of a native deity, adopted in Roman times and articulated in the language of the invader with the words 'To the Holy God Viridios'.[4] His grave's discovery symbolizes our link with that time; as the earth fell away from the inscription, so the words could be read because we use the same letters today. The old man's death came towards the end of the time of, or not long after, the Roman era in Britain when a strange juxtaposition of Christian ways and older pagan customs was finding some sort of strange equilibrium. He was buried apparently as a Christian, a religion that found its way to Britain through the conduits of Roman trade and communications, but with the reassuring presence of an older spiritual force known to the native population for far longer. Perhaps he lived at a time when Ancaster was still recognizably a Roman town, though evidently the shrine of Viridios had fallen into ruin. Perhaps he lived at a time when the Roman era was already no more than a childhood memory, if even that. What is certain is that he lived at a time when the remains of the infrastructure of Britannia were a very great deal more visible than they are today and must have profoundly affected his perception of the world around him. The old man's life is known to us only through its end but he is a reminder that Roman Britain was a real human experience in an infinite number of different ways for millions of individuals.

Cunorix was buried sometime between the mid-fifth and mid-sixth centuries at Wroxeter, a civitas capital that was by then a shadow of its former self. Some semblance of urban order remained well into the fifth century, with timber public buildings occupying footprints in and among the remains of the tile and masonry structures from the city's heyday. His tombstone reads, 'Cunorix, son of Maqui Coline'. It was neither wholly Roman nor wholly native since the names are mostly Irish and the text is only in a form of Latin.[5] Cunorix, whose name means something like 'hound king', lived in a Britain where Roman buildings must still have been in great evidence, even if many of them were now in ruin. His Wroxeter must have been something of a shanty town, but recognizably Roman, with make-do timber dwellings and other gimcrack structures dotted in and around the derelict masonry and skeletal remnants of the old public buildings. Elsewhere by this time the ruins of Lullingstone villa were probably still visible and Nettleton's octagonal podium was cluttered with the debris from the collapsed temple. A large and well-appointed villa at Dinnington in Somerset was excavated in 2004, revealing that at least a century's worth of anonymous and unknown residents, perhaps descendants of the fourth-century owners, continued to use the old villa house. However, the once fine mosaics now served as threshing floors before the roof finally collapsed around the end of the fifth century and the house was finally abandoned.

Not everything decayed into oblivion. In 685 St Cuthbert visited Carlisle and was impressed to see that the aqueduct still worked and fed an operational public fountain.[6] In the late 1100s Gerald of Wales wondered at the startling vestiges of 'hot baths, the remains of temples and theatres' at Caerleon, formerly the fortress of the II Legion, by then around a thousand years old.[7] Still later, vast stretches of Hadrian's Wall were standing and available for farmers and others to help themselves to stone well into the nineteenth century. This means that the remains of the Roman era must still have been hugely conspicuous in the fifth century, even if for many people living at that time it had become increasingly mythical.

The legacy of the Roman era in Britain is hard to measure because much of its presence in today's society has arrived in more recent centuries by other routes rather than being handed down directly from Roman Britain. Indeed, one of the curiosities of the period is just how little direct influence there seems to have been. It is a remarkable fact that, insofar as we can ascertain, organized town life ceased to exist. The great villa estates almost certainly remained, used for farmland, but the grand houses themselves slowly, but surely, fell into ruin. The process was protracted and lasted for decades, but the disruption of the material record is far more abrupt. Coinage more or less fell out of use and even the manufacture of pottery seems to have stopped.

Although this book has looked at many lives of Roman Britain, from men and women of total insignificance to others of great status and importance, they only represent an utterly minuscule proportion of the original. Over a 360-year period tens of millions of individuals were involved in experiencing life in Roman Britain yet we know of only a few hundreds by name, if even that.

The Western Australian town of Albany was one of the earliest settled parts of that state, thanks to its outstanding natural harbour. A book of old photographs, taken here in the mid-1800s to the early 1900s, shows soldiers on their way to the South African war in 1899, settlers standing proudly outside their houses, farms or shops, and here and there the Aboriginal people reduced to the status of largely anonymous curios posing with their weapons.[8] There is something strangely reminiscent of Roman Britain in these images of an imperial dominion. That photographic record is almost entirely dominated by immigrants of all sorts; when the indigenous people appear it is, of course, only through a medium brought by the immigrants. So it is for Roman Britain, a remote province of the Roman Empire. Claudia Severa and Sulpicia Lepidina might just as easily be two immigrant wives in Albany, clutching the hands of their infant children, outside Claudia's home on her birthday while staring at a camera as it recorded that moment in their lives on a glass plate negative. In one picture, a fully laden baker's cart waits outside the baker's shop, its wooden wheels about to endure another day of rattling along Australia's early roads; one is instantly reminded of Octavius and his concerns about sending out his wagons on northern Britain's damaged roads. Behind the cart, four boys are caught in a moment of blurred movement as they grin at one another. One, however, stares fixedly at the camera, his name and destiny now lost to the ages. Of course we have no such photographic record for Roman Britain, but the correspondence and all those other inscriptions, references and artefacts in a very real way serve to fulfil the same role.

Moreover, we see almost every one of these people of the past only for a fleeting instant whether through photographs or inscriptions. Almost everything else about their lives is lost to us. We do not know where Claudia Severa and Sulpicia Lepidina came from or what they looked like. We do not know whether either of them grew old enough to be able to reminisce about their days as young wives in remote military outposts, or whether they succumbed to disease or post-partum complications as so many of their peers would have done. Their lives and graves are otherwise entirely lost. Bruccius and Caratius Colasunus emerge abruptly from the fog of time to hurl their statue of Mars, made for them by Celatus the coppersmith, into the Foss Dike and then disappear just as quickly.

Does that invalidate any attempt to look at who these people were and try to work out a little of what their lives were? No, because they are all we have – it is the record left to us and it is something of a miracle that it exists at all. We might indulge the conceit that our age will be different, but will it? The Romans lived in an era when by the standards of the time an enormous amount of data was generated; it was after all a world run according to the rule of law with edicts, taxation, or censuses, all of which were recorded in an epigraphic panopticon. Almost all of that has gone, especially documents like the Vindolanda tablets which must once have been ubiquitous, with every official building, fort and rural estate drowning in paperwork. Our own age now produces data in unprecedented quantities yet almost all of it exists only in electronic form, reliant on software and computers to access and understand it. It would take very little for it to be wiped out and lost forever. It may well be that in several thousand years' time our own era will be proportionately no better, or even worse, represented in whatever record survives than Roman Britain.

It is also worth remembering that for every one of the people mentioned in this book Britain was at least for a time their home. They were like us. They had jobs, families, hopes, fears, joy and disappointments and their experiences were conducted in the same place we live in today. Yes, some rivers have moved and the vast processes of erosion, deforestation, enclosure and urbanization, and the coming of the railways and cars have altered Britain forever. But the evidence for the

Romano-British is still buried in our world and around all of us today and although much has been transferred to museums, new material is found almost every month. At the point of discovery the artefact or record makes that sudden transition from the world of Roman Britain to our own time. Nothing is more potent on those occasions than the evidence for a real person, a real life. Roman Britain is within us and around us. It is also an inevitable fact that some of us, perhaps many of us, are descended from a very small number of Romano-British individuals, though not a single one of us will ever be able to trace that lineage. It is an obvious point, though often overlooked, that every one of us had ancestors who lived in that time. At on average around twenty to twenty-five years per generation, around seventy generations have passed since the Roman era in Britain.

Every year that passes sees more individuals from Roman Britain's population recovered from the ground in the form of records on tombstones, religious dedications, writing tablets and graffiti. But in relative terms the numbers are tiny. All the people who have been described in this book, and those who still wait their turn to emerge from the shadows, must be seen to stand for the myriad and nameless others who passed all or some of their real lives in Britannia seventeen to twenty centuries ago. The rest are lost to the ages. And it will probably be much the same for most of us in time.

Quisque suos patimur Manes.[9]

'Every one of us suffers his (or her) own fate in the afterlife.'

ROMAN NAMES AND ROMAN MONEY

Names

A Roman citizen normally had three names: the *praenomen*, the *nomen* and the *cognomen* (the *tria nomina*). The best known is Gaius Julius Caesar. The *nomen* was the name of the *gens* to which the closest modern equivalent is our word 'clan' or 'house'. It identified different families all united by a common descent. The actual family or branch was indicated by the *cognomen*, and the individual person by the *praenomen*, thus 'Gaius of the Julian clan, family Caesar'. The *cognomen* could be derived from any one of many sources, including a forbear's nickname. 'Caesar' in fact means 'hairy', though Julius Caesar himself was bald.

While this seems simple enough in practice, Roman names are much more complicated. Sons often bore the same name as their fathers, resulting in confusingly identical names applied to several people. One Roman solution for a larger clan was to use two cognomens and thus assist in distinguishing one family or branch from another.

Names were not acquired exclusively through genetic descent. In Roman law adoption was indistinguishable in legal validity from normal parentage. A boy or man who was adopted by a Roman citizen acquired his adoptive father's name. A freed slave retained his old slave name as the *cognomen* but acquired his former Roman citizen master's *praenomen* and *nomen*. Thanks to this process it is quite possible to find people in remote provincial frontier locations with names that hark back to great Roman families of Republican times such as Aulus Cluentius Habitus on Hadrian's Wall (see chapter 5). How they inherited them in any one case is now impossible to tell.

Women were generally known by the female version of the *nomen* without any other appellation. Thus, women of the Julian clan were normally simply known as 'Julia', or in the family of Marcus Tullius Cicero as 'Tullia'.

Slave names were awarded by masters according to their fancy. These included names which alluded to the slave's place of origin, mythology, personal characteristics, or appropriate Roman virtues or terms, among others. Thus the freedwoman 'Regina' had a Latin name that means 'queen'. It is unlikely to be the name she acquired at birth unless she was born into slavery.

In a remote province like Britain few people apart from immigrant soldiers, administrators, traders and selected elite natives were likely to be Roman citizens until the edict of universal citizenship issued by Caracalla in 212. The British or provincial names from other parts of the Roman world which turn up in the record frequently exhibit Latinized versions of native names, such as Sulinus the sculptor at Bath whose name seems to have been derived from the god of the sacred spring, or Sennianus the *mortaria* potter at Water Newton. In some cases native names were absorbed into the three names of a Roman citizen where the old native name was retained as the *cognomen*. In exceptional instances, such as Lossio Veda, the Caledonian expatriate in Colchester, native names survived intact in what seems to be their original form.

Money

Some inscriptions make explicit references to Roman money and there are other occasional references in the text. Until the late third century AD the system was based on the following:

1 gold aureus = 25 silver denarii
1 silver denarius = 4 brass sestertii

1 brass sestertius = 2 brass dupondii
1 brass dupondius = 1 copper as

Values are almost unknown to us. But we do know that until the late first century AD a legionary soldier received 225 denarii per annum, and after that date 300. Prices also generally elude us but at one end of the scale a pottery lamp might cost 1 as, while a slave girl cost 600 denarii.

In the early third century a double silver denarius, now called an antoninianus, was introduced. By the late third century this denomination, now heavily debased, was almost the only circulating coin. In the fourth century the coinage system was repeatedly reformed and our knowledge of values and even denomination names is minimal. The gold coin then made was known as the solidus and the silver coin a siliqua. Their precise relationship is unknown. Vast numbers of base metal coins circulated with huge variations in module size over time, many of which were local counterfeits.

Over the period the coins most likely to be hoarded were the gold and silver coins, for example in the Dorchester and Hoxne hoards.

DATES IN THE HISTORY OF ROMAN BRITAIN

55 BC — Julius Caesar makes his first unsuccessful foray into Britain.

54 BC — Julius Caesar makes his second unsuccessful foray into Britain.

Caesar does no more than fight a few skirmishes in southern Britain on these occasions but he introduces the Roman world to the Iron Age tribes that made up prehistoric Britain. In fact, there has been commercial and social contact with the Mediterranean nations for centuries. The events set off years of diplomatic dealings with the tribes of Britain. The smart ones realize the Romans are the most powerful and influential force around, and that having Roman support could be decisive in their own success in local intertribal feuds and wars. This will be their undoing because they never act together.

43 AD — Verica of the Atrebates is ousted, probably by dynastic rivals, and flees to Rome for help. This gives Claudius the pretext he needs to invade Britain. Aulus Plautius leads the invasion of Roman Britain on the orders of CLAUDIUS (41–54), and serves as the first governor. He conquers southern Britain and arranges a triumphal march into Colchester for Claudius. The legions involved are probably II Augusta, IX Hispana,

XIV Gemina, and XX, as well as part of VIII Augusta. Auxiliary troops make up the rest. The force could have been as big as 40,000+ men. The II heads for the South Midlands and south-west, the IX for the north, the XIV into the West Midlands. XX is based at Colchester.

47–52 Publius Ostorius Scapula becomes governor. Colchester is made the first colony of veteran troops and the XX Legion goes west. Scapula marches against the tribes in south Wales, and defeats a rebellion by the Iceni in East Anglia.

52–57 Aulus Didius Gallus becomes governor. He holds the Welsh tribes in check and finds the Brigantes of northern Britain, Rome's allies, are splitting between the feuding king Venutius and his queen Cartimandua. NERO (54–68) becomes emperor.

57/8 Quintus Veranius Nepos becomes governor but dies in post.

57/8–61 Gaius Suetonius Paulinus becomes governor. He sets out to destroy the Druid stronghold in Anglesey, headquarters of the resistance to Rome. In 60 Boudica leads the revolt of the Iceni, joined by some of the Trinovantes. They defeat *part* of the IX Legion. The Iceni burn Colchester, London and St Albans. Suetonius Paulinus marches back with the XIV and XX Legions and defeats Boudica, wiping out the rebels. No tribe will ever threaten Roman Britain again this way. Suetonius Paulinus keeps the army mobile and garrisons the south. For its part the XIV is renamed XIV Gemina Martia Victrix, and this is probably when XX became XX Valeria Victrix. Paulinus is opposed in his punitive policy by the new procurator, Gaius Julius Classicianus, who is more concerned to mend fences and build a new future. When a naval force is lost, this gives the government the pretext to withdraw Paulinus.

61–63 Publius Petronius Turpilianus becomes governor. Much later on the Roman historian Tacitus accuses him of laziness, but Turpilianus was probably repairing the damage in Britain and reforming Roman government.

63–69 Marcus Trebellius Maximus becomes governor. He, too, is accused of laziness by Tacitus but faces a mutiny by the XX

Legion. In 68 NERO commits suicide and the Roman civil war breaks out. GALBA (68–9) rules briefly. Trebellius seems to have fled to side with VITELLIUS (69) in the Roman civil war.

69–71 VESPASIAN (69–79) wins the civil war and establishes the Flavian dynasty. Marcus Vettius Bolanus becomes governor. He rescues Cartimandua from the Brigantian feud. The Brigantes are now drawn into the Empire. By this time XIV has been withdrawn and replaced by the II Adiutrix Pia Fidelis. The new legion spends time at Lincoln, replacing IX, which heads off to build a new fortress at York. The II Augusta will soon be at Caerleon.

71–74 Quintus Petillius Cerealis becomes governor. He annexes much of what is now northern England, and may have founded the legionary fortress of the IX Legion at York.

74–77/8 Sextus Julius Frontinus becomes governor. He conquers the Silures in Wales. This is almost the last Roman war in Wales. Around this time the spa at Bath is being developed. Since Frontinus was later placed in charge of aqueducts in Rome, he might have been responsible.

77/8–83/4 Gnaeus Julius Agricola becomes governor. In his term he finishes off the Welsh war, conquers northern Britain, reaching as far north as the north-east tip of Caledonia (Scotland), and circumnavigates Britain. He encourages the erection of public buildings, temples and houses, as well as the use of the Latin language. He is recorded on an inscription from the new forum at St Albans (Verulamium). The historical accounts of Tacitus end here and thereafter we have much less detail. During this time the II Adiutrix Pia Fidelis moves to Chester, while the XX is in Scotland.

79 Accession of TITUS (79–81). Eruption of Vesuvius in Italy.

81 Accession of DOMITIAN (81–96).

84 DOMITIAN recalls Agricola, abandons Caledonia and pulls back the Roman army to what is now northern England. During this time the II Adiutrix Pia Fidelis is withdrawn. Britain now has three legions: II Augusta (Caerleon), IX Hispana (York), and XX Valeria Victrix (Chester).

96 Accession of NERVA (96–8). Gloucester is founded as a colony, but in fact this probably took place under Domitian – Domitian was 'damned' after his murder and his achievements suppressed by his successors. Lincoln was probably also made a colony at this time.

98 Accession of TRAJAN (98–117). Around this time the Vindolanda writing tablets are produced.

Second Century (AD 100+)

100s Around this time the IX Legion disappears. It is last recorded on an inscription from York dated to 107–8. It may have been lost in Britain around the time Hadrian became emperor but nothing for certain is known.

117 Accession of HADRIAN (117–38).

119 HADRIAN visits Britain. He orders the building of Hadrian's Wall by the governor Aulus Platorius Nepos (*c.* 121–4). He also encourages public building. The great basilica of London is built about this time. The south of Britain is now a settled world with towns, roads, markets, villages, industries (e.g. pottery) and rural farmsteads. The north and west is a military zone with three legionary fortresses: Caerleon (II Augusta), Chester (XX Valeria Victrix) and York (VI Victrix). The latter was brought by Aulus Platorius Nepos.

129–130 Forum and basilica at Wroxeter, Viroconium Cornoviorum, is dedicated in the name of Hadrian, who had probably instigated its construction during his visit a decade earlier

138 Accession of ANTONINUS PIUS (138–61). A new war is fought in northern Britain. Antoninus orders a new wall, made of turf, to be built further north – roughly between where Glasgow and Edinburgh are now – by his governor Quintus Lollius Urbicus (*c.* 138–42). The wall is known now as the Antonine Wall.

140–161 The last known major public building inscription from Britain is set up: Marcus Ulpius Januarius, *aedile* at the town of Petuaria (Brough-on-Humber), donates a new stage for the town theatre.

161 Accession of MARCUS AURELIUS (161–80).

163 War breaks out in northern Britain again. The governor Sextus Calpurnius Agricola (*c.* 161–5) is sent against 'the Britons'. Hadrian's Wall is reoccupied and the Antonine Wall abandoned.

170s Marcus Aurelius creates an alliance with the Sarmatian Iazyges tribe (their territory was partly equivalent to modern Ukraine). They give him 8,000 cavalry, and the emperor sends 5,500 of them to Britain, though whether it was to reinforce the garrison or to train them up at a safe distance is unknown.

180 Accession of COMMODUS (180–92), the emperor immortalized in the movie *Gladiator*.

184 Tribes cross Hadrian's Wall from Caledonia and defeat a legionary contingent.

The garrison of Britain, outraged by the way Commodus has delegated his power to the praetorian prefect Perennis, elect one of their number, Priscus, to be emperor. Priscus declines so the garrison sends a 1,500-strong delegation to Rome. Terrified, Commodus allows the praetorians to lynch Perennis. He sends Pertinax to govern Britain and impose some discipline. The British legions eventually mutiny and leave Pertinax for dead. He escapes.

192–197 COMMODUS murdered. All hell breaks loose. PERTINAX becomes emperor at the beginning of 193 but is murdered on 28 March after 86 days. He is followed by DIDIUS JULIANUS, who lasts 66 days. Now the civil war starts. The new British governor, Clodius Albinus, is one of the candidates to be emperor. In the east PESCENNIUS NIGER is proclaimed emperor but is defeated by SEPTIMIUS SEVERUS in 194. Severus has convinced Albinus to be his successor and associate while he wipes out Niger. By 195 Albinus realizes he has been tricked when Severus declares him a public enemy. Albinus takes much of Britain's garrison and sets off for Gaul to meet Severus. In 197, near Lyons, Albinus and his army are wiped out. SEPTIMIUS SEVERUS (193–211) is the victor.

Third Century (AD 200+)

205–208 Much military rebuilding in northern Britain.

208 SEPTIMIUS SEVERUS arrives in Britain to lead the reconquest of Caledonia to toughen up his sons, CARACALLA (211–17) and GETA (211–12). The campaign is a struggle and inconclusive.

211 SEPTIMIUS SEVERUS dies of exhaustion at York. CARACALLA abandons the conquests, kills his brother (and joint emperor) the next year and embarks on a reign of terror. Britain is quiet now, and the years ahead are marked by a vast amount of new military building on the northern frontier. In this time, the villas of the southern lowlands start their slow climb to wealth and greatness. In the towns, the age of public building is all but over. The rich are beginning to spend the money on themselves.

During this time Britain is divided into two, so that no other governor would ever be able to mount a rebellion. Britannia Superior is the south, ruled from London. Britannia Inferior is the north, ruled from York – the commander of the VI Legion there now becomes its governor.

259 Gallic Empire: POSTUMUS seizes control of Britain, Gaul and Germany to create the Gallic Empire.

268 Gallic Empire: murder of Postumus, accession of MARIUS followed by his almost immediate murder. Accession of VICTORINUS.

270 Accession of AURELIAN.

Gallic Empire: murder of Victorinus, accession of TETRICUS I and his son TETRICUS II.

273 Suppression of the Gallic Empire by Aurelian.

275 Murder of Aurelian. Accession of TACITUS.

276 Death of Tacitus, accession of FLORIANUS, death of Florianus, accession of PROBUS.

282 Murder of Probus, accession of CARUS.

283 Elevation of Carus' sons CARINUS and NUMERIAN to the rank of Caesar. Death of Carus, accession of CARINUS (West), and NUMERIAN (East) who is murdered later this year.

285 Murder of Carinus. Accession of DIOCLETIAN.

286 Appointment of MAXIMIANUS by Diocletian to rule the West.

CARAUSIUS, commander of the British fleet, seizes control in Britain and part of northern Gaul. This is the first 'British Empire'.

293 Murder of Carausius and accession of ALLECTUS in Britain.

Diocletian appoints junior partners (Caesars) to assist him and Maximian: Galerius (East) and CONSTANTIUS I (West). This system is known as the Tetrarchy.

296 Defeat and death of Allectus by the army of Constantius I. Britain passes back under control of MAXIMIANUS (Augustus) and CONSTANTIUS I (Caesar).

Fourth Century (AD 300+)

During this time a few of the villas grow to a great size. This is the age of the fabulously wealthy, though by Empire standards Britain remains a backwater. No Roman Briton will ever have an Empire-wide reputation.

305 Abdication of Diocletian and Maximian and elevation of CONSTANTIUS I to Augustus in the West, with SEVERUS (Caesar).

306 Proclamation of CONSTANTINE the Great at York following the death of his father, Constantius I, there. This disruption of the Tetrarchic system leads to protracted feuds and wars involving Maximian and his son Maxentius.

308 Settlement at Carnuntum passes control of the West to LICINIUS (Augustus) and CONSTANTINE I (Caesar), while Galerius (Augustus) and Maximinus (Caesar) hold the East. The feuds continue unabated because Maximian and Maxentius, and Maximinus, try to recapture power.

By around this time, perhaps by 296, Britain is divided into four: Maxima Caesariensis (the south-east and East Anglia), Britannia Prima, governed from Cirencester (Wales, the south-west and West Midlands); Britannia Secunda, governed from York (the north); and Flavia Caesariensis, governed from Lincoln (north-east Midlands and Lincolnshire).

312 Battle of the Milvian Bridge: Constantine defeats Maxentius, using troops partly raised in Britain. The West is now under the exclusive control of CONSTANTINE I, while Licinius controls the East.

313 Edict of Milan guarantees total religious toleration.

324 Constantine I defeats Licinius.

337 Death of Constantine I and accession of his sons: CONSTANTINE II (Britain, Gaul and Spain), Constantius II (the East), and Constans (Italy, Africa and Central Europe).

340 Murder of Constantine II by Constans. Britain passes under control of CONSTANS.

343 Constans visits Britain.

350 Revolt of MAGNENTIUS in Autun and murder of Constans.

353 Suicide of Magnentius following defeats. CONSTANTIUS II becomes ruler of the whole Empire. Paulus, an imperial secretary, is sent by Constantius to purge Britain of any Magnentian supporters, which he does with ruthless efficiency.

360 JULIAN, cousin of Constantius II, proclaimed emperor in Gaul.

361 Death from fever of Constantius II.

363 Death of Julian. Accession of JOVIAN, formerly commander of the imperial guard.

364 Death of Jovian. Accession of VALENTINIAN I (West) and his brother Valens (East).

367 Barbarian conspiracy overruns Britain.

GRATIAN appointed joint Augustus in the West with VALENTINIAN I.

Arrival of Count Theodosius in Britain – he restores Britain's defences.

375 Death of Valentinian I. GRATIAN now rules jointly in the West with his brother VALENTINIAN II.

378 Death of Valens. Gratian and Valentinian II rule the whole Empire.

379 Appointment of Theodosius to rule the East.

383 Death of Gratian. MAGNUS MAXIMUS, senior officer in the British garrison, proclaimed emperor in Britain and straightaway invades Gaul.

Theodosius' son, Arcadius, is made joint emperor in the East.

387 Valentinian II flees from Maximus to the East.

388 Magnus Maximus defeated and executed in Italy by THEODOSIUS.

392 Murder of Valentinian II.

393 Theodosius' son HONORIUS is made joint emperor.

395 Death of Theodosius. The Empire is divided between his sons: HONORIUS (West) and Arcadius (East).

Fifth Century (AD 400+)

407 Proclamation of CONSTANTINE III in Britain. He moves to Gaul, taking much of what was left of Britain's already denuded garrison.

408 Constantine III takes Spain (he will be defeated and killed in 411).

410 Honorius, with scarcely the resources to defend Italy, instructs Britain to look after its own defences. Around this time the Thetford and Hoxne treasures are deposited, not to be found until the late twentieth century.

From now on Britain continues to live the Roman way but it had been gradually fading for decades. The towns lapse into ruin, the villas are slowly abandoned – natural disasters or normal crises like house fires were no longer followed by repair. We know very little about what went on but it is plain the end was slow. There was no abrupt disaster. The Christian Church in Britain remained in contact with the continent, especially during the great crisis of the Pelagian heresy. In 429 the British Church appealed to the Church in Gaul for help in suppressing the heresy. St Germanus of Auxerre arrived to deal with the problem and visited the shrine of St Alban during this visit.

During the fifth century are the first recorded arrivals of the ANGLES, to be followed by the SAXONS. In 446 the Britons appealed for help and in 449 the Saxon invasions became critical. The Britons and their Church are forced westwards, with their culture surviving in the place names of Wales and the south-west, and the Welsh and Cornish languages that preserve some Latin words. Southern Britain becomes ENGLAND, the pagan land of the Anglo-Saxon kingdoms.

GAZETTEER

The prime location for anyone wishing to see the original sources for himself or herself has to be the British Museum in London. Here, within the space of a few yards in the Roman Britain gallery on the first floor, are the Lullingstone wall-paintings and busts, the great treasures of Mildenhall, Thetford, Hoxne and Water Newton, the Vindolanda tablets, the tomb of Classicianus, and a host of other finds, including the Thruxton mosaic, and casts of the Regina tombstone and the altar of Marcus Aurelius Lunaris. The Museum of London has an excellent collection of artefacts which include the Austalis tile, the Ulpius Silvanus tauroctony and the Tiberinius Celerianus inscription.

Other recommended locations in southern Britain must first include the Castle Museum in Colchester where the Facilis and Longinus tombstones are displayed along with the Colchester samian potters' efforts. The Verulamium Museum, just outside St Albans, currently houses artefacts from the Roman town of Verulamium. The villa at Lullingstone lies close to the junction of the M20 and M25 motorways near Eynsford and is easily reached from London. Here the entire villa house and its mosaics are on display all year round.

Elsewhere in Britain museums with items mentioned in this book abound, though the distribution of Roman inscriptions in Britain tends to reflect the distribution of the army; consequently the best places are in the west and north. The most useful places to visit in the south-west are the Corinium Museum in Cirencester, where the collection includes the enigmatic fourth-century Jupiter column, and the Roman Baths Museum in Bath, where an important collection of inscribed stones sits alongside the remains of the temple of Sulis-Minerva, the temple precinct and the baths. Along the Welsh frontier zone, the Legionary Museum at Caerleon has an impressive collection, as does the Grosvenor Museum in Chester: the homes of the II Legion Augusta and the XX Legion Valeria Victrix respectively, it is no surprise that there are numerous inscriptions on display recording the lives and works of the Roman army. In between is the site of the Roman town at Wroxeter, where the Cunorix tombstone can be seen.

Northern England is inevitably home to some of the finest collections of Roman inscriptions. Lincoln's museum, called The Collection, has material from the city's time as the home of the II Legion Adiutrix Pia Fidelis and the IX Legion Hispana, and then as a colony, as well as the Ancaster inscriptions of the god Viridios. York's Yorkshire Museum has items from the legionary fortress of the IX Legion Hispana, succeeded there by the VI Legion Victrix, as well as the adjacent colony. To the east, Hull and East Riding Museum displays the Brough inscription by Marcus Ulpius Januarius and the Rudston villa's idiosyncratic Venus mosaic. Heading on further north, the museums attached to the forts along Hadrian's Wall, such as Birdoswald, Housesteads, Vindolanda, Chesters and Segedunum (Wallsend) all have items from their vicinities. No journey to the area should omit a visit to the Great North Museum at Hancock to the west of Newcastle-upon-Tyne where finds from mostly the eastern half of the Wall are stored. Some others are on display in the brand new museum in Palace Green Library, which is just next to Durham cathedral. Finds from the western half of the Wall are mainly stored at the Tullie House Museum in Carlisle. Outposts of the northern frontier are also well served by the excellent museum at Arbeia (South Shields) where Regina's tombstone can be seen, and the Senhouse Museum at Maryport where altars dedicated by the commanding officers are on display. Antonine Wall material is mainly to be found in the Hunterian Museum in Glasgow and the National Museum of Scotland in Edinburgh.

Readers should also be aware that there are numerous other local museums with artefacts and other records of life in Roman Britain, for example at the fort of Ribchester (Lancashire), the Clifton Park Museum in

Rotherham which houses the finds from the fort at Templeborough, or the villas at Chedworth (Gloucesterhire) and Rockbourne (Hampshire).

In today's internet world there is no point in providing contact details for any of these places, or weblinks because they constantly change. Readers should start with the list here and consult a search engine for current links in order to find out what is open, when, and where. There is, however, no guarantee that anything mentioned in this book will be on display at any time in any of these places.

A NOTE ON SOURCES

Most of the core basic material for *The Real Lives of Roman Britain* can be found in the various volumes in the *Roman Inscriptions of Britain* series (see the Select Bibliography). These can be divided into volumes I and III which deal with inscriptions on stone, with volume I containing those found and reported up till 1955 and volume III containing those from 1955 until 2006. Volume II is divided into a subseries of fascicules which deal with inscriptions on portable objects such as mosaics, pottery, silver vessels, jewellery, tiles, and so on. Every inscription is accompanied by an illustration where possible (some exist only as antiquarian descriptions), a transcription, translation and brief discussion, as well as references and cross-references. Inscriptions found since these were published, and of whatever class, are for the moment to be found in the annual journal *Britannia*, published by the Society for the Promotion of Roman Studies. However, all these volumes are not only expensive but also bulky and thus unlikely to be suitable or even available to a school classics department or an individual. The London Association of Classical Teachers' volume 4 (4th edition), *Inscriptions of Roman Britain*, edited by Valerie Maxfield and Brian Dobson, is an excellent alternative and includes some of the texts used in this book.

Of course some individuals featured here are to be found only in ancient written sources such as Caesar's account of the *Gallic Wars*, Tacitus' *Annals* and *Agricola*, Suetonius' *Twelve Caesars*, Dio's *Roman History*, and a few others. The most convenient sourcebook for anyone seeking to find out more is Stanley Ireland's *Roman Britain: A Sourcebook* which features, in translation only, a litany of original sources for Roman Britain including texts, inscriptions and coins. Many of the historical texts are also available in the Penguin Classics series, though this does not include Dio for the period concerned. Nevertheless, there is no real substitute for the Loeb Classical Library and its inimitable series of volumes featuring the Greek or Latin text and a parallel translation. The internet has made texts like Bede's *Life of St Cuthbert* and others easily accessible; inscriptions are also becoming accessible this way, a useful source being http://db.edcs.eu/epigr/epi_en.php (at the time of writing).

What becomes rapidly apparent to anyone studying the epigraphic sources in more depth and, better still, examining the original material is how much work has been done to deal with the very real difficulties caused by damaged, incomplete or ambiguous inscriptions. Roman inscriptions tend to be heavily abbreviated, often to save space. Roman writing tablets frequently feature phenomenally abstruse texts where even word divisions are sometimes difficult to identify, let alone letter forms; few are complete and many are almost impossible to read. The result can *in extremis* be a text that defies conclusive interpretation even when the original slab or document survives more or less intact. Others are simply tantalizingly incomplete, requiring a speculative restored text to make sense of what has survived. Without the work done to date, the entire subject would be a shadow of its current self.

Nonetheless, there is no doubt that some scholars have perhaps been on occasion rather too confident that their readings and restorations are correct. The result has sometimes been that very precise assumptions are formed which become commonly accepted as facts. The case of the Classicianus tombstone is one of the best examples. Roger Tomlin's 1995 reassessment of the inscriptions found up till 1955 and published by Collingwood and Wright in 1965 showed that many were more ambiguous than at first had been assumed and that other readings are often possible, given the abbreviations and formulae used. *RIB* 162 at Bath, originally read as recording the death of an infant girl called Mercatilla, is a very good example. Apart from the single word *alumna* ('foster daughter') every other word requires expansion and despite the brevity of the text, indeed perhaps because of the brevity, it can be read several different ways.

The Vindolanda tablets

It would be as well to discuss the Vindolanda writing tablets more specifically. Much is made of these celebrated documents but it would be an enormous mistake to believe that the archive is a voluminous series of lucid, detailed and conclusive texts. The reality is that most of the Vindolanda tablets are very fragmentary and many amount to little more than perfunctory, damaged and incomplete lists. They are usually exceptionally difficult to read and have relied for their interpretation on experts who have themselves often had to make assumptions or inferences about missing words and other difficulties of comprehension. These problems are compounded by the fact that the Roman writers of the tablets seem to have been often little more concerned about Latin grammar than the proverbial schoolchildren of more recent centuries.

Moreover, most of the Vindolanda tablets belong to a very short time in Romano-British history, essentially from the mid-90s to around ten years later. For the most part they are the surviving remnants of an attempt to burn an archive, probably when the resident unit was moved on. They are thus literally no more than vignettes, mere glimpses, and we cannot really know how representative they are. With all due respect to the scholars who have been privileged to work on the tablets and undoubtedly done sterling work, it is a fact that much of what has been published has to be taken by the rest of us in good faith and on trust. In some cases different readings or refinements of interpretation may well be made in time.

ABBREVIATIONS

AE	*L'Année épigraphique* (Paris, 1888–). Some of this material is now available on the internet from the same source as *ILS* below.
Britannia	A journal of Romano-British and Kindred Studies published by the Society for the Promotion of Roman Studies, 1970 and later. Note that volume numbers are in Roman format up to volume XL, and from 41 on in Arabic.
CIL	*Corpus Inscriptionum Latinarum* (Berlin, 1863–) in sixteen volumes. Some of this material is now available on the internet from the same source as *ILS* below.
ILS	*Inscriptionum Latinae Selectae*, ed. H. Dessau (3 vols, Berlin, 1892–1916). Now available on the internet with full search facilities at http://db.edcs.eu/epigr/epi_en.php.
JRS	*Journal of Roman Studies*, published by the Society for the Promotion of Roman Studies.
RCHM London	*Royal Commission on Historical Monuments (England): An Inventory of the Historical Monuments in London, Volume III: Roman London* (His Majesty's Stationery Office, London, 1928).
RCHM York	*Royal Commission on Historical Monuments (England): An Inventory of the Historical Monuments in York, Volume I: Eburacum, Roman York* (Her Majesty's Stationery Office, London, 1962).
RIB	*The Roman Inscriptions of Britain*: see Collingwood and Wright (1965), numbers 1–2314 revised by Tomlin in a 2nd edn (1995); for inscriptions reported 1995–2006 see Tomlin, Wright and Hassall (2009), numbers 3001–3550, and for non-stone inscriptions see Frere and others (1990 and later dates, see Select Bibliography), numbers 2401–2505. Note that stone inscriptions are also available online at http://db.edcs.eu/epigr/epi_en.php.
SHA	*Scriptores Historiae Augustae*, available in the Loeb Classics Series, Harvard University Press, vols I and II; also in translation, *The Lives of the Later Caesars*, trans. A. Birley (Penguin Classics).
Tab. Vindol.	Bowman and Thomas (1994 and 2003).

NOTES

Introduction

1. This man was either a member of the senatorial family of the Atilii (Ateilius is simply a variant spelling) or one of their freedmen himself. Part of the Latin text is ambiguous, hence the variant reading.
2. *CIL* 6.9545.
3. McCarthy (2013).
4. One curse tablet from Bath may be a transliteration of a Celtic text.
5. *Select Papyri* 112 (this can be found in the Loeb series No. 206, *Select Papyri*, vol. I).For Regina, see pp. 129 ff, for Lossio. Veda, see p. 127, and for Similis see *RIB* 192.
6. Virgil, *Eclogues* 1.66; Catullus 11.
7. Tacitus, *Agricola* 11.
8 *RIB* 236.
9. *RIB* 363.
10. *RIB* 373 and 375.
11. *RIB* 3061 and 3071.
12. *RIB* 684.
13. Richard Dawkins in *Unweaving the Rainbow* (2006) elegantly makes the point about the extraordinary odds against any one of us being born.

Chapter 1 Cold Contact: The Coming of Caesar, 55 BC–AD 41

1. Caesar, *Gallic War* 5.12ff.
2. Diodorus Siculus 5.22.
3. Strabo, *Geography* 4.5.1ff.
4. Cassius Dio 40.1.
5. Cassius Dio 39.53.
6. Cicero, *Letters to Quintus* 2.16.4.
7. Cicero, *Letters to Quintus* 3.1.13.
8. Caesar, *Gallic War* 4.33.
9. Cicero, *Letters to Quintus* 3.1.

10. Augustus, *Res Gestae* 32.
11. Cassius Dio 53.22.5, 25.2.
12. Stead (1967).
13. Priest and Clay (n.d.)
14. See for example Cunliffe (2012), 350.
15. Cunliffe (2012), 353.
16. Suetonius, *Caligula* 44.
17. Cassius Dio 60.19.1. Those who wish to pursue Verica in more depth may find Henig (2002) an interesting trawl.
18. The Romans utilized many old tribal centres, or nearby locations, as places in which to establish towns to serve as centres of local government for a tribal area or *civitas*. Named for the tribe involved, these civitas capitals were equipped with public buildings on a Roman model such as a forum and basilica. The process allowed the Roman government to delegate local administration to existing elite groups and thus incorporate them into the Roman system, rather than alienating them.
19. See *British Archaeology* (July/August 2014), 41, where this piece is illustrated.
20. The vast majority of known coins abbreviate the names to TINC, TINCOM and EPPI or EPPIL.
21. Augustus, *Res Gestae* 32. Usually given as 'Tincommius' but the name is damaged. This old reconstruction of the name is now known from coins found in the Alton Hoard in 1996 to be wrong, and should read 'Tincomarus'.

Chapter 2 Quislings and Rebels, AD 41–61

1. Suetonius, *Claudius* 26.2.
2. Birley (1979), 35.
3. Thirty-four were found originally, and three more seem to have been found separately. Robertson (2000), 6, no. 22. A gold aureus was the highest value coin normally available in the Roman world. An ordinary legionary earned the equivalent of 9 aurei per annum at this date.
4. *ILS* 2648.
5. The tombstone of Lucius Valerius Geminus, a veteran of II Augusta, found at Alchester may be evidence that the II Legion was based there at some point (*RIB* 3121). See chapter 3.
6. Barley (1983), 96–7.
7. Horace, *Odes* 1.4.1.
8. *RIB* 200.
9. *RIB* 3121.
10. In the Roman social hierarchy, families of senatorial status came first and had wealth equivalent to 1 million sesterces. Equestrians came second and had wealth equivalent to 400,000 sesterces. Equestrians usually rose to serve in a number of senior administrative posts as prefects or procurators.
11. *ILS* 2696.
12. The name can also be read as Longinus, son of Sdapezematygus.
13. *RIB* 201.
14. *RIB* 159.
15. Tacitus, *Agricola* 12.
16. Cartimandua's tale can be pieced together from Tacitus: *Histories* 3.45, *Annals* 12.36, 40, *Agricola* 17.
17. Caratacus' story can be pieced together from Cassius Dio 60.20 and Tacitus, *Annals* 12.33–8.
18. *RIB* 294.
19. *Agricola* 14 and *RIB* 91.

20. Roller (2003), pp. 1–3.
21. Sear (1982), 549, no. 5573.
22. See Tomlin (1995) in Collingwood and Wright (1995), 758; *-dumnus* and *-dubnus* are entirely interchangeable – there is no significance in the differences between Tacitus and the Chichester inscription.
23. *RIB* 92.
24. Russell and Manley (2013).
25. See chapter 4.
26. *Britannia* XXVII (1996), 455, no. 48; *RIB* 21.
27. Petronius, *Satyricon* 71.
28. See Tiberius Claudius Paulinus, chapter 6 below.
29. *RIB* 219.
30. *RIB* 2404.7–10 (Mendips), 2404.41–5 (Derbyshire).
31. For example, *RIB* 2404.47 (Protus), 2404.51 (Abascantus), 2404.59 (anonymous partnership).
32. See Tomlin's note to *RIB* 3121 in Tomlin, Wright and Hassall (2009), 128.
33. *RIB* 620.
34. *RIB* 621.
35. *RIB* 639.
36. Caesar, *Gallic War* 6.16.

Chapter 3 Roman Britain's Boom Years, AD 61–161

1. Tacitus, *Annals* 14.33.
2. Tacitus, *Annals* 14.38.
3. *RIB* 12.
4. Tacitus, *Annals* 11.23–24.
5. In RCHM London (1928), 171, no. 6.
6. Grasby and Tomlin (2002) have produced a plausible reconstruction of the complete text.
7. Tacitus, *Annals* 3.42.1ff.
8. Tacitus, *Annals* 14.38–9.
9. Cassius Dio 63.22.1ff.
10. *RIB* 2491.82. The name Boduacus shares its prefix with Boduogenus; see the skillet maker below in this chapter.
11. *RIB* 2491.147.
12. See Caecilius Musicus the freedman in chapter 6.
13. *RIB* 2490.6.
14. *RIB* 707.
15. See chapter 6 and the story of Tiberius Claudius Paulinus.
16. *RIB* 2487.1, 2, 3 and 6.
17. *RIB* 2488.1.
18. *RIB* 250, 674, 3201. The Vindolanda man is recorded on *Tab. Vindol.* II.299. Interestingly, Volusia Faustina also appears as the name of a slave woman who buried her husband, the surveyor Helicus, in Rome. Clearly names with imperial associations could be held by persons of the least exalted status. *CIL* 6.9620.
19. *RIB* 87. A kinsman of his also made a dedication to Hercules at Silchester recorded on another inscription (*RIB* 67), reinforcing the impression that this was a prominent Silchester family.
20. Tacitus, *Agricola* 21.
21. Tomlin (2003).
22. A writing tablet from Pompeii (*CIL* 4.3340.155) refers to the sale of slaves 'on 13th December next . . . at Pompeii in the Forum publicly in the daytime'.
23. *RIB* 2443.7.

24. See the remarkable tale of the ransomed slave woman bought back by the centurion Cocceius Firmus in chapter 4.
25. See in chapter 6, for example, the interesting question of the villa at Yewden.
26. *RIB* 21.
27. *RIB* 3014.
28. *RIB* 678.
29. Marsden (1980), 129.
30. *RIB* 2414.37.
31. *RIB* 274.
32. Sozomen, *Ecclesiastical History* 2.4.
33. *RIB* 2503.127.
34. *RIB* 9.
35. *RIB* 2501.172.
36. *RIB* 2501.307.
37. de la Bédoyère (1988), 46, and fig. 36.
38. Bennett (1978), 393–4.
39. Hull (1963), passim but especially pp. 20ff.
40. Tyers (1996), 132.
41. Rivet and Smith (1979), 463.
42. Castle (1978), 388.
43. *Aeneid* 5.369ff.; *Iliad* 5.9ff.
44. Rivet and Smith (1979), 494.
45. *RIB* 2504.29.
46. Tomlin (2011), 446.
47. *RIB* 152.

Chapter 4 Life on the Frontier

1. *Britannia* XXIII (1992), 147.
2. *RIB* 526.
3. *RIB* 2213.
4. Plutarch, *Moralia* 419e; *RIB* 662–3.
5. Tacitus, *Agricola* 30–2.
6. Suetonius, *Domitian* 10.
7. *RIB* 2334, generally condemned as a forgery but not by all – since the stone cannot be located the arguments are unresolvable.
8. Henig and Nash (1982). Amminus may be derived from Adminius, the name of a son of Cunbelinus, exiled during Caligula's reign (37–41). For Togidubnus, see chapter 2.
9. Russell (2006).
10. See for example Magilton (2013).
11. Tacitus, *Germania* 2.
12. *Tab. Vindol.* II.164.
13. *Tab. Vindol.* II.310.
14. *RIB* 369. See chapter 6.
15. *Tab. Vindol.* II.343.
16. *RIB* 2445.6.
17. Cassius Dio 56.20.
18. Quoted in Adkins (2003), 84.
19. *Tab. Vindol.* II.291.
20. *Tab Vindol.* II.118 with *Aeneid* 9.473.
21. *RIB* 2491.14.
22. See the Aelia Severa story in chapter 6.
23. *Tab. Vindol.* II.233.
24. See Bollihope Common, chapter 6.

25. *ILS* 2926 (Aquinum).
26. Juvenal, *Satires* 2.161.
27. *RIB* 816.
28. Birley (1979), 63.
29. *RIB* 2401.1.
30. *RIB* 2401.11.
31. This information is recorded on a diploma: *CIL* 16.49.
32. *AE* 1956.249.
33. *CIL* 16.160.
34. See Birley (1979), 103.
35. *SHA* Hadrian 10–11.
36. *SHA* Hadrian 11.2, '*in qua multa correxit*'.
37. *SHA* Hadrian 5.2
38. The word used is *divideret*; it means something more forceful than the literal English equivalent 'divide'.
39. Recorded on a military diploma found in Hungary, *CIL* 16.69, which had been owned by an auxiliary veteran discharged in Britain by Nepos' predecessor Quintus Pompeius Falco by that year. The diploma gives a date of 17 July 122 and states that the units listed are currently under the command of Nepos in Britain.
40. *ILS* 2726.
41. *RIB* 2426.1.
42. *RIB* 1340.
43. *RIB* 66.
44. See Bassus/Bassianus at Beauport Park in chapter 6.
45. *RIB* 2401.8.
46. For example *Tab. Vindol.* III.581, line 96, *adventu consularis*, 'on the coming of the (pro) consular', i.e. a man who had served as consul.
47. *RIB* 1347.
48. *RIB* 1415, 1879, 1972–3.
49. *RIB* 1442.
50. *RIB* 1431.
51. Quintilian 11.3.8; Cicero, *Republic* 2.10.20, *Laws* 1.1.3.
52. *RIB* 2491.96.
53. *RIB* 2034, *ob res trans vallum prospere gestas*.
54. *SHA* Antoninus Pius 5.4.
55. *RIB* 2160.
56. *RIB* 2182.
57. *RIB* 2174–7; Justinian, *Digest* 49.15.6.
58. *RIB* 2183.
59. *RIB* 2409.36. It is conceivable that the die was a souvenir owned in antiquity and thus came from Italy or Gaul, but there is no special reason to doubt its authenticity as a Romano-British find.
60. Pausanias 8.43.3–4. The description is cryptic and ambiguous and may be confused with trouble elsewhere in the Empire.
61. *SHA* Marcus Aurelius 8.7–8.
62. *RIB* 2142.
63. *RIB* 1322.
64. *Britannia* 45 (2014) 434, no. 4. For another engineer, see p. 101. The expansion Elius Taominus is approximately paralleled by Elius Feluminus on *RIB* 2324. This stone, although genuinely ancient, was probably imported to Britain in modern times and is thus of unknown provenance. For Egyptian Tao- names, see the Loeb Classical Library *Select Papyri* volume I, p. 219, and volume II, pp. 353, 495. However, the name may simply be unique.

Chapter 5 Gods and Goddesses

1. *RIB* 3149. Sextius is restored from SEXT in *RIB*, where the alternative possibility, Sextilius, is also considered. If so, *RIB* notes that this man might be one and the same with Sextilius Marcianus, *primus pilus* (senior centurion) with the XXII Legion at Mainz in the year 192. The latter records that he was formerly a centurion with the X[. . .] Legion, perhaps XX (*CIL* xiii 6728).
2. *RIB* 1920.
3. *RIB* 2501.156.
4. *RIB* 2443.13.
5. Herodian (1.12.1) specifically blamed its impact on Rome because of the overcrowding and the movement of peoples. The plague's recurrence was also referred to by Cassius Dio (73.14.3–4, not Book 72 as cited in many sources erroneously; it can be found on p. 101 of volume IX in the Loeb series of Dio's history), killing up to 2,000 daily in Rome in 189.
6. The reasons for this are discussed by Tomlin (2013), 390, n. 24.
7. Ammianus Marcellinus 23.6.24.
8. *RIB* 3001.
9. *RIB* 2091 See also the recently discovered altar of Eltaominus, an engineer at Binchester, below, p. 93.
10. *RIB* 627.
11. *RIB* 1534.
12. Various names are listed from *RIB* 1522 onward.
13. *RIB* 1329.
14. *Britannia* XXXV (2004), 344–5.
15. *RIB* 1124, 1129.
16. *RIB* 3151.
17. *RIB* 758.
18. *RIB* 1545.
19. Quintilian, *Institutes* 2.17.21 and 11.1.61ff.
20. Virgil, *Aeneid* 5.123.
21. Rivet and Smith (1979), 372.
22. *RIB* 1600.
23. *RIB* 1599.
24. Sauer in Goldsworthy and Haynes (1999), 53.
25. *RIB* 143–4.
26. *RIB* 156.
27. *RIB* 3170 and also 3171.
28. *RIB* 3180.
29. *RIB* 3053.
30. *RIB* 164.
31. *RIB* 162. Although Mercatilla is a possible expansion for the child's name and is cited in some works, there are other possibilities such as Mercuria (Tomlin, 1995, 760, correcting Collingwood and Wright, who also observes that if MAGNI is a man's name then it must be Magnus, not Magnius as originally thought).
32. *RIB* 140, 149.
33. *RIB* 151 and 105 respectively.
34. Cunliffe (1988), p. 114, no. 5
35. Cunliffe (1988), p. 122, no. 10.
36. Cunliffe (1988), p. 226, no. 94.
37. Cunliffe (1988), p. 146, no. 30.
38. *RIB* 3049.
39. R.S.O. Tomlin in Woodward and Leach (1993), 113–30, citing five exemplar tablets. Others have been published sporadically in *Britannia* since then.
40. See M.W.C. Hassall and R.S.O. Tomlin in *Britannia* XXVI (1995), 376–8, nos 3 and 4.

41. See Tiberinius Celerianus in chapter 3 above.
42. Cunliffe (1988), p. 128, no. 14.
43. Cunliffe (1988), p. 232, no. 98.
44. Johns (1997).
45. *RIB* 712.

Chapter 6 Death, Disruption and Decline in the Third Century

1. *RIB* 1234; see also Cassius Dio 79.14.1–5.
2. *ILS* 2089.
3. Caesar, *Gallic War* 5.14.
4. Cassius Dio 77.16.5.
5. Tacitus, *Annals* 12.37. The story is discussed in chapter 2.
6. Cassius Dio 78.1 and Herodian 3.15.4.
7. B.C. Burnham, 'Roman Britain in 2005', *Britannia* XXXVII (2006), 394.
8. *SHA* Caracalla 5.1–3. The name of Gaius Julius Marcus survives only on *RIB* 2298, and 997 (partial).
9. *RIB* 369.
10. Pliny the Elder, *Natural History* 34.17
11. *RIB* 311.
12. *RIB* 1280.
13. *CIL* 13.362; see also R. Saller, 'The Family and Society', in Bodel (2012).
14. *RIB* 179.
15. *RIB* 3036.
16. *RIB* 3031.
17. *RIB* 1091, 1092.
18. *RIB* 191.
19. Claudian, *Panegyric to Stilicho* 2. Claudian's Britain, for all its ethnic identity, was seeking Roman protection.
20. *RIB* 683.
21. *RIB* 685.
22. *RIB* 1065.
23. The Tigris unit is listed in the *Notitia Dignitatum*, a late Roman listing of military units most easily accessed in Rivet and Smith (1979), 256. They, however, do not offer a conclusive translation of *Arbeia*.
24. *RIB* 1171.
25. *RIB* 155.
26. Cassius Dio 68.7.4.
27. *Imagines clipeatae*, 'shield portraits', were an established Roman stylistic convention often used to depict esteemed ancestors. The person's head and shoulders protrude from a circular frame.
28. As cited in the BBC2 television programme *Digging for Britain* (2010 and 2011) involving Dr Simon Mays and colleagues.
29. *RIB* 1041.
30. *RIB* 1042.
31. *Britannia* 42 (2011), 343.
32. *Britannia* VIII (1977), 430, no. 18.
33. *ILS* 4751.
34. *RIB* 2495.1, where '*vrit*' is rejected for the reasons cited but no meaningful alternative is offered, implying that the word must mean something else that no one has ever heard of. Conversely, Birley (1979, 136) accepts *vrit* without a murmur.
35. Ovid, *Metamorphoses* 10.296.
36. *RIB* 653.

37. *JRS* XI (1921), 102. A facsimile is displayed at the British Museum.
38. *RIB* 3027.
39. A further 23 coins were subsequently reported from the site, bringing the total to over 2,600.
40. Abdy, Brunning and Webster (2001).
41. Robertson (2000), 103–4, no. 470.
42. *RIB* 605.
43. *RIB* 1883, 1885, 1886.
44. *RIB* 2232, 2224–6.
45. *RIB* 3218.
46. Body no. 305, see C. Wells, 'The Human Remains', in McWhirr, Viner and Wells (1982), 171.
47. Tacitus, *Annals* 14.7.
48. *RIB* 2441.7; RCHM York, 135 no. 149.
49. Juvenal, *Satires* 3.278–301.
50. Crow (2004), 78.
51. Constantius, *Life of St Germanus*; Gildas 10–11; Bede, *Ecclesiastical History* 1.7.
52. Cary and Scullard (1975), 547.
53. *RIB* 3045.
54. Burial 4 at Neatham, see Millett and Graham (1986), 58.
55. Millett and Graham (1986), 130, no. 491.
56. Mountford (2014).
57. Reece in Price (2000), 205–9.
58. Corney (2003), 15.
59. *Aeneid* 5.262; *Eclogues* 4.6–7; de la Bédoyère (1998).
60. *RIB* 2291.
61. *RIB* 2291.
62. The reader is advised to consult Burdette (2008), pp. 136–9 for remarkable tales of modern hoards of American silver dollars and the documented eccentricities of the hoarders. The Diary of Samuel Pepys also contains a farcical attempt both to hoard coins and then recover them which would be totally impossible to extrapolate from any find of a coin hoard (13 and 19 June, 10 October 1667).
63. *RIB* 1912.

Chapter 7 Roman Britain's High Summer, AD 307–410

1. Ausonius, *Epigrams* 107–12.
2. *RIB* 2053.
3. Egerton Phillimore, ed., 'Pedigrees from Jesus College MS. 20', *Y Cymmrodor* (Honourable Society of Cymmrodorion) VIII (1887), 83–92.
4. *RIB* 103. In fact the surviving text reads no more than CIVIS R(. . .).
5. Ammianus Marcellinus 14.5.6–8.
6. Neal (1974), 6 and 103.
7. Mars Nodens (sometimes called Mars Nodons) is also attested on inscriptions found at Cockersand Moss in Lancashire (*RIB* 616–17).
8. *RIB* 2448.3.
9. Pausanias 2.27.
10. Wheeler (1932), 100.
11. *RIB* 305.
12. Rivet and Smith (1979), 499.
13. Davey and Ling (1981), 106–10.
14. See Cosh and Neal (2005), 257.
15. Barrett (1978), 308–9.

16. Sidonius, *Letters* 2.2.6 (Loeb edition, vol. I, pp. 422–3).
17. The various theories are outlined by Cosh and Neal (2009), part 1, 266–7.
18. Most notably by Thomas (1998, 2003).
19. *RIB* 2448.7.
20. Barrett (1978), 312.
21. Sidonius, *Letters* 2.2.7.
22. Thomas (1998), 50.
23. See the brilliant review by McKee and McKee (2002) which systematically and logically dismantles the theories.
24. *RIB* 2448.8; Cosh and Neal (2005), 134ff.
25. *RIB* 2448.9.
26. *RIB* 2448.11.
27. Cosh and Neal (2009), part 1, 246, citing Cunliffe (2003).
28. Cosh and Neal (2010), pp. 394–5. The mosaic is also illustrated in *Current Archaeology*, no. 157 (1998) on the front cover.
29. The treasure is fully published in Johns and Potter (1983).
30. Horace, *Odes* 3.18.
31. Virgil, *Aeneid* 7.86–8.
32. B. Mason, 'The Prophet of Gases', *Science Now Daily News*, 2 October 2006.
33. Johns and Potter (1983), 73.
34. *RIB* 2420.33–4.
35. *RIB* 2414.5–6.
36. *RIB* 2414.1.
37. *RIB* 2414.2.
38. *RIB* 955.

Chapter 8 Looking Back on the World of Giants, AD 410 and After

1. The sources for Patrick are itemized in the *Oxford Dictionary of the Christian Church* (1957), 1026.
2. Johns (2010), 201.
3. Hobbs (2006), 44–45.
4. *RIB* 3171.
5. Wright and Jackson (1968).
6. Bede, *Life of St Cuthbert* 27.
7. Gerald of Wales (Giraldus Cambrensis), *Itinerary through Wales*, ch. 5: 'thermas insignes, templorum reliquias, et loca theatralia'.
8. Dowson (2008).
9. Virgil, *Aeneid* 6.743.

SELECT BIBLIOGRAPHY

The entries in this bibliography are divided into two sections. The first part covers the principal sources for the texts of inscriptions from Roman Britain. There is so much literature available on Roman Britain that the remaining bibliography is largely restricted to books specifically referred to in the text; there is no intention here to create a definitive general list.

Classical references

The reader will notice that throughout the book a number of references are made to classical authors such as Tacitus or Ammianus Marcellinus. Anyone wishing to follow these up will find the texts are generally available in the Loeb Classical Library series published by Harvard University Press; these feature the Latin or Greek text on the left page and the English on the right. Some, for example Tacitus, are easily available in translation in the Penguin Classics series. However, it is often much easier these days to find the texts online, for example on the LacusCurtius website provided by the University of Chicago. As is the normal convention the references in this book feature the long-established numerical subsections of each ancient text which are applicable to any edition, online or print, and will enable the reader to identity each of the references made here in their original context.

Inscriptions and writing tablets

Bowman, A.K. (2004) *Life and Letters on the Roman Frontier: Vindolanda and its People*, London.

Bowman, A.K., and Thomas, J.D. (1994) *The Vindolanda Writing-Tablets (Tabulae Vindolandenses II)*, London. The most important letters also cited in Bowman (2004).

Bowman, A.K., and Thomas, J.D. (2003) *The Vindolanda Writing-Tablets (Tabulae Vindolandenses III)*, London. The most important letters also cited in Bowman (2004).

Collingwood, R.G., and Wright, R.P. (1965, 1995) *The Roman Inscriptions of Britain, Volume I: Inscriptions on Stone*; 2nd edn 1995 with 'Addenda and Corrigenda' by R.S.O. Tomlin, Stroud. This is the definitive publication of inscribed slabs, altars and so on. Hadrian's Wall and associated sites are represented on pp. 349–649 inclusive. For indexes to this work, see Goodburn and Waugh (1983) below.

Frere, S.S., Roxan, M., and Tomlin, R.S.O., eds (1990) *The Roman Inscriptions of Britain, Volume II, Fascicule 1: The Military Diplomata etc. (RIB 2401–2411)*, Stroud.

Frere, S.S., and Tomlin, R.S.O., eds (1991) *The Roman Inscriptions of Britain, Volume II, Fascicule 2: Weights, Metal Vessels, etc. (RIB 2412–2420)*, Stroud.

Frere, S.S., and Tomlin, R.S.O., eds (1991) *The Roman Inscriptions of Britain, Volume II, Fascicule 3: Jewellery, Armour, etc. (RIB 2421–2441)*, Stroud.

Frere, S.S., and Tomlin, R.S.O., eds (1992) *The Roman Inscriptions of Britain, Volume II, Fascicule 4: Wooden Barrels, Tile Stamps, etc. (RIB 2442–2480)*, Stroud.

Frere, S.S., and Tomlin, R.S.O., eds (1993) *The Roman Inscriptions of Britain, Volume II, Fascicule 5: Tile Stamps of the Classis Britannica; Imperial, Procuratorial and Civic Tile-Stamps; Stamps of Private Tilers; Inscriptions on Relief-Patterned Tiles and Graffiti on Tiles (RIB 2481–2491)*, Stroud.

Frere, S.S., and Tomlin, R.S.O., eds (1995) *The Roman Inscriptions of Britain, Volume II, Fascicule 7: Graffiti on Samian Ware (Terra Sigillata) (RIB 2501)*, Stroud.

Frere, S.S., and Tomlin, R.S.O., eds (1995) *The Roman Inscriptions of Britain, Volume II, Fascicule 8: Graffiti on Coarse Pottery; Stamps on Coarse Pottery; Addenda and Corrigenda to Fascicules 1–8 (RIB 2502–2505)*, Stroud.

Goodburn, R., and Waugh, H. (1983) *The Roman Inscriptions of Britain, Volume* I: *Inscriptions on Stone, Epigraphic Indexes*, Gloucester.

Maxfield, V., and Dobson, B. (2006) *Inscriptions of Roman Britain, Lactor 4* (4th edn), London. A selection of Romano-British written records which includes Vindolanda tablets, diplomas, and stone inscriptions.

Tomlin, R.S.O. (1995) 'Addenda and Corrigenda', in Collingwood and Wright (1995).

Tomlin, R.S.O. (2011) 'Inscriptions', *Britannia* 42, 446–7.

Tomlin, R.S.O. (2013) 'Inscriptions', *Britannia* 44, 390.

Tomlin, R.S.O., Wright, R.P., and Hassall, M.W.C. (2009) *The Roman Inscriptions of Britain, Volume III: Inscriptions on Stone Found or Notified between 1 January 1955 and 31 December 2006*, Oxford.

General works

Abdy, R., Brunning, R.A., and Webster, C.J. (2001) 'The Discovery of a Roman Villa at Shapwick and its Severan Hoard of 9,238 Silver *Denarii*', *Journal of Roman Archaeology* 14, 358ff.

Adkins, L. (2003) *Empires of the Plains: Henry Rawlinson and the Lost Languages of Babylon*, Harper Perennial, London.

Barley, N. (1983) *The Innocent Anthropologist*, Penguin, London.

Barrett, A. (1978) 'The Literary Classics in Roman Britain', *Britannia IX*, 307–14.

Bennett, J. (1978) 'A Further Vessel by the Aldgate-Pulborough Potter', *Britannia IX*, 393–4.

Birley, A. (1979) *The People of Roman Britain*, Batsford, London.

Bodel, J., ed. (2012) *Epigraphic History: Ancient History from Inscriptions*, Routledge, London.

Burdette, R.W. (2008) *A Guide Book of Peace Dollars*, Whitman, Atlanta.

Castle, S.A. (1978) 'Amphorae from Brockley Hill', *Britannia IX*, 383–392.

Corney, M. (2003) *The Roman Villa at Bradford on Avon*, Ex Libris, Bradford on Avon.

Cosh, S.R., and Neal, D.S. (2002) *Roman Mosaics of Britain, Volume I: Northern Britain*, Society of Antiquaries, London.

Cosh, S.R., and Neal, D.S. (2005) *Roman Mosaics of Britain, Volume II: South-West Britain*, Society of Antiquaries, London.

Cosh, S.R., and Neal, D.S. (2009) *Roman Mosaics of Britain, Volume III: South-East Britain*, Society of Antiquaries, London.

Cosh, S.R., and Neal, D.S. (2010) *Roman Mosaics of Britain, Volume IV: Western Britain*, Society of Antiquaries, London.

Crow, J. (2004) *Housesteads: A Fort and Garrison on Hadrian's Wall*, Tempus, Stroud.

Cunliffe, B.W. (1988) *The Temple of Sulis Minerva at Bath, Volume II: The Finds from the Sacred Spring*, Oxford University Committee for Archaeology Monograph No. 16, Oxford.

Cunliffe, B.W. (2003) 'Roman Danebury', *Current Archaeology* 188, 344–51.

Cunliffe, B.W. (2012) *Britain Begins*, Oxford University Press, Oxford.

Cunliffe, B., and Davenport, P. (1985) *The Temple of Sulis Minerva at Bath, Volume 1: The Site*, Oxford University Committee for Archaeology Monograph No. 7, Oxford.

Davey, N., and Ling, R. (1981) *Wall-Painting in Roman Britain*, Britannia Monograph Series, No. 3, Society for the Promotion of Roman Studies, London.

de la Bédoyère, G. (1988) *Samian Ware*, Shire, Aylesbury.

de la Bédoyère, G. (1998) 'Carausius and the Marks RSR and INPCDA', *Numismatic Chronicle* 158, 79–88.

de la Bédoyère, G. (2003) *Defying Rome: The Rebels of Roman Britain*, Tempus, Stroud.

de la Bédoyère, G. (2013) *Roman Britain: A New History*, Thames & Hudson, London.

Dowson, J. (2008) *Old Albany*, Albany Chamber of Commerce and Industry, Albany, Western Australia.

Goldsworthy, A., and Haynes, I., eds (1999) *The Roman Army as a Community*, Journal of Roman Archaeology Supplementary Series No. 34, Portsmouth, Rhode Island.

Grasby, R.D., and Tomlin, R.S.O. (2002) 'The Sepuchral Monument of the Procurator C. Julius Classicianus', *Britannia* XXXIII, 43–76.

Henig, M. (2002) *The Heirs of King Verica*, Tempus, Stroud.

Henig, M., and Nash, D. (1982) 'Amminus and the Kingdom of Verica', *Oxford Journal of Archaeology* 1.2, 243–6.

Higgins, C. (2013) *Under Another Sky*, Jonathan Cape, London.

Hobbs, R. (2006) *Late Roman Precious Metal Deposits c.* AD *200–700: Changes over Time and Space*, Archaeopress, Oxford.

Hull, M.R. (1963) *The Roman Potters' Kilns of Colchester*, Report of the Research Committee of the Society of Antiquaries of London No. XXI, Society of Antiquaries, London.

Ireland, S. (1986) *Roman Britain: A Sourcebook*, Croom Helm, London.

Johns, C. (1997) *The Snettisham Roman Jeweller's Hoard*, British Museum, London.

Johns, C. (2010) *The Hoxne Late Roman Treasure*, British Museum, London.

Johns, C., and Potter, T. (1983) *The Thetford Treasure: Roman Jewellery and Silver*, British Museum, London.

Kent, J.P.C., and Painter, K.S. (1977) *Wealth of the Roman World* AD *300–700*, British Museum, London.

McCarthy, M. (2013) 'Where is the Romano-British Peasant?', *British Archaeology* (November–December), 47–9.

McKee, H., and McKee, J. (2002) 'Counter Arguments and Numerical Patterns in Early Celtic Inscriptions: A Re-examination of *Christian Celts: Messages and Images*', *Medieval Archaeology* XLVI, 29–40.

McWhirr, A., Viner, L., and Wells, C. (1982) *Cirencester Excavations II: Romano-British Cemeteries at Cirencester*, Cirencester Excavations Committee, Cirencester.

Magilton, J. (2013) '*RIB* I, 2334: An Alleged Inscription from Chichester Reconsidered', *Britannia* 44, 85–92.

Marsden, P. (1980) *Roman London*, Thames & Hudson, London.

Meates, Lt-Col. G.W. (1979) *The Lullingstone Roman Villa, Kent, Volume I: The Site*, Kent Archaeological Society, Maidstone.

Millett, M., and Graham, D. (1986) *Excavations on the Romano-British Small Town at Neatham, Hampshire 1969–1979*, Hampshire Field Club, Gloucester.

Moorhead, S., and Stuttard, D. (2012) *The Romans Who Shaped Britain*, Thames & Hudson, London.

Mountford, L. (2014) 'The Remains of Romano-Britons', *British Archaeology*, no. 135 (March–April), 22–5.

Neal, D.S. (1974) *The Excavation of the Roman Villa in Gadebridge Park, Hemel Hempstead 1963–8*, Society of Antiquaries, London.

Painter, K.S. (1977) *The Mildenhall Treasure*, British Museum, London.

Price, E. (2000) *Frocester: A Romano-British Settlement, Its Antecedents and Successors*, Gloucester and District Archaeological Research Group, Stonehouse.

Priest, V., and Clay, P. (n.d.) *The East Leicestershire Hoard*, University of Leicester, Leicester.

Rivet, A.L.F., and Smith, C. (1979) *The Place-Names of Roman Britain*, Batsford, London.

Robertson, A.S. (2000) *An Inventory of Romano-British Coin Hoards*, Royal Numismatic Society Special Publication 20, London.

Roller, Duane W. (2003) *The World of Juba II and Kleopatra Selene*, Routledge, London.

Russell, M. (2006) *Roman Sussex*, History Press, Stroud.

Russell, M., and Manley, H. (2013) 'Finding Nero: Shining a New Light on Romano-British Sculpture', *Internet Archaeology* 32 (http://dx.doi.org/10.11141/ia.32.5).

Sauer, E. (1999) 'The Augustan Army Spa at Bourbonne-les-Bains', in Goldsworthy and Haynes (1999).

Sear, D.R. (1982) *Greek Imperial Coins*, Seaby, London.

Stead, I.M. (1967) 'A La Tène III Burial at Welwyn Garden City', *Archaeologia* 101, 1–62.

Thomas, C. (1998, 2003) *Christian Celts: Messages and Images*; 2nd edn 2003, Tempus, Stroud.

Tomlin, R.S.O. (2003) 'The Girl in Question: A New Text from Roman London', *Britannia* XXXIV, 41–51.

Tyers, P. (1996) *Roman Pottery in Britain*, Batsford, London.

Wedlake, W.J. (1982) *The Excavation of the Shrine of Apollo at Nettleton, Wiltshire, 1956–1971*, Society of Antiquaries, London.

Wheeler, R.E.M. (1932) *Report on the Excavation of the Prehistoric, Roman, and Post-Roman Site in Lydney Park, Gloucestershire*, Research Report of the Society of Antiquaries of London No. IX, London.

Woodward, A., and Leach, P. (1993) *The Uley Shrines: Excavation of a Ritual Complex on West Hill, Uley, Gloucestershire 1977–9*, English Heritage, London.

Wright, R.P., and Jackson, K.H. (1968) 'A Late Inscription from Wroxeter', *Antiquaries Journal* 48 (part 2): 296–300.

INDEX

For sites, the modern English name has been preferred unless the site is commonly known by its ancient name, e.g. Vindolanda. Names of Romans are generally indexed here by the *nomen* (the middle part of the Roman citizen's full name), thus Valerius Genialis, Sextus, for Sextus Valerius Genialis. However, where the individual is clearly of native origin the name is indexed by the identifying *cognomen*, thus Catuarus, Tiberius Claudius. Likewise, Romans best known by their *cognomina* such as Agricola and Cicero are indexed similarly. Needless to say, there are many examples of Roman names which are either incomplete or have additional names.

PICTURE CREDITS

Plate 1 is a photograph by Irene de la Bédoyère; all other photographs and drawings are by the author. The drawings at the start of each chapter portray the following: